ZIGZAG:
A LIFE ON THE MOVE

Other Books by James Houston

ZIGZAG

A Life on the Move

JAMES HOUSTON

[A DOUGLAS GIBSON BOOK]

M&S

Canadian Cataloguing in Publication Data

Houston, James, 1921–
   Zigzag : a life on the move

ISBN 0-7710-4208-6

1. Houston, James, 1921–   – Biography. 2. Authors, Canadian (English) – 20th century – Biography.* 3. Designers – New York (State) – New York – Biography.   I. Title.

PS8515.079Z53 1998   C813'.54   C98-931299-2
PR9199.3.H68Z478 1998

The publishers acknowledge the financial support of the Government of Canada through the Book Publishing Industry Development Program for our publishing activities. We further acknowledge the support of The Canada Council for the Arts and the Ontario Arts Council for our publishing program.

Typeset in Goudy by M & S, Toronto
Printed and bound in Canada

A Douglas Gibson Book

McClelland & Stewart Inc.
The Canadian Publishers
481 University Avenue
Toronto, Ontario
M5G 2E9

1 2 3 4 5   02 01 00 99 98

For my sons,
John and Sam Houston

Contents

I

The Paper Bag

Leaving the Arctic was about the most difficult thing I ever had to do. I had cast the die myself and had known for some time that I was going. Toward the end of April, 1962, I sent a message from my Baffin Island home south to Ottawa to the Department of Northern Affairs in Canada's Federal Government, saying that I intended to resign. I wasn't really emotionally ready for it, but now I felt I had to go.

I had been offered a position in the South as Assistant Director of Design at Steuben Glass, with a breathtaking office on the second floor of their new building looking out on the corner of 5th Avenue at 56th Street, right in the middle of Manhattan Island. I was very excited, yet apprehensive, about the prospects of undertaking such different work. This job offered more than three times the salary I had been earning in the Arctic. Beyond that, my new boss, Arthur A. Houghton, Jr., who knew just about everyone worth knowing in the United States, offered a wonderful sponsorship in that overwhelming city of New York. It was at a time when the Kennedy administration was just beginning, and New York was a neat, clean city throbbing with exciting, new ideas. Living in a brownstone in mid-Manhattan after a dozen years in the Arctic was bound to make a dramatic change in my whole life.

As I prepared to leave the Arctic, part of me felt that after all those wonderful years, I was sneaking out on Inuit who had befriended me and shown me a better way to live. I had been with the *Kingarmiut*, the people at Cape Dorset, coming and going for the past nine years. It had simply been the best of times for me. But now, Terry Ryan had been with us for nearly two years, and I knew that he was in position to continue helping the West Baffin Eskimo Co-operative move forward. My wife, Allie, had departed for England about eight months earlier to put the boys in school. She and I had separated and did not expect to get together again.

Closing up the government house that I had helped to build at Cape Dorset was a sorrowful task. I started giving away my Arctic essentials to the printmakers and carvers in the co-op. My big, octagonal tent was one of the hardest things to part with, because leaving it seemed to cut me off forever from that joyful, nomadic way of life. My hunting companion, Osuitok, was delighted to have my high-powered rifle with the scope, along with a case of ammunition. After that, I asked the other hunters and their wives to make their choice of sleeping bags, parkas, wind pants, skin boots, everything, including my Swedish Primus stove. I left the dogs till last. Osuitok would take care of them, along with the big sled. Years later, I returned to Cape Dorset for one of many visits and said to him with the pure delight that recognition gives, "Why, there's our lead bitch, Lao." "*Kasak*, almost," Osuitok nodded. "It's her great, great granddaughter."

The Arctic weather in late May of 1962 turned fine and the Royal Canadian Mounted Police flew over in their single-engine Otter on skis. We had a glorious send-off party. One of my best friends, Big Red Pedersen, who until recently had been with the Hudson's Bay Company, had joined our co-op. Red was a powerful six-foot-four. He raised his arms in a farewell toast and leapt into the air with Danish joie de vivre, punching his two large fists through the plywood ceiling. The patch marks are still there for you to see!

I had a wonderful time at that party, but later I went and stood alone outside watching the white dawn rising with the moon still glowing bone-white over Kingait Mountain. *This is the end*, I thought. *It's like watching yourself die, without really doing it.* I could see the yellow police plane resting peacefully beyond the barrier ice. There was not a breath of wind. The time had really come now, no blizzards or ice fogs to prevent it, no excuses. I was going after all these years.

Fletch, the mounted police pilot, came out the back door in his underwear and skin boots to check the weather. He shuddered and hurried back inside, for that fine, spring weather had a sharp razor's edge that on a sultry summer's day I sometimes try to recreate in my memory.

Later in the morning, ice fog started to roll in over the hills, drifting off the open waters of the polynyas, a huge pool opening in the sea ice which is kept open by winds and tidal action. Seals, walrus, and polar bears have always been drawn there. That is the reason Inuit hunting families chose to live near Kingait in the first place.

Osuitok came in the house and smiled at me. "*Sila piungituk uva-tiaruapik*, weather's going to get bad soon," he said.

His wife, Nipisa, made us some coffee, and when that was finished, the pilot came into the room and stared out the window. "Well, it looks like now or never, pal. Let's go."

Now the time had really come. I thought of rushing out the door and hiding in the hills. But as I looked outside, I could see Inuit gathering near the lazily rolling flag that Osuitok had just raised. They looked to me like people assembling for a funeral. My Arctic years had come to an end, years of dog-team traveling, hunting, dancing, lovemaking, printmaking, laughing, arguing, peacemaking, crying, singing, helping the young get food to eat, helping the old get the stones put on them. All of that was ending for me. Grabbing my bags with lots of help from others, we went out the door.

"You going to lock it?" asked the other policeman.

"God, no!" I said. "There's no need to lock anything here. I threw the keys away the day this house was finished."

Osuitok was standing quietly at the corner of the building with Nipisa. "Here," he said, "it's a poor carving, but I made it for you."

It was a marvelous jade green stone carving of a walrus, the very best that I have ever seen. (In 1997, I saw another fine carving by Osuitok on sale in a Vancouver gallery for $11,000.00.)

"I'll carry it," his wife said, and opened her hood for Osuitok to lay it inside.

We walked in silence to the police plane – men, women, and children. I had the feeling that I wasn't going to make it, that I might collapse and die while moving with the others through the rough ice.

"Ayii, Saomik, hey, Left-Handed," called a powerful voice.

I stopped beside the plane. The police pilot looked at me sadly, the way people do when they know you're going to have to bear unbearable news, then he climbed inside.

"Saomik," Kiaksuk said. "Left-Handed, I have a little message for you."

It was only right, of course, that he, Kiaksuk, the oldest man among them, should speak for everyone. The others stared silently at me, and if I looked back at them, they smiled in a sad way that made me look at my feet. *You hold on, you weakling,* I said to myself. *These families will remember how you act right now.*

"Left-Handed, we have something for you, *tujuusiat illunatinni,* a small gift from many here."

He held out a small brown-paper bag. It was old and crumpled with what looked like seal-fat stains that made irregular, shiny blotches. I wondered what was inside, thinking probably a super carving. Kiaksuk laid it in my hands. It had no weight. It was nothing like a carving. Light as a feather, it seemed to contain nothing, to be just a crumpled bag.

"Look inside," said Kiaksuk proudly.

The paper bag

I opened the bag and reached in. Inside was a clutch of small, tightly folded letters many people had penciled in Inuktitut. I drew out a handful of one- and two-dollar bills, each one wadded up tight. There were a lot of them in that little paper bag – thirty-three Canadian dollars.

"What are these for?" I asked.

"A gift for you," Kiaksuk said. "Everyone gives them to you. You're going away, everyone says, to try and make more money."

Kiinaujat was the word he used, meaning paper with a face on it, money.

"If at first you don't have enough money in that foreign place, we thought to give some to you. *Tavvauvutit,* good-bye," he said, and shook my hand.

Seeing all of them only in a blur, I shook hands with everyone, including babies in the hood, then climbed weakly aboard the plane. I pulled my hood over my face and left that unforgettable place that had for so long been my home.

2

Fast Immigration

The United States Consul General's Office in Montreal was at that time directly across Peel Street from the Mount Royal Hotel. I had stayed there for several nights, trying to recapture my city bearings, arranging for an exhibition at the Guild, and worrying about the great leap south I was about to take. My last night I slept badly, plagued by dreams, rose early, packed the hotel soap in my bags, had breakfast in the coffee shop downstairs, shuffled my fistful of papers, and marched across to the Consul's Office the moment that it opened. No one else was visible except a trim, attractive-looking, dark-haired girl who sat primly behind her desk. She didn't smile or even look at me before she began our interview in rapid French. When I answered her in my French, she frowned and wrinkled her nose, reluctantly forced to allow our conversation to convert to English.

After examining my letters, she grimaced, rose, snatched open one of the office's doors, and spoke angrily inside, again in French. I looked around. The office seemed full of doors. A male voice answered her very sharply. "*Cochon!*" she said, and slammed his door, then got back on my case.

I needed a green card to immigrate with the right to work in the United States. She ordered me to go a few blocks away and return only when I had three duplicate photos of my head, *not smiling!* I crept out and searched for the St. Catherine Street address. Click, click, click. I rushed back, small pictures clutched in my hand.

"Read this, sign!" she screamed in a voice no Inuk, male or female, would even dream of using on another human being. It was a shock being in the outside world again, having a hostile encounter with an attractive-looking girl. Well, after all, she was a civil servant. I signed.

Frowning, the beauty rose, turned her back on me, and disappeared. It took her a long time to return. She was carrying more papers and a green card with my picture and signature freshly encased in shining plastic. (I realize, after all these years, that this whole green card episode can now take years; my case at that time took less than two hours.) This petulant girl did not indicate in any way that my interview was over, but simply frowned and shoved my papers and the new green card across her desk. I signed again. She rose and disappeared behind one of the many office doors.

Was I finished? Was I free to leave? I looked at my watch. It was nearly noon and I had to check out of my hotel, cab to the airport, and catch the plane. Where was she?

"*Excusez-moi, mademoiselle,*" I called.

No answer. God, had she gone to lunch?

I paced over to the window and above the buildings caught a glimpse of the clear blue sky. "*Mademoiselle,*" I called, "I'll be late for my plane. *Mon avion sera parti.*"

No answer.

Pocketing my new green card, I tiptoed to the door that she had entered. I tapped, then taking the handle, I boldly opened it. There she sat before me on what I soon realized was a toilet. She let out a primordial scream and tried to throw the paper roll at me! I slammed that door, found the right one, and escaped down the stairs. Across the street, I checked out of the Mount Royal in a panic and caught a cab to Dorval Airport, looking back to see if we were being followed by the Montreal Police. No. Well, here I was on my way to New York City.

I fell asleep as the plane was taking off and woke when the hostess shook me. The travelers and the greeters elbowed me as I passed through La Guardia airport, letting nothing stand in the path of their progress. With my green card and special passport, I cleared Customs with ease, grateful that the Citizenship and Immigration girl in Montreal had hardened me for all of this quick and aggressive civilization. I cheerfully began wading through the crowds as I searched for my baggage, then my friend.

3
Houghton's New York

I had first met Arthur A. Houghton, Jr. when he came into the Arctic in 1959 with a party of eight, the first tourist party I had ever seen in the far North. Now he gave me a loud hail above the confusion near the incoming piles of luggage. We got into his waiting car and were driven into Manhattan. He lived at No. 3 Sutton Place in a large, red brick house six blocks straight east of the Steuben building and just north of the United Nations. I did not immediately understand the grandeur of that fine, ivy-covered old house that had once belonged to J. P. Morgan's daughter. A huge, block-long garden behind it was bordered by the East River, which reflected thousands of shimmering lights as it flowed peacefully beneath the huge span of the Queensboro Bridge. Houghton shared that garden with Ari Onassis and Randolph Hearst's best friend, the film actress Marion Davies (a very pleasant person). Inside, I found that my elaborate, Louis XV bathroom had a toilet disguised perfectly as a kind of throne on a raised dais hidden in a truly historic wing chair covered in petit point roses. The chair's seat, when I guessed its function, could be lifted with quiet dignity. I believe in retrospect that throne suggested a good deal of what I would so willingly encounter in my new life.

Chair

Somerset Maugham was quoted in *The New Yorker* magazine as having said that there were two truly memorable aspects of New York City at that time: one, the United Nations building, and two, Peacock, Arthur's English butler. Peacock had a traditional facade that was utterly impenetrable, not only to me, but to Houghton.

For my Manhattan stay, my mother had sent down from Canada a box of many things, including my old-fashioned, pre-war dinner jacket with its wide satin lapels. It was English and as heavy as an overcoat. Over time, the hot spots under the arms and crotch had turned a faint, mossy green. When I unpacked it, the pants looked like an accordion that had been salvaged from the bottom of my army kit bag. I pulled the petit point cord by the bed that rang for Peacock, who soon glided in like a dignified if aging Noel Coward. I asked if I could have my costume pressed in time to appear at dinner that night. He gave me a pained, English look. But after showering, I was pleased to see it neatly pressed.

During drinks and then dinner, Arthur and his elegant wife, Betty, were the soul of kindness. Knowing how little else I knew, they kept the conversation centered on the Arctic. After our unusually small dinner for four, they personally escorted me into the elevator that rose to the fourth floor and showed me to my bedroom located at the front of the house. To my surprise, Arthur turned on something that made an awful whirring, growling sound. "Goodnight. Sleep well!" they called out. "Coffee in the library early. Breakfast at eight." Smiling warmly, they departed.

I suffered the groaning noise for a few minutes, then rolled out of bed, found the offending dial behind the draperies, and turned the racket off. I began to read a book left by my bed, which was entitled, *The Making of Fine Glass*. God knows I needed to learn more about glass if I was to design glass sculptures for Steuben to sell. Not long afterward, I heard a tap, and the door opened. It was Arthur and Betty again.

"Don't you find it stuffy in here? There is an air conditioner in this room," Arthur explained, correctly guessing that I'd never owned or used one in my life. He crossed the room and turned the racket on again.

I waited politely until I thought they'd left the floor, then hopped out of bed again and turned it off. Not long after, I heard a firmer tapping on my door. They entered, this time in their dressing gowns.

"Is that damned thing malfunctioning, Houston, or did you turn it off?"

"I turned it off," I admitted sheepishly.

With a positive thrust, Arthur turned it on full force. "Air conditioners are considered a great blessing in this city. Keep yours on," he commanded. "That way you won't hear the police sirens and the screaming and shooting in the streets. Goodnight!"

Whenever I stayed at Sutton Place, Peacock brought duplicate papers to the library for the coffee session that preceded breakfast. It was the first time I had ever felt newspapers still warm from ironing. It gives them that smooth, friendly feeling of a woman's silk nightgown, appropriate for reading in your dressing gown.

Arthur took four morning newspapers and read them all: *The New York Times*, *The Wall Street Journal*, *The Washington Post*, and

The Post, which I thought a highly questionable tabloid filled with gossip – sometimes about his friends and himself.

As I took up my paper, I noticed that Houghton had finished his *Times* and had rapidly moved on to *The Washington Post*. He had a lively interest in all that went on in the nation's capital, especially items concerning President Kennedy and his brother, the Attorney General, whom he did not favor, and the CIA and FBI, plus gossip and the obituaries.

He looked up at me with alarm when he saw that I was still on page 2 of the *Times*. He stared at me with an eagle eye, took a quick sip of coffee, and said, "Houston, you're not going to get anywhere if you continue to read papers at that rate." I admitted to him that I had totally lost the habit of reading newspapers after I went away from Toronto as a teenager to join a Scottish regiment in 1940. He thought this outlandish. I assured him that to keep up with the news, I intended to listen to the morning and evening newscast. He snorted at that, declaring that I would miss all the second line items of daily news which were essential for every New Yorker to know. "Come over here. I'll show you how to read the papers."

He looked at the front page quickly, absorbing the titles of the articles only, then said, pointing to one, "Our Mayor, John Lindsay, says he's going to take on that threat of a garbage strike." He shook his head. "You'll meet him Friday. He and Mary are coming to dinner."

He whipped open pages 2 and 3 and scanned each heading. Nothing caught his interest. Continuing at a furious speed until he found an item concerning Corning Glass Works, of which he was the major shareholder, he nodded approval, then went fast forward to the stock quotations, took in what interested him in a moment, and finally checked the obituaries. "There, that's that," he said, and rushed to the back of the paper to check on the placement of one of David Ogilvie's Steuben ads.

Then, after a bite of cinnamon toast, he took up the next paper. He had mastered the art of running his eye down a column of type and instantly seeing names, places, and other key words that would interest him. These were the areas that he would swiftly absorb. The rest he ignored.

I was smiling at a half-naked girl's photo in my tabloid when he asked, "Do you know her personally?"

"No," I said, and laughed.

"You keep away from girls like that. She's got old Jerry all tied up in court. Tall Yale man, famous squash player, you'll see him at the club. He's living there now, they say. His wife won't let him in their house, not even to get his salmon rods. Now that woman's going too damn far!"

I thought on that in the bath. I decided to take three papers – the *Times*, the wildest tabloid, and *The Montreal Star*, a day old, but available at the St. Regis Hotel a block's walk from Steuben.

After dressing quickly, I took the elevator down to breakfast in the dining room overlooking the East River. Betty joined us. I had coffee, juice, one egg, and a few strips of bacon – needed, Inuit believe, to grease the joints.

Arthur rose from the table at precisely 8:50, and we met Ryan, his chauffeur, who had previously driven for Her Majesty, Queen Elizabeth. Ryan opened and closed the door of the black Rolls Royce. I wondered if Osuitok would be out with our team that morning, as we rolled the few blocks across Manhattan to the office.

4

The Office and Beyond

The Steuben building on 5th Avenue at 56th Street was a glass tower, twenty-seven floors of new and impressive beauty. It had been designed by the famous architect, Wally Harrison, who had just done the United Nations building. The larger Seagram building had not yet been built.

The Steuben showroom was on the ground floor of what I thought the most elegant corner in New York, though Tiffany and Cartier, each a block away, might wish to argue that. The showroom was a place of plush gray carpeting and white flowers with masterful lighting and gunmetal mirrors carefully placed to display the heavy crystal in the grandest style. When I looked at some of the prices, I nearly collapsed. I was a long way from the Canadian Arctic, and not just in miles.

Arthur introduced me to half a dozen attractive-looking salespersons: one a Belgian countess, another the daughter of the world's first female Prime Minister, Mrs. Banderanaiake of Sri Lanka.

"Come on, we'll take the little elevator upstairs and ask Sally what's going on today."

Arthur's office on the third floor looked out on 5th Avenue at 56th Street. It was simply and elegantly furnished with rough tan silk on the walls, with two gold-framed Fragonard sketches (another twenty hung along the hall). On the south wall over the sofa was one of the rarest fifteenth-century Spanish maps of the New World.

I was grateful to see Sally Walker again. She was a ranking tennis player and the Executive Vice President of Steuben who had come into the Arctic in 1959 with Arthur's party of eight when Arthur and I had become friends, and the trail that led to this office had begun. He suggested that we three have lunch together, then hurried me down to the second floor, the Design Department, which featured an impressive library, with a large, round table used for design meetings. Jack Gates, a tall, good-humored architect from Harvard, came out of his office to greet us, and together they introduced me to the other eight persons who made up the Design Department.

I was a total unknown, an outsider coming in as the Assistant Director of Design, an idea that I imagined might not be altogether popular. However, most Americans are great about putting the best face on everything – at least at first – knowing that for one reason or another, you may only last a month or so.

I liked the look of Steuben and everyone in it. Imagine all this luxury after twelve years of very different circumstances! Two thousand miles straight north of Manhattan Island, about fifteen hundred humans then lived on Baffin, the fifth largest island in the world, while Manhattan, one of the smallest islands, had a working population of over twenty million. Many of these folks were semi-nomads, too, having their bedrooms, as they say, somewhere out in the other five boroughs or even farther in the countryside.

What would I come to think of these designers in their large, well-lighted spaces? What would I think of Manhattan in a year, if I had the stuff that would allow me to remain that long?

During lunch, Houghton and Sally told me that they would more than understand if I just decided to chuck the whole damn thing and rush straight back to my Arctic solitude. They knew that I had been happy there, and that lots of people just couldn't stand New York. I got the message and thought, I'll keep my bags half packed.

"Where do you plan to live?" Houghton asked me. "Do you need any help to choose a place?"

"No, thanks," I told him. "I've got it all worked out in my mind."

It seemed to me that I was for the first time in my life earning a huge salary, more than I could spend, for to my surprise items in the New York stores cost considerably less than they did in Canada.

After lunch, I marched boldly westward to a large but somewhat older-looking hotel on 7th Avenue called the Wellington. I chose that hotel simply because I admired the Duke of Wellington and his military prowess at Waterloo. I asked the man at the desk if they had any small suites.

"For how long, sir?" he asked.

"Oh, a month or two, or perhaps till winter. Hard to tell."

He showed me three suites. The second one seemed perfect – a bedroom with a bathroom, so necessary in these parts, and a manly looking sitting room with a chesterfield (always called a sofa in the U.S.), and two red leather wing chairs, plus a telephone, a good-looking desk, and another dreaded air conditioner. On the walls there were several bland pictures, which I planned to change, perhaps for one of the Duke himself in a scarlet tunic, or better still, some bold Inuit prints. It all appeared fine. I felt duty-bound to reappear at Steuben or I would probably have taken it then and there.

When I returned to the Design Department, I told Jack Gates of my good luck in finding such a place.

"I wonder if you'll really like it over there," he said to me. "You could probably find something more suitable here on the east side of town. Don't sign anything until I speak to Arthur."

Arthur seemed alarmed when he spoke to me, alarmed because I was even contemplating accommodations on the west side of 5th Avenue. He suggested that I stay a day or two longer at his house, while he thought it over, although I knew he had the theory that guests, like fish, after four days begin to smell.

"I may have just the place for you," he said next day. "One of our salesgirls who now lives in Greenwich, Connecticut, has a small apartment on East 63rd near Park Avenue. She says she won't be using it during the summer and you'd be welcome to it."

The monthly rent she asked after she had showed me around was far less than the cost of the hotel suite, and the location was much more pleasant.

It turned out to be a perfect apartment. I unpacked and spread my few possessions in the bureaus and the closets. I found a good place to have breakfast on Madison Avenue, and staggered to work through the oppressive heat. That evening, I turned on the air conditioner in the apartment. This one seemed noisier than Arthur's, but it cooled the air. I turned on the nightly news and tried to convince myself that I could scarcely hear the maddening, humming sound. The three-quarter bed was soft and I slept nearly as well as I had in any snowhouse, hoping I would learn to handle life in this big city and the hardships of New York.

Next morning, I rose early, eager to start work. I took a shower. What a privilege! Even in the last years in the government house in Kingait, if I wanted to take a bath, I would have to melt enough ice to partly fill the tub, then carry pails of water to it. Worst of all, after the bath I would have to bail out the tub, being careful to leave in no water that might freeze and crack the tub. We kept the house up there at about 50 degrees F. to make visiting Eskimos, not to mention us in our heavier clothes, feel comfortable indoors. So, as you can imagine, not a helluva lot of bathing went on during the long course of the winter. The saving grace in the Arctic cold is that one almost never perspires, which, of course, one does in warmer climates, and that makes the frequent bath essential.

When I had the unfamiliar shower suitably adjusted, I stepped in and drew the curtain, feeling like someone who has just discovered that man could live well even on the moon. I started singing, which had been an earlier bathing habit of mine.

I had just finished the first chorus of "Then we will come and eat up ducks, *On Ilkla Moor baht 'at,*" when a female voice through the wall of the next apartment took up the next verse, and together we sang the chorus!

Shower

I turned off my shower to hear the soprano voice singing in her shower, invisible, of course, but oh so sweet and close beside me.

I turned on my shower again and tried "Drink to me only with thine eyes." I heard her laugh!

I was trembling when I opened my apartment door and there she was just closing hers.

"Are you a friend of the wonderful person from that apartment? Where is she?"

"Greenwich," I told her. "Don't know when she'll be back. Some say never. She's going to get married out there."

"Do you want to come in and join me for a drink?"

I started quickly toward her door.

"Oh, I mean after work." She laughed. She had that quick look of a Montrealer, but I could tell by her unfamiliar accent that she was a homegrown American.

"Sure," I said, "what time?"

"Six-thirty on the dot," she said, and went back inside her apartment to get something.

I hurried in a sweat along the eight short blocks to work.

That evening after she had poured us drinks, she said, "That damned ad agency's got me all wound up today. Are you any good at giving a neck and back massage?" She started taking off her shirt.

"I'll do my best!" I told her. "Here's to you!" We took a good, quick drink.

Hell, New York wasn't going to be anything like as tough as those Ottawa civil servants swore that it was going to be. If I could survive in 50 below, I guess I could manage it here in this apartment – with the air conditioning on, of course!

5

The High Life

Before World War II, my father had been part of a Canadian firm that dealt in the importation of British yard goods. When he judged that I had reached my full growth, he ordered me an English-cut dinner jacket. There were lots of black-tie, formal events in Toronto before the war. Then, because of my being in uniform from 1940 until war's end in 1945, this dinner jacket was tucked away in mothballs. I used it only a few times before going to the Arctic and only a few times on my trips to Japan and Europe. My dinner jacket had been cut from a piece of fine, heavy material (probably a bargain in 1936) that was suitable, my father said, for Canadian winters and drafty Scottish halls.

Arthur Houghton, when I first knew him, donned black tie practically every evening – except Sunday, of course, when dinner clothes were never worn.

It was warm that first summer in New York, and I could feel little trickles of sweat crawling buglike down my back at cocktail time. Testing the thickness of the sleeve, Houghton said, "That weight will never do around here. Why don't you get someone who knows the tailors around town to advise you? Buy two new dinner jackets. You can keep one at your apartment and the other at the office. There's a clothes closet and a shower there. That way, you can either go home to dress or change after work and leave directly for any party. And, by the way, do you have an alarm on your wristwatch?"

"No, I didn't know they made them."

"Well, they do, and it will keep you from being late. I saw an ad in the *Times* for one this morning. They cost about a hundred dollars. Your friends here say you must have lost your sense of timing somewhere in the Arctic, and you need to get it back if you're going to attend meetings and be on time for parties."

The whole concept of time as we so-called civilized folk think of it is repugnant to lots of North America's aboriginal people. I have many friends among them who seem to possess an altogether different concept of time. They reject the idea of time as their master who will force them to rush to be at some place at a given moment on the clock. Time is thought by them to be something passing, something that you should live with and enjoy during the long or brief course of your life.

A long, dark winter does not hang heavy over the heads of Inuit because it is a natural part of their lives. Missionary teachers years ago used to try and beat our sense of time into native children. But it didn't work. It only caused the resisting children to grow into adults who still resisted having their lives ruled by the clock. Instead, Inuit hunters might go out for thirty or forty hours until they have secured the meat they need, then return to camp, eat, and lie down and sleep until they're tired of it. I call that being in control of time.

Nevertheless, I bought the watch with the alarm and ordered two dinner jackets of the lightest material I could find. The keeping of one in the office closet worked both ways. It meant that when I returned from some far-too-late adventure, I could go directly to the office, shave, take an early shower, slip back into my business suit, and appear to be an early riser driven to the drawing table by the inspiration of some new glass design.

One reason I wore black tie so often was that I attended endless theater benefits with the Houghtons or their friends I had met at dinner parties. Hostesses were often looking for an extra man. I was told by some hostesses that it was not considered good form to give a dinner party for eight to ten or twelve persons, asking only husbands and wives, and certainly it was almost unforgivable to hold a dinner party with an unbalanced table.

Sometimes, I would walk home after work and flop down on my bed. Then the telephone would ring and a familiar voice would say, "Oh, James, we haven't seen you for, well, a week or more. I was wondering if you'd join us for dinner."

"Oh, thank you," I'd answer, reaching for my date book. "When?"

"Tonight. I know it's very short notice, but come on. It's for a friend. Cocktails at 7:00. It might be hard to get a taxi. Don't be late, James. Good-bye."

Cocktails at 7:00, I would think. Oh, God! I'd shower, dress, and catch a taxi. It was New York life and another wonderful party. No doubt about it. I was starting to get the hang of Manhattan and it was a marvelous city – opposite in almost every measurable way from life in the Arctic.

I welcomed the difference most of the time. It was novel to dress up in New York in the same sense that it is novel for strangers coming into the Arctic to dress up in local garb – caribou skin pants and parkas, knee-high sealskin boots. Strangers were delighted with the lightness and the warmth of Inuit clothing of earlier times, just as I was with the look of my new city costumes. On other occasions, however, I got things wrong. Once I asked a girl I knew in Canada to come down to New York for a few days, saying that we would go to a Broadway play that we were both eager to see. I told her to be sure to bring a long dress.

On the night of the performance, we two dressed formally and went out to dinner. She registered surprise when my wrist alarm went off and we taxied to the theater, arriving on time. As we entered, I noticed a rough-looking couple, he in a tweed jacket, she in blue jeans. We headed down to the better seats. I looked around me. Not a single person was in formal dress.

"I feel kind of funny in this long dress," my friend said.

"People always wear dress clothes to the theater," I said weakly.

As the curtain rose, she turned and looked at me as though the strain of New York had broken my mind. The truth was that since my arrival, I had never gone to any theater unless I was first invited out to dinner, then attended a benefit performance as the guest of my hosts. This had happened to me so often that I had assumed that all New Yorkers dressed for the theater. Ah, well, it's hard to learn a whole new lifestyle in a month or even a year.

Arthur and Betty Houghton, my true sponsors in New York, lived a very active social life. I also came to know a good many other people. It did not take me long to realize that during the season in New York, mid-autumn through late spring, countless dinner parties were given, most in private homes or clubs such as the River Club, the Colony Club, the Century, etc. These parties would usually consist of twelve or fourteen persons, and it was remarkable that almost always you could count on seeing the same faces. If I did see a new man or a couple, I could bet that they were not just other New Yorkers, not just persons from the west coast or elsewhere in the United States, but Europeans, most likely English. That may sound boring, but I never found it so. It was comforting to me to find a circle of reliable friends. It was almost like being part of an Inuit camp. And all in all, I had to admit that the food and drink were mostly better.

Imagine that, a shower at the office and dressing in black tie almost every night for a lavish, four-course dinner, when not so long before I had been unwashed for a month, out traveling the coast with Osuitok and Charles Gimpel, the Englishman Inuit called *Ukjuk*, bearded seal, because of his bushy sideburns. Then, I'd been dressed in sealskin boots and a none-too-clean parka, scratching when I felt the urge, and wondering if I'd eat a raw fish or a chunk of bully beef.

Would this new life make me soft? You bet it would. Was it being any fun? Damned right it was. Did I plan to change my ways? Well, not right then I didn't. I was on the town, as some New Yorkers like to say, and I was enjoying it to the hilt.

It was a thrilling thing to change worlds, change habits. It made everything seem new. And I certainly would not have been able to do that so painlessly without Arthur, who acted in the old-fashioned sense as my patron.

I have recently been accused in the Canadian press as having patronized Inuit artists. I hope that is true. I certainly see nothing wrong with being a patron, or the beneficiary of a patron. Leonardo da Vinci and Michelangelo certainly had patrons in the popes and kings. If Arthur's help didn't make me a better artist or a better author, it certainly gave me a new lively and varied life for which I'll be forever grateful.

Arthur said to all of the Steuben designers, "Don't just sit at your desks or stand in front of the glory hole. Take at least one day off each week and go to refresh yourselves at a museum." To me he said, "America has some splendid art galleries and museums. You should go out and see as many as you can. You'll surely gather good ideas."

I did fly around America a bit and view the important museums, but as I think back on it, I didn't experience as many of them as I should have. I visited many of the major museums in Europe and saw splendid glass collections. I needed to wake up to a whole new world of glass and precious metals.

Just as Pootoogook had helped me to find my way into Arctic life on west Baffin Island, so Arthur had helped me enter the rare complexities of Manhattan Island and weekend country life at his estate on the eastern shore of Maryland. That zigzag may seem simple to you, but it is, I believe, at least as complex and different as Eskimo life. Anyone making a similar jump needs help.

When I think of it now, I realize that I used to be far too casual about dinner parties, luncheons, even business breakfasts. New York is anything but a casual place on such matters. Often, I let the notepad slip on which I made scrawls when writing times and places. But my new wristwatch alarm helped me arrive at meetings on time. And because I had learned to shower, shave, and dress in record time, I fancied I was becoming a New Yorker. No more thinking, *I'll just lay here inside this snowhouse in this warm sleeping bag and reread my only book, then sleep until this damn weather changes.*

One night out on the town, I couldn't find a cab, but walked fast up to Park Avenue – or was it 5th Avenue? I frisked myself as I came to the corner and found my note. I had difficulty reading it beneath the street light. Well, the apartment number was 820. That was clear enough. It was not at all uncommon in New York to see people out walking to neighboring apartment buildings dressed in dinner clothes.

Yes, I had it right. I gave the doorman my name, and he rang my hosts, then directed me to a small, walnut-paneled elevator with a velvet seat. When the elevator door opened, I tapped on the only door in the foyer. I checked my watch. I was right on time, but I noted that beyond the door, there was an unexpected silence.

I tapped again and the door opened cautiously. It was my host and behind him my hostess, both elderly and both dressed in their bathrobes.

"Oh, James, come in," my hostess called from behind her astonished husband.

"Oh," I gasped, looking at my watch. "Am I early?"

"No, no," they said. "Come right in."

It dawned on me that we three were alone. "Aren't you having a party tonight?"

"Well, yes, we could have one," the hostess said gamely, "now that you've arrived."

"Oh, God, forgive me. I'm leaving right now. I've got my dates mixed up."

"Should you be someplace else, James?" Ann said thoughtfully.

"No, no. 820, that was clear."

"Well, we were just about to have some supper. Stay with us. It's our man's and the cook's night out, but we'll be alone. You can tell us about the Arctic and we'll tell you about the Gobi Desert."

They grabbed my arm and insisted, and like an Eskimo, I giggled and stayed. Sherman broke out a bottle of champagne and Ann brought in caviar, followed by tinned soup and salad. We laughed together at my blunder and their ragged bathrobes, and I enjoyed one of my best evenings in New York.

Next day at work, I had a call from another hostess who said, "James, we missed you last night at the party. What happened?"

"I don't know," I said. "I thought you lived at 820 5th Avenue."

"No, my dear, next time try us at 520 Park Avenue."

"I was getting desperate."

"Not to worry, dear," she said, "it worked out more or less, except I had to sit next to a dreadful woman. We thought after the Arctic that you could find your way across town somehow. Not to worry, dear, we'll send a car for you next time."

Dinner parties, especially at first, were a problem in New York. It seemed to me that everyone had lots to talk about, and I felt so limited. They would look at me and say they had had lunch with a well-known senator that day, and that Lawrence was sleeping at his club and not at home, and that so-and-so had gone to meet our man in Paris.

When I looked blank, they'd cock their head at me. "Mr. Houston, how long were you away in the Arctic? You must have fallen absolutely out of touch."

But I soon discovered that I had little to complain about. I found that the ladies seated on either side of me were eager – well, perhaps that is too strong a word – were polite enough to ask about and listen to various aspects of the Inuit world.

Of course, it is absolutely necessary to turn with the table and talk to the lady seated on your other side. This is crucial. The other trick is never to allow yourself to dwell on your one-and-only subject for too long. I learned to watch the lady next to me if I was speaking. If I saw her start to squirm or begin to square away her silver, I'd take it as a positive sign to dummy up and turn the table.

When Nelson Rockefeller was divorced from his first wife and remarried, it caused a great stir in New York. Rockefeller was not only New York's Governor, but it was known that he intended to run for the Presidency of the United States on the Republican ticket, and much was being said about his recent marriage. Arthur called me on short notice and asked if I would join them in a small dinner party for six. He said it was almost the first time that Nelson and his new bride, Happy, had been out to dinner since their marriage, and that he didn't know Nelson's new wife or how the conversation might go. He said that if the atmosphere grew tense during dinner and the conversation broke down, he would ask me a question about Inuit, and I was to immediately leap into the gap with a story. "Tell the one about Eskimo marriages," he said, for he felt that subject would ease the strain and put the dinner party on a lighthearted track.

Believe it or not, the conversation between soup and salad did falter. The hostess started to look wild-eyed and Arthur gave the secret signal. I launched into the story. The guests laughed merrily and the whole thing seemed to work.

A year later, I attended a dinner party. When Happy noticed the silence at our end of the table, she said, "Mr. Houston, tell the one about the Eskimo newlyweds." Knowing my subject, I launched straight in. The Inuit again had saved the day.

A Canadian girl I knew, who had lived longer in New York than I had, was married to a man whose job took them to the head office in London. They excitedly moved to the most elegant square in Mayfair. When we went to visit them several years later, she seemed happy enough with her new life and her new house. But when I asked her how she liked living in England, she said, "Oh, fine," then paused. "James, a person has just got to face it. When you're out of New York, you're nowhere."

A lot of people felt that way about New York in the sixties.

6

Missile Threat

Walking home along Madison Avenue in the autumn of 1962, I was part of a crowd that stopped and listened to a radio announcement coming through the open door of a shop. It was President

Kennedy's voice announcing for the first time awesome details of the Cuban missile crisis.

The very threat of the use of atomic missiles gave me, like everyone else, a sense of horror. It would not be like World War II where individuals would have time to organize and fight. Instead, this presented to me a picture of a mushroom cloud followed by a nuclear holocaust. I was dumbstruck by the fact that so many people who had heard the news continued walking along the street, calmly discussing the thoughts that had occupied their minds before this stunning revelation.

I had a date that night with a girl I knew well. Her family had escaped the spread of Nazism in 1938 and had gone to live in the south of Ireland. There, she had told me, she was obliged to be a Roman Catholic in school and to learn the Irish language. Often, for the fun of it, she spoke and sang to me in Gaelic. What was left of her family had regathered to live in Switzerland.

We went together to a small party in Greenwich Village. When I tried to discuss the Russian placement of missiles in Cuba and President Kennedy's quick response, I discovered that everyone had heard the news, but few had paid serious attention to it on that first night. Only one person seemed upset – that was the girl with me. She said she felt unwell and asked me to take her uptown to her apartment.

We both went in, and as I watched in surprise, she hauled two large suitcases from the closet and began to pack. She asked me if I would start telephoning the airlines and reserve the first seat I could to Switzerland that night. After trying several airlines, I found one. They said there were a lot of sudden requests that night. She quickly wrote a check to cover that month's rent and left it on the table.

"Are you certain you want to do this? And so fast?"

"Oh, yes, I'm going tonight. My father and his whole branch of the family were killed because they didn't heed the warnings soon enough. My mother warned me, 'When you decide to move, in troubles related to war, move fast! Waiting even for one day can make you too late.'"

I took her out to Idlewild Airport, which was all too soon to have its name changed to Kennedy in memory of the slain President. I kissed her good-bye as she boarded her flight, and I never laid my eyes on that dear girl again.

7

Steuben Design Meetings

Design meetings at Steuben seemed casual enough to me, at first. As I studied the setting in the boardroom on the third floor, I thought of our occasional West Baffin Eskimo Co-operative meetings in the printmaking room, with a handful of Inuit artists in attendance, smoking and smiling. There the discussion usually centered around carving, printmaking, and the pleasures of hunting on firm ice during clear, windless days. They never mentioned the weeks of winter weather, with violent, bone-numbing winds. Cold was a subject rarely discussed. When I did mention the fact that it was cold in the raw workroom where we held our meetings, the oldest, wisest man, Kiaksuk, said, "*Uppinarani*, no wonder. Look at that big iron anvil under the table. You must know that anvil gives off cold just the way a stove gives off heat." After thinking about that for a while, I got my mind back to our Steuben meeting.

The first questions seemed light and easy. "What about Steuben's window designs?" There was an expectant pause around the table. "What do you think, Houston?" Arthur Houghton asked.

"Oh, the window designs. Ours look a bit cold and bare, too stiff and formal for me."

Lots of sly smiles around the boardroom table. No further comment on the windows.

New subject. "What about the back room behind the large showroom? What about the feeling back there?"

Dead silence at the table.

"Houston, what do you think?"

"I think it looks funereal, too casket-velvet gray. Why don't we try some rich red velvet on those walls, my favorite color, like the Morgan Library?" I added, knowing Arthur was mad for libraries, books, and J. P. Morgan.

The others looked at each other appalled, then stared at me again. Didn't I know that such decisions were to be made by Arthur and someone else in charge of window design and back showrooms? No, I didn't, and if so, why tempt me to give a bad answer? Understanding Steuben certainly did not come to me as quickly as I had hoped it would. Beneath the friendly veneer of local manners, New Yorkers guard their territory as boldly as a rough-legged hawk. This was no gentle Eskimo camp down here with everyone willing, even eager, to help each other. Hell, this was rougher than the army. It took me some time to understand that!

Arthur was President and what he said went at all times. At least, that gave the glass, the decor in the sales rooms, and the Steuben ads a unified image in what I believe will be well remembered as a notable era in the history of American advertising and of glassmaking.

I soon discovered that Arthur was such an overwhelming force that none of us designers ever bothered to fight each other. That was understood as unnecessary and would only have led to trouble. Everyone felt they had their own designing to do, and it affected no one else until judgment day. That came about once a month in the second floor library when we would gather with Arthur, Jack, and Sally to examine drawings of proposed designs for the following year and show glass test pieces we had made during our recent work session at the factory in Corning.

We designers were always free to experiment with any ideas of glass forms that we could imagine, then present them at design meetings in New York. What to say of my fellow designers at Steuben in the New York office? I came to like them all – in varying degrees.

Jack Gates, the Director of Design, after I came to know him, turned out to be one of my favorite persons in the world. He had been trained as an architect at Harvard, and at Arthur's request came to Steuben. I was his assistant. His sense of humor was, to my ear, one of the best imaginable. He hadn't designed any glass for years, and when Arthur asked him what he thought of all the monthly creations, he would invariably answer, "Well, . . . what do you think of it, Arthur? I'm with you."

Sally watched everyone's reactions carefully, but she rarely if ever disagreed. We all appeared of one mind in that elegant crystal and velvet setting. With a system like that, you can see why we in Design all got along together. As for the administrative part of the New York office, it seemed pretty much the same. And in Corning, the head of the factory would ask Arthur what he thought the cost of a particular piece of glass should be, then cry out, "Arthur, there's a coincidence. That price is exactly what the factory plans to charge!" It was the same with Public Relations and Advertising. Everything ran smoothly and I think far more sociably than is usually true when people are encouraged to be openly more competitive. Once I got used to the unspoken idea that my colleagues had territories to defend, we all got on with one another, more or less, like nomad hunters and the women in their Arctic hunting camp – at least that's how working in New York first seemed to me.

Steuben, like virtually all New York firms, used to give a large Christmas party. Amory Houghton, Chairman of the Board of Corning Glass, and his cousin, Arthur, would host the whole affair up in the 5th Avenue Club, an elegant space in the Steuben building next door to the present Trump Tower, with a wonderful penthouse view of that remarkable city. At the Christmas party, everyone who worked for Steuben in New York was welcome, and others were flown from Corning on the company plane to join us. It was difficult to get near the beautifully designed bar because of a double phalanx of glass packers from the basement who would gather there in a solid ring, drinking Dom Perignon champagne exclusively, and occasionally passing back a glass to one of the prettier girls who cleaned the offices. God knows I was seeing American democracy at work – except that as these parties peaked, the glass packers would start elbowing and jostling and calling the management and designers a lot of very unattractive names. These seasonal festivities finally got so out of hand that Houghton, who was too late to have the bartenders hide the hundred-dollar bottles of Dom Perignon, nevertheless canceled future Christmas parties. Wild Christmas parties, it was agreed, had caused a lot of divorces and car crashes before they started to ease off. It was the beginning of the end of an era in Manhattan.

8

Going up to Corning

A chauffeur-driven car arrived in front of my apartment at 6:30 in the morning. When the bell rang, I was in my underwear, trying to pack. My very different sense of Arctic timing was still running me.

The car had not been sent because this was Steuben's common method of transport. Oh, no, it arrived because of Arthur's firm conviction that I was completely confused by the city and had lost all my sense of direction, along with my sense of timing. Arthur believed that there was no way I would get to the New York Marine Terminal in time to catch the Corning plane unless I was nabbed and forced out of my apartment and put on the plane by his chauffeur, Ryan, an excessively punctual person.

What to do about the damned air conditioner in my apartment? It was going to be a boiling hot morning outside, but the apartment was nicely cool. I decided to leave the air conditioning on so that the place would remain comfortable, ready for my return three weeks later.

The plane flew north to the Finger Lakes region, and Jim Thurston, who was in charge of Steuben sales, met me at the small country airport that served the upstate towns of Corning and Elmira in western New York. He drove me to the factory, an amazing-looking building with a special long heat vent on the roof. Attached to that building is the Corning Museum, widely acknowledged to be the world's best glass museum.

The warm-hearted Thurston introduced me to Bob Levy, who was in charge of our factory. I realize now that over the years, Levy had seen lots of new designers like me. Some of them had lasted, others had not. At the time, he seemed busy, detached, and utterly uninterested in me. He was a baldheaded, snub-nosed, hard-driving man who looked all business in his short-sleeved white shirt and narrow necktie. His glasses reflected sharply as we shook hands.

"Where would you like me to start?" I asked him.

The glory hole

"I'll show you the blowing room floor first, let you get the feeling of the heat from the glory hole. Arthur warned me that you're fresh out of the Arctic. This should help to thaw your ass." When he laughed, he looked not at me, but at my new-found friend, Jim Thurston, who studied his shoes. (I learned right away that "the glory hole" was a centuries-old term to indicate the red-hot glass-maker's furnace. The opening of such a furnace is round to accommodate turning the glass.)

For the rest of that day, I hung awkwardly around the blowing room and then the adjoining cutting room, shifting my weight from one foot to the other, afraid to move around much, for dour-looking men were passing me with blowing irons whose tips still glowed a menacing, fiery red. Women in the cutting room wore bandanas round their heads, long rubber gloves, and rubber aprons. They edged carefully around me, carrying glistening, thousand-dollar crystal pieces. Everything there was water and fine clouds of sand-like pumice. The cutting room was where the glass was ground and polished. It was a strange stage set of a room. It looked like a Piranasi drawing with shafts of overhead light beaming down through the haze of pumice grinding compounds. The worker holding the glass to be cut angles it against one of the various grinding wheels, some of which are vertical, the others horizontal, all spitting wet and large as seventeenth-century corn-grinding stones.

Almost everything here would make you think of a much earlier era in glassmaking, and that was planned. Steuben wished to create their heavy-leaded Bavarian crystal in the traditional manner. Science seems to improve our lives or endanger us in surprising leaps. But that was not the way with Steuben. We do not have any evidence that our glass today is of significantly better design than glass created during the fifteenth-century German and Italian Renaissance. Our crystal, heavy and clear, presents a thrill and challenge for a combination of artisans working together to present something shining and desirable that will last for centuries.

9

The Glory Hole

When I first came to Corning, it was the beginning of summer and I was impressed with the fresh, lush green of northern New York State. It is a rolling, hilly country, with groves of pines and hardwoods. The Chemung River curves gracefully through the town south of the five Finger Lakes. It is even more spectacular in autumn, with flaming scarlet and yellow maples.

In the middle of Corning stood the Baron Steuben Hotel. I stayed there, sometimes for a month at a time, in the old days when I was learning glassmaking. Alas, the hotel has now been renovated into an office building. (This and a lot of other things have changed during the period that I came and went from Corning for almost forty years.)

Elsie, the waitress at the Baron Steuben, was the greatest permanent fixture that hotel ever had. She was a short, thin, pale-faced woman, old, but how old, I could not guess, for her hair was a vibrant henna red. Elsie was the absolute soul of motherly care and kindness. She had very little small talk, but a great deal of determination to see that Gates, Waugh, Thompson, Pollard, Houston, and any other designers staying at the hotel behaved right and ate right. We usually arrived off the plane from New York when the dining room was almost empty. If any one of us dared to order a second double martini or another double scotch, they'd get a thin single, no mistake about that, and it could easily take Elsie until coffee time to deliver it.

Gates would say, "Well, Elsie, tonight I'm going to have some beef, done medium, but not before I've had that second drink. Damn it, Elsie! Where is that drink?"

Elsie would nod, write nothing down, then ask me for my order. "I'll have the same, but rare, Elsie. I'm not kidding. I mean red rare."

She'd wrinkle her nose and look at me in utter disgust. "Eskimo culture," she'd grumble, then nod and write down nothing. Sometimes Jack would feel it necessary to order for Sidney Waugh, but she paid not the slightest attention.

Limping off favoring her arthritic hip, she would swing open the kitchen door and we could hear her call to the cook, "The gang's all here. Don't worry, I'm ordering for them. Mr. Gates, beef very well done. Mr. Houston's steak, cook it kinda medium, with no blood showing. Potatoes, peas, and a bit of bacon for Mr. Waugh, he won't eat it anyway. I'll get cognac and coffee for Mr. Pollard and for Mr. Thompson bourbon straight up. They're just in off Mohawk's evening plane. They're tired, and they all ate too many peanuts and had a drink or two along the way."

When Elsie died, we knew Corning and the Baron Steuben would never be the same without her.

In the mornings, it used to be my habit to rise early and walk along the street that led to the wide, concrete bridge spanning the Chemung River. Just to breathe the fresh air and to look up at the wide blue sky was great after the enclosed life of New York's tall buildings. At first, it seemed like a wild holiday to me, though I quickly grew fond of Manhattan and enjoyed it more and more.

As had been prearranged from New York, I shared the Steuben factory's one design office with John Dreves. He had been in residence there for a long time. His job was to control the quality of design after the designers had departed, and the decision had been made to create a certain number of pieces. Some designs Steuben made were one of a kind. There were others limited to two or three, or a dozen, or perhaps fifty or one hundred. Some pieces were unlimited. Whatever the head office decision on the limitation in numbers of a glass edition, it had to be strictly adhered to.

Arthur was immensely fond of architecture, as was Jack Gates, himself a trained architect, so they were both dead keen on applying architectural principles to every piece of glass. They insisted that every person even remotely concerned would receive tight, detailed blueprints of the glass. Sidney Waugh, who had received the *Prix de Rome* and was Steuben's most famous designer of that period, detested this over-formalized practice. His response was to order dozens and dozens of his blueprints, which he would then send to everyone, including the cleaning ladies and the workers in the packing room. All of this seemed strange to me since the gaffers at the glory hole themselves seemed to pay so little attention to these carefully drawn plans.

My early attempts at glass design were much sketchier. I made hundreds of rough drawings of pieces that I soon discovered might or might not be developed into glass. Some of them simply proved impossible to make. Part of this was because of my newness and the unique nature of clear glass. Because you can see right through it, many designs that might work in wood or clay or stone or metal would fail in glass. But, if luck is with you, the clarity of glass can make a design vibrant with the feeling of life because of the almost magical flow of ever-changing lights that emerges from within a solid piece of crystal.

At first, when I walked on the factory floor, I found myself driven off by the intense heat of the glory hole. Then I timidly approached again, clutching my sheaf of drawings. An amphitheater full of summer visitors watched us intently.

Hausler
Steuben 1962

"Wait, wait!" Jack Holtzman, the foreman, shouted. "They've just called from New York, saying you're to try out your first designs during the night shift – unless you want to use the back furnace where no one can see you."

I trudged sadly away from the visitors' gallery, still hoping that my first design would be sensational.

That night when I joined the shift, I learned that I was to work with Sammy Carlinio, a famous American-Italian "gaffer" – the head glassmaker of a four-man shop. Sammy showed me where to get my own coffee and to put five cents in a box to pay my share.

"What are we going to make?" Sammy asked me with a big smile. Then with the others in the shop, we started looking at my drawings of a polar bear.

"I picked this first because it's easy to make," I told them.

"May be hard to make," Sammy groaned. "Don't start thinking pieces that look small and easy are really easy. We'll see. How many minutes of glass do you want for this bear?"

"I don't know," I said. "You measure in minutes?"

"Yeah. You'll soon see. Here, this is small – not much glass needed. One and a half minutes," Sammy yelled to our bit gatherer. The furnace was roaring like a herd of walrus and glowing like a view of hell. I felt it melting me like grilled cheese.

The bit gatherer brought up a steel cup that would hold exactly one and a half minutes of glass and filled it from the ever-flowing, white-hot stream of molten glass. He stuck the five-foot pontil iron into the cup, pulled it out with the glass adhering to it, and handed it to Sammy.

Arctic Fisherman

Sammy quickly thrust the glass inside the roaring glory hole and started turning it, reheating it while singing his favorite aria from the opera *Carmen*. Sammy could sing really loud and he was at his best only when the glassmaking was going well. What a wonderful gaffer, what a wonderful person he turned out to be, so willing to help me learn the ancient skills of glass.

The intense heat in front of a glory hole in the old days, without overhead fans at noon on a summer's day, seemed intolerable, so hot that you could not perspire because the heat dries it too fast. At first, I marveled at these men who could take the heat, but, hell, in another way it's just like Inuit hunters being able to withstand cold. They get used to it and accept it.

My first attempt, the polar bear that had been so easy as I had drawn it on paper, turned out to be impossibly difficult! We tried again and again to shape its body as its head grew too red, too yellow, then too white-hot and drooped down like an icicle. Meanwhile, the bear's tail end, which had been stuck to another solid iron, grew so cold that it finally cracked off like an ice cube in a pan when you lift it out of a refrigerator into a hot kitchen. My polar bear just froze on its rear end, blew off, and smashed to pieces when it hit the floor.

Sammy stopped singing and said, "Well, Jamie, you've had your first try at glass. Let's try to make your dinosaur tomorrow. Don't worry, it's bigger and should be easier. You'll have better luck next time."

I had been afraid to start the dinosaur. It was a lot bigger than the bear and had four legs that Sammy called bits and a head to attach to the long, curved neck. I bought some children's Plasticine, and in my hotel room that evening, I made a model of the dinosaur to give it a full, round shape, to show Sammy in the morning.

"This big guy's going to be easier than that little bear," said Sammy. "How much glass do you want?"

I guessed, "Four minutes."

By the time Sammy got the glass from the stick-up boy, I was sweating like a distance runner and trying to ease away from the blast of heat emerging from the glory hole. During the reheat of the dinosaur's body, Sammy started singing again, this time "The Toreador's Song." Soon he had the glass out, swinging the iron like a drum major in a band, lengthening the glass then reheating it again, slowly moving it like a clock pendulum until we agreed that the body length looked just right.

In the end, this brontosaurus, though we made several of them, did not match my feelings or my model. So we knocked it off into the iron pan of hot, rejected glass. I would try again another day. Unless a piece of Steuben is good enough to display and sell, we always smash it and try to make another one. Sometimes we have to give up altogether and just go on to another design.

I O

Partial Eclipse

Steuben had sent out a request to some of America's finest poets, asking them to create a new poem from which Steuben designers would attempt to make a piece of glass reflecting the spirit of the poem. My first real challenge came when Houghton called from New York and asked me to pick a poem from among the works submitted.

I chose "Partial Eclipse," by the American poet, W. D. Snodgrass. I was to create in crystal the feelings that came to me from his poem. I thought hard about the visions that came to me when reading the poem and made endless drawings. Finally, an image forced its way into my mind. I imagined ancient human fear and wonder on seeing a solar or lunar eclipse up in the endless sky.

I showed my drawings of "Partial Eclipse" to Dreves in the design office in Corning. He shook his head. Steuben had never combined its glass with any other material. "Gold and glass. They'll never let you even try a thing like that."

Another telephone call came from New York, asking me what poem I planned to try. I told them I was wrestling with a new kind of design that might go with "Partial Eclipse." They warned me that

I'd better hurry. They wanted to include it in the exhibition. So I folded up and sent them my best version of "Partial Eclipse" drawings, clearly marking the twin figures behind the solid blank of glass, which I intended to be in gold. Gold at this time had long been pegged at thirty-five dollars an ounce. Soon after they received the drawing, Arthur called. "Go ahead. See if you can make it." *There*, I thought, *most people love the sight and sound of gold.* I told Dreves, who shook his head in disbelief, then scheduled a four-man shop for me next day at 6:00 a.m.

Sammy Carlinio was gaffer on the shop. The rest of the crew looked like they wished to God they were home in bed. I had a sheaf of drawings, but no one was in any way interested in seeing them. Suddenly, the gatherer reappeared and handed Sammy a gather of glowing glass on the end of a hollow blowing iron which he kept constantly turning in his hands. Sammy took it from him and thrust it in the glory hole, heaved a sigh, looked sadly at me, then removed the ever turning glass from the glory hole. How was he going to make this piece, I thought? He hasn't even seen my drawings.

Sammy gave a quick dart of breath into his end of the blowing iron, and suddenly, the round, solid glob of glass on the end of the iron ballooned. Sammy looked around, then shook it out by dangling the iron downwards and swinging it quickly back and forth. The glass elongated and became pear-shaped. He shoved it in the glory hole again, reheated it, and pulled it out. No joking now. The whole shop looked sad, except for the gatherer who remained like an Eskimo hunter, alert and watchful. What was he looking for? What was going on?

When Sammy withdrew the gather of glass this time, he wet his cherry paddle and started to flatten the bottom of this glass balloon.

"What are you making?" I shouted at him over the roar and heat of the glass furnace, for he had still not even glanced at my drawings.

"Wait a couple of minutes, you'll see," the bit gatherer growled in my ear.

I looked around. The sun was rising out through the eastern wall of windows. I had had no breakfast, and breakfast was my most important meal. This shift would end at 2:00 p.m., too late to go uptown for lunch. There were no fast food places in Corning yet. Dammit! Nothing was going as I had hoped it would.

Finally, Sammy readjusted his peak cap to shade his eyes. He looked into the intense heat of the glory hole, then pulled out the glass. Now he opened the stem end of the pear-shaped globe with the flattened bottom. Reaching in, he increased the size of the neck and shaped it carefully, almost reverently. Then, heating it again, he let it dangle, lengthening the neck.

"He's a big guy. That ought to fit him fine," the stick up shouted to Sammy as he carefully cracked off the glass.

The whole shop looked nervously around. The foreman had his back to them. The bit gatherer quickly dug a hole in the red box full of pure white sand, then carefully covered the new piece with his foot.

Urinal

"What the hell's that?" I yelled at Sammy.

He took me by the arm and led me away from the roar of the glory hole. "That's for Jimmy. The poor bugger's in the hospital. We don't know what's wrong with him, but glassmakers, they take care of each other. That's a kinda pisspot, you know, a urinal, they call them in the hospital. We always make a special one, you know, to fit the guy. Someone from the shop will take it up to him tomorrow after it cools. You don't say anything about that to the foreman. He knows we'll make one and send one up to Jimmy, but he's not supposed to know who did it. Come on, pal, it's time for a break. You don't wanna make any serious glass without first a cuppa coffee. You put a nickel in that paper cup over there and then pour yourself a cup outta that beat-up pot. I told my wife I was going to be working with you this morning and she sent you down her special bologna and pickle sandwich. Here, good, home-made garlic bread. You'll like it."

Oh, I felt better after the acid-tasting coffee and the real Italian sandwich that made up for it. *This is going to be all right*, I thought. *I'm working with men here who share their food like Inuit hunting companions. It's going to be fine.*

"Let's have a look at your drawings," Sammy said, and after we had examined them and talked about how to do it – with the others crowded round – we began to make it with Sammy, who suggested four minutes of glass.

Sammy Carlinio was a powerful man with broad shoulders and bulging biceps. He needed all his strength to hold onto such a weight of glass at the end of a long iron bar for up to forty-five minutes; that requires both muscle and determination. *Partial Eclipse* was to be a solid gather, no air blown inside.

One of the interesting aspects of making glass is that the piece you're working on must be in constant turning motion. The hot glass only remains on the iron because it is held there by centrifugal force. This means that as it starts to stretch and take shape, anyone working with lead crystal must be prepared to think fast and make instant decisions. I have always enjoyed making very fast sketches from life, of animals or humans. That, I believe, is why hot glass suits me well.

After the glass had been laid on a charred, wet cherry board, after many reheats, we finally managed, with the aid of a flat, wet cherry paddle, to shape the piece to match my drawing. When we tried to measure the piece of hot glass near the paper, it burst into flames, and I lost my eyebrows. (Those were the days before safety glasses were mandatory.) We carefully laid the piece inside the kiln to slowly cool. It was to be two days before we removed it from the kiln and I could see what we had made.

I had met a goldsmith in New York, and over lunch I had explained my plans to use gold in *Partial Eclipse*. He recommended I do my metal sculptures in lost wax, and he gave me some. I shaped and sculpted two human figures, using much the same methods as the Inuit stone carvers. I took this hard wax sculpture, the size of the first joint of your thumb, to him for casting. When I got it back,

I searched to find a hardware store – no easy task in midtown Manhattan. Finally, I discovered a good one, where I bought some ordinary files and emery paper and started to file and shape, then polish the figures.

Now, with the glass safely cooled and looking fine, I could hardly wait to fix the 18K. gold to the glass and set the finished piece in a proper light. When I did this, I was thrilled with the look of the clear crystal and gold materials shining so richly together. Arthur and Jack said I was the first Steuben designer to combine glass and metal in this way. *Partial Eclipse* glowed like magic when I set it on a light box. The piece, exhibited with all the others, was quickly sold. I hated to see it disappear into some household somewhere, never to be seen again by me.

II

Glassmakers

Master gaffers of a shop, who shape the hot glass, are, I have observed, men of very quick natures, by instinct fast and nervous. They talk fast, smoke fast, gulp their coffee, and maybe bite their nails. Accomplished glass engravers, on the other hand, are inclined to be slow and thoughtful. You ask one of them a question and they may take a while to think it over before they answer. Copper wheel engraving is itself a slow and lengthy process. Both gaffers and engravers are craftsmen, each determined to achieve their own special goals. Fifty hours on a single glass design is common to the engraver, with little room for error. With the gaffer at the glory hole, it's one great, creative, rhythmic rush before the glass can freeze up at the iron and crack off onto the floor. If the piece is good, it is treated like a treasure; if not, it is thrown away and another one is quickly undertaken.

JHouston 62

Before my time, a great Czechoslovakian glassmaker had come to work at Steuben. Joe was a legendary figure admired by highest management as he was by the shop men and designers. Even the floor sweepers respected this man as the absolute best. He was in some ways perceived as a kind of Robin Hood. He tolerated no foolishness, nor could he be suppressed by dukes or kings, for he had boundless talent and an uncertain disposition, with no patience for fools of any rank.

If this master gaffer were working on a piece of glass and any member of his shop failed to pay attention during the fast, exciting period before the final crack-off, he would stop and raise his blowing iron high above his head, then slam it down onto the concrete floor, causing the iron to hop from end to end, tolling like a church bell, while the broken glass flew everywhere. Then, without a word and bright red in the face, Joe would fling his tools into his box, snatch up his lunch pail, and march off the blowing room floor. Still stiff with rage, he would bicycle home.

For several days, they said, no one in Joe's household would dare to answer the telephone. Then, only after several diplomatic visits from the blowing room foreman to his home, would this great gaffer finally agree to reappear at the glory hole.

You had to be a world-class gaffer to pull off a temper tantrum like that, then continue to be admired by all for holding to your own high glassmaking standards in a very imperfect world.

Leonard Parker was an excellent gaffer of relatively even temperament. He was a splendid, homegrown American glassmaker, who was anything but a common occurrence in the world of fine glass. He was a lean man of medium height, naturally somewhat nervous, with abundant talent, not a raw, wild nature, but a sober man. He understood the qualities of glass not in a scientific way, but in the way of an inspired master craftsman.

We worked together in front of the glory hole several days a month for over a dozen years before he retired. Leonard's wife used to telephone me in New York. The thrust of her conversation would go like this:

"I suppose you've already made your drawings, Jim, and you know what you're going to try to make with Leonard when you're up in Corning this time?"

"Yes, I've got lots of drawings, Marge. Maybe one or two of them will work."

"Well, Jim, will you do me a favor?"

"Sure . . ."

"Promise me you won't tell Leonard. I know he'll telephone you and ask what you're planning to make, what the piece is going to look like. That's enough to set him off, Jim. Leonard will start that very night wandering up and down the hall. I'll see him pass the bedroom door, twisting his wrists, pretending he's got the glass on his pontil iron, calling out to his stick up for the bits, making and remaking that piece. Promise me you won't even give him a hint, Jim. Will you do that for me, please?"

"Don't worry, Marge, I won't tell him all that much."

But when Leonard phoned, I could never resist. When I arrived on the blowing room floor at 5:40 a.m. after walking from the Baron Steuben – unable to find any breakfast at that hour – Leonard would be fussing around in front of the glory hole, rooting in his work box, laying out the various tools he planned to use. Most of the tools had been handmade by him; others were made by Corning, but reshaped to each gaffer's requirements. He would nod at me, but give no other sign of recognition. I would draw off a paper cup of poisonous-tasting coffee left over from the night shift, then go into the little side room off the hall used by the designers when up in Corning, almost always at different times. There I would unroll my drawings, sit down, and nervously re-examine them, my excitement rising, wondering which one of them I dared try first.

Leonard would come in with Jimmy, his bit gatherer. They'd light cigarettes and without comment stare over my shoulder at the drawings as I shuffled through the best ones, wanting to hear their reaction. Usually Jimmy would snort and I'd turn and look at him.

"Well, that fuckin' thing's impossible to make!" he'd say.

"The hell it is," Leonard would say. He was always as hopeful as I was. "Where are we going to stick it up to put the tail on?"

Leonard would ask, then say, "Oh, I know. You keep your eyes open, Jimmy. You might learn something today."

Those were the days before Steuben used a spot heat torch, and we both knew Jimmy might be right. Some pieces were just impossible to make. Quite often we'd try and fail, but try again. After the ten o'clock lunch break, we'd approach the problem in a different way and succeed or fail. For me, the real excitement came when we were ready to take the glass out of the glory hole for the final shaping and the last reheat.

If everything had gone just right, Leonard would hold the piece upright on the end of the iron for us and the ring of glassmakers who had gathered to take a final look. Hot glass gives off a kind of magical sparkle and may not ever look quite that fine again.

Leonard would look at Jimmy, who would say, "Jesus, I never thought you'd make it!"

"Yes, we're going to keep that one!" I'd say.

Sammy Carlinio had come to America with his parents when he was young. He was a bombastic glassmaker, with the flamboyant nature of an Italian opera singer. He would sometimes cross himself before we started to make a major piece, and he often sang loudly while he was forming the glass. Sammy, as a gaffer, was always friendly to his ever-changing helpers that made up the shop around his glory hole, and was never very demanding of his men. He would sing grand arias, reheat, and wait. Sammy perhaps didn't really feel in full control. He seemed to think that glassmaking was a divine art beyond any of us mortals and that God would, if He saw fit, allow something miraculous to flow into the glass.

Once we had a new Czechoslovakian glass engraver at the Steuben factory, a giant of a man who had been asked to come to Corning. He understood no English and was completely deaf and dumb. A young woman came with him. She spoke both Czech and English and had promised to help him get established in a small apartment in Corning. She remained with him for a week or so, coming each day to Steuben's engraving room to interpret for him, since he could lip-read in Czech, but no other language. I was there when she kissed him good-bye and tearfully asked us all to help him whenever we could.

In a strange way, he seemed to help all of us. He had a shy, warm smile and such a gentle eagerness to make contact and learn that he soon became everyone's friend. And, of course, he was already an outstanding copper wheel engraver and was acquiring more knowledge about North America every day. It was probably the combination of his smile, huge size, gentleness, and perhaps his silence that captured everyone. Too much talk can be a troublesome thing. He made quick drawings to explain himself, a method I, too, had utilized early in my speechless days among the Inuit, when I found that sketches can explain almost every need.

12

Manhattan Work Ethics

A lot of different things about New York amazed me, none more than the enthusiasm with which Americans took up an idea. They had hope, and dreams, and drive! I was a great student of all the marvelous, ever-changing articles to be seen in shop windows along Madison Avenue as I walked to work most mornings, for I hoped to grab some indirect idea or inspiration from them. Occasionally, I'd see something from an entirely different material that might be converted to a successful idea in glass. Lots of the inspirations I received would not possibly convert to glass because of the nature of the material. But, still, a good idea might be twisted around until it worked.

If I already had a glass idea in mind, I would turn east a block to Park Avenue so I could think. There are few shops on Park Avenue and even fewer interesting people. In the morning, it is a place of no distractions, a perfect street on which to mentally develop new designs.

At my drawing board during the day, I would try to create and re-create sketches of this new, and I hoped, exciting object to be. If the idea definitely would not work in glass, I would sometimes say to a likely person at one of the clubs, "What do you think of this idea?" I'd pull a drawing of it from my pocket and explain it.

"Come look at this," that man would say to a friend. "Do you think you could make a thing like this in production?"

"Damned right, and I know just the person who could sell it. Would you be willing to split the profits three ways? I know a decent lawyer who could help us draw up a contract."

"Let's try it!"

Now I have also heard lots of conversations like that in Canada. Next morning, I thought, well, that was fun to discuss, but it's probably the last I'll ever hear from them.

But this was New York. By 10:00 a.m. next morning, the people in last night's conversation started to call me. "Are you making progress with the design?" they asked. "Are you thinking more about the materials and the patenting?" They explained that the lawyer they'd talked about, a Harvard man, had already started on a rough draft of a contract. "Could we test, and try to market that idea this year?"

In Canada, almost nothing ever worked like that for me. Some good ideas in many fields were bandied about as possibilities and usually ended with the question, "Where the hell would we ever raise the money? Certainly not the banks!"

What a damned pity. Much of the reason that so few ideas and products are developed there is because of a lack of belief, a lack of drive and a too-tight fist on money. Canadians usually have to borrow money from someone in the United States, and that often has huge strings attached. Our New York schemes didn't always work, but they usually led to something rewarding. The greatest sin of all is not to try.

13

Museums

"Be sure to take a day off every week to visit the museums here in New York, especially the Metropolitan Museum," Arthur told me. "Go and introduce yourself to the Director. I've told him you'll be coming soon. Soak up all you can. These collections belong to you, to all of us. Enjoy them. Learn from them."

That was music to my ears. I had been too long away from museums. Taking some time off to visit galleries and museums had long been a ritual with Steuben designers in the fifties and sixties, and I eagerly fell in with the custom.

I had grown up in Toronto when my father had been very keen on taking me to the Royal Ontario Museum. It was gray-stoned and large, very dignified, with many suits of armor, which I liked. After standing and admiring one, I would walk what seemed like half a block past almost pictureless walls to stop and admire another suit of armor. The Royal Ontario Museum was a very sterile museum in those days, with none of the tax-free gifts of pictures and other collected rarities that had been the making of all the great American museums. But I'm pleased to say that the Royal Ontario Museum collection of Eskimo and Indian artifacts and art was very exciting to me, as was the great Oriental collection amassed by Bishop White, a Canadian missionary who worked in China.

But the Met was overwhelming, the size of its collections vast. I felt that I could never get enough of it. When I told Arthur that, he said, "Time for you to go to the Frick, the National Gallery in Washington, to Williamsburg, and further afield. I'd like to suggest the Green Vaults, but they're behind the Iron Curtain in East Germany." (Arthur had for a period right after the war been curator of the Rare Books Division at the Library of Congress in Washington and was considered perhaps the leading rare book collector in the United States.) Arthur told me I should educate myself. "Go to the major museums," he said, "concentrate on the visual arts, the Philadelphia Museum and Boston, the Fogg and the Peabody at Harvard, the Field Museum in Chicago." As President of the Metropolitan Museum, Arthur gave me introductions to directors or curators all the way. Finally, I traveled, with Steuben's blessing, to the DeYoung Museum in San Francisco and the County Museum in Los Angeles. It was all a great education.

I was put up as a member of the Grolier Club in New York, an especially fine place to give a party on a Saturday afternoon, where you could invite all your friends, and in that bachelor way acknowledge with thanks so many dinner parties. I became a member of the Council there and even helped mount one of its exhibitions, "Jesuit Relations," a subject that had always interested me.

One of my favorite quotes is by Father Jerome Lalemant, *The Jesuit Relations*, 1659, describing the Iroquois:

They come like foxes
through the woods.
They attack like lions.
They take flight like birds,
disappearing before
They have really appeared.

14

The Magnetic North

The Canadian army and Inuit in the Arctic managed to permanently instill in me the habit of rising early. Inuit got up early not only to relieve their kidneys, but to gauge the wind and weather outside. There they would make their judgment whether to go hunting or go back to bed and wait for a more favorable day.

In the spring of my second year in New York, I was comfortably installed in my lower half of a brownstone on East 69th Street near the Hungarian church. My clock said 5:00 a.m. and I was awakened by a strange sound that I thought must be the tail end of a dream. I could hear them, maybe twenty of them, coming up from the East River. I leapt out of bed and ran to my front door, jerked it open, and ran out into the middle of the empty street in my pajamas. There, not high above me, was a flock of more than a dozen Canada geese. Perhaps nervous of the buildings on either side of them, they had not formed a wedge, but they continued straight west along 69th Street until they crossed 5th Avenue. *Did they land on the pond in Central Park*, I wondered, my mind still clinging to their rich, double-pitched, honking sounds. *Never mind*, I thought, as I walked back into the apartment, my slippers flopping. *Those Canadas, those plump, cool weather lovers are heading north again along the coast of Arctic Quebec and Baffin Island to nest. By God, I'll tell Linda I'm going north with them.* And I did!

Arthur Houghton had said in asking me to come south and work that he thought it would prove immensely difficult for me. And in some ways he was right. He told me I should go north any time that I felt the compulsion to go, and that I need inform no one but the wonderful big Linda, our head secretary in Design, telling her that I had gone north again and would be back when I got back. Imagine any company as thoughtful as that! They never even docked my pay, but hoped I would return with new ideas for glass.

I returned to the Arctic twenty-six times over the next thirty-six years, thanks to organizations like the Canadian Eskimo Arts Council, the Canada Council, Paramount Pictures, the Glenbow-Alberta Museum, the American Indian Art Center, and *Polaris*, a Swedish tour ship that plied the Arctic from Spitsbergen, to Iceland, to Greenland, to Baffin Island, and on to Walrus Island in western Hudson Bay.

The brownstone on East 69th was only eighteen blocks from work – counting both uptown and cross-town blocks. I walked briskly between the two places each morning, unless it was unbearably hot, raining, or snowing really hard. Walking is a sure way to stay warm, and wearing a wool suit makes it unnecessary to wear an overcoat. Wind is not at all the problem in New York that it is in the Arctic, since by picking the right streets and the right side to walk in midtown, you can remain protected from the wind by the large buildings. Nevertheless, friends at work and some people in the street did view me, coatless in midwinter, as a crazed outsider. But one good thing about Manhattan Island is that the people working there are hardened to all kinds of outlandish behavior. If you fall down in the street heart-struck or dead drunk, they have learned to step over you or walk around you to avoid causing themselves delay, or worse than that, perhaps a lawsuit if they do become involved.

Taxi cabs in those days were not expensive, but in other ways they were a challenge, worse in my mind than any rain or wind or snow. During rush hour traffic, it would take me fourteen minutes to walk to work and on average as much as twenty-two minutes if I took a cab. The Vietnam War was beginning in earnest, with incredibly bloody TV pictures on the morning news. If I got a cab, I would often have to sit in a dense fog of cheap cigar smoke and listen to the driver's violently expressed views on the U.S. government. I often yelled at the driver, demanded to be let out, then paid and walked the rest of the way, trying to put my morning thoughts in order.

Once, just after the new year in 1964, I was hurrying to work along East 58th when I was stopped cold in my tracks by one of the world's most deliciously pungent odors. Someone had thrown a match or cigarette butt into a trash can and had set afire a small pine Christmas tree. I stood there, inhaling the sweet, burning smell of the needles as they gave off their acrid smoke and filled me with memories of that familiar, sub-Arctic wilderness that stands in silence west of Hudson Bay.

To hell with this, I thought. *I'm going north again. The sun will be coming back there in a month or so. What in the name of God am I waiting for?*

I waited until March to go back to Baffin Island, this time with the Canadian Eskimo Arts Council. We stayed a while at Kingait, my old, beloved home, but I realized that there it could never be the same again for me. For the first time, I saw myself as an awkward outsider in Abercrombie & Fitch store-bought clothing and clumsy white military snow boots, something between a New Yorker and a country bumpkin.

I have seen huge changes in the Arctic over the last fifty years from the days when a government icebreaker came to deliver mail and X-ray health services once a year, to check on the Hudson's Bay post settlements, and to do instant dentistry – extractions only, no time for fillings. Today there are small airstrips and weekly, ski-wheel flights into most of the Arctic communities. Has this made it better or worse? If you had known it the way it used to be, I'm sure you, like everyone else, would have preferred it in the old style. But the Arctic is not a museum, nor its people native-dressed, historical dummies. Everyone has to get along with life more or less as it comes flying at us.

The dog teams have all but disappeared, replaced now by snowmobiles, with an amazing impact on the walrus population that I'll explain later. Flying in and out of the Arctic in that middle period between the early 1960s and 1990s was a very expensive game, and pilots on charter in small planes usually landed on the ice where they would hop out, shudder, stomp on the ice, then check their wristwatches and ask whether you planned to stay thirty minutes or a full hour. Even the Mounted Police pilots hated risking their planes by staying overnight. So I was more than grateful to any government or film project that could fly or ship me into the country and back out again, if only to try and catch what was left of the savor of the old life again.

15
Oscar

Even in the early sixties, fundraisers for American museums, zoos, and arboretums had begun to brush up their techniques. They had discovered that to write a form letter that begins "Dear Friend of the Animals (or Fish or Flowers)" will not guarantee a check for thousands of dollars in the return mail.

How to get at those sometimes generous people? Arthur Houghton was generous, but he was not a man likely to leap up and trek out to some local zoo. The Arctic, yes. Africa, certainly. But not a nearby zoo.

Well, how about Houston? He works with Arthur. They're friends. They fish at Boca Grande with the other friends.

So it came about that George Merck, an important fundraiser for the Bronx Zoo and also a friend, called to ask me if I would go out to visit a creature at the zoo. He assured me that Dr. Carelli, the Director, would be there to greet me. Was 8:30 in the morning, before the zoo opened to the public, too early for me? Dr. Carelli asked in our telephone conversation. He assured me he had something that was rare and remarkable for me to see. "We'll send a car to meet you at 8:00 a.m.," he said.

It was a dank, foggy morning when I arrived at the zoo. Dr. Carelli, an enthusiastic mammologist, took time out for a swift cup of coffee before we left his office and hurried through a concrete tunnel thick with that stale urine smell of incarcerated animals. Then, thankfully, we were in the open air again.

"There he is," cried the director. "There's Oscar! He's new here. You'll be seeing photos of him in the newspapers."

On the opposite edge of a large, round, concrete basin lay Oscar, a young walrus pup, just sprouting tusks and weighing perhaps five or six hundred pounds. Oscar raised his head and studied both of us with interest.

"Oscar, *ciao!*" Dr. Carelli called. "He may mistake us for the man who feeds him!" He smiled and clapped his hands. "We've come to visit you, *carissimo*," Dr. Carelli called.

Oscar's answer was like a choirboy starting high, then throttling down to a deep-throated grunt as he started trustingly across his concrete pool toward us. I was reminded of the large herds of walrus I had seen lying together on drifting ice or hauled out to rest on the smooth rocks that had been polished by the ancient Arctic glaciers eons ago. The walrus I used to know had been nervous at the very sight of mankind, for they had always been hunted by Inuit for food. Later, they had been pursued by the insatiable American and Scottish whalers more than a century ago when the whalers had killed almost all the big whales and continued to search for smaller whales and walrus oil.

Oscar

But this young walrus, Oscar, knew no fear. He loved people. In fact, I was told he was bonded to the keeper who fed him. Oscar came swimming and grunting toward us, landed, and raised up on his elbows to look me squarely in the eye. His clam-seeking moustache was nothing but a youthful stubble, and from a foot away, his breath smelled like a nearly fresh clam broth.

I was impressed by Oscar's friendliness. But this attempt to stand so tall on his elbow joints with his front flippers splayed wide soon proved tiring for him. Oscar gave another grunt and flopped down onto his ample belly. That was when the worst thing happened. As he came down, one of his small, banana-sized, ivory tusks caught inside the pocket of my new English trenchcoat. Oscar and I started tussling with each other, both overeager to correct this small mistake, but our timing made that simple act impossible, and Mr. Asquith's sewing refused to give a stitch.

I think Oscar was the first to realize the fix that we were in. He gave a desperate grunt, then panicked. So did I. Showing off his superior strength, Oscar turned and dragged us both, hopping up and down together, toward his slippery, disc-shaped, concrete pool. The water at its center was probably not above my head, but plenty enough to do me in, I judged.

As we bounced together into the water. Dr. Carelli raced after us, yelling in Italian and tugging at my trenchcoat belt. Oscar would hump up and lunge forward. I would hump down and try to lunge backward on top of Dr. Carelli. Oh, how I dreaded going further into Oscar's woklike pool, and I was already crotch-deep in very cold water. Suddenly, a stroke of Inuit cunning hit – or was it New York street smarts? When Oscar goes up, try going down and side-ways. On the next jump, it worked! I felt one last, tremendous tug at my pocket. Oscar's tusk jerked free, and he dove into the deepest center of his pool and lay there, holding his breath much longer than I ever could. Dr. Carelli half dragged me, wet to the waist, back to his office to cling to his radiator and drink more coffee.

We are always getting hell from the professional environmen-talists and wildlife types who still send people like me masses of those mindless form letters about saving every bird, animal, and fish in the world. Forty years ago when I was, among other things, a Game and Fisheries Officer for the Northwest Territories, walrus greatly feared the approach of man and would not willingly allow you within rifle shot of them. In recent years, however, I have returned to the Arctic aboard *Polaris*, from which the passengers, with an environmentalist, would put out in rubber Zodiacs. To my amazement, we could cruise almost close enough to touch the walrus, ignoring the huge bull as he gave us red-eyed glares and grunts in case we even thought of wooing away the chubby females in his harem.

Who or what had brought about this wondrous change? Well, you might say North Americans did by exporting snowmobiles into the Arctic. Eskimo families and their big dog teams must have jointly consumed perhaps a thousand tons of walrus meat each winter in the eastern and central Arctic. No game officer had to order this to halt. It just stopped. The dog teams that had been so all important to Inuit food-gathering societies had been the very measure of a successful man, and had suddenly faded into history. The arrival of the snowmobile about 1963-4 must have felt exactly like the appearance of the automobile. This new, bright yellow mechanical toy of every Arctic family's choice needed gasoline, not walrus meat, to feed it.

There were other effects. Gasoline flown into Arctic settlements then cost more than five dollars a gallon, twenty times what it cost in New York. The hunters who were able to purchase one of these motor-driven wonders began to contemplate other ways of surviving to afford the gas to run them. Why not an increased trade in their carvings? Not in walrus ivory, but in stone or ancient whale bone abandoned by the foreign whalers. So that change from walrus meat to gasoline started to direct Inuit energies toward carving. It quickly drew them in from their remote, seal-hunting fiords to the newly developing settlements. The dog teams disappeared as quickly as the chainsaw scream of the snowmobiles increased. Next thing you know, Canada, like Fairbanks, Alaska, will have presented their once totally self-sufficient hunting families with smog.

16

Excalibur

Pictures of King Arthur and his famous sword, Excalibur, were in my head before I could read. Families do this for their children perhaps as part of some ancient storytelling tradition. I remember days at our summer cottage when dark clouds would appear and the north wind went wild. This "three-day blow" was often accompanied by cold rain. Several of my friends would gather at our cottage, or the Burgess', or Sheriff's cottage. These three mothers were known to us as willing and imaginative readers. My Aunt Mary, who lived in Beaverton, was an author as well as a good storyteller, but she lived too far along the edge of the lake. So the local mother readers, especially in bad weather, always won.

King Arthur I remember now through the wonderful illustrations of N. C. Wyeth. For me, at the heart of that grand legend stands the image of the sword Excalibur, magically held in the anvil stone. Even much later, during the war, I dreamed of it. Had the true sword rusted? Was its blade tipped on an angle, or had it been driven straight down in the stone? What was the trick to it?

Even as I was preparing to leave the Arctic to go to New York and start making glass, I tried to imagine and make small sketches of various objects I hoped to make. One of the first ones, I thought, would certainly be Excalibur. Actually, I'm glad I waited. *Excalibur* was the third piece I attempted and proved to be so difficult that it almost broke my heart. It was the first time that I had ever worked with the great gaffer, Leonard Parker. Perhaps because of the extreme difficulties involved in trying to create this piece, we two drank far too much black coffee at 5:30 a.m. and became lifelong friends.

My drawings of *Excalibur* had always shown it as a solid piece of crystal, which I preferred to blown glass. This would represent the anvil stone. That shape was not too difficult to make, but would take some serious cutting later. As for the sword, I had been up studying broadswords in the armory room of the Metropolitan Museum. I made many drawings of the ones that I preferred, finally selecting an impressive, two-handed, English broadsword. I thought there would be nothing to the trick of sticking a small copper sword blade into the hot glass. Oh, how wrong I was!

Working together, Parker and I tried to perform this task twenty times. But the hot, molten glass would dent in, as when you stick your finger into a jar of honey, and would then sag completely out of shape as the test sword was withdrawn.

I was, at first, encouraged, and I took the best (though distorted) glass stone to experiment on, and had concave cuts made on one side. I took the idea in to a design meeting in New York. I set my miniature model of a broadsword in the hole, its hilt now bound with shining brass to represent the 18K. gold that I intended to use. Arthur and Jack Gates were excited by this piece. Arthur, perhaps because of his name, had always been attracted to the Arthurian legend. I explained the problems that still remained, making them sound easier than they were. The two of them urged me to keep trying, and during the following week I flew back to Corning.

On the early morning shift, Parker and I launched into what seemed like a marathon of endless attempts, and we failed in them all. We worried about the temperature of the glass. I searched the Corning Museum to find other examples of metal penetrated into glass, but found none. We stuck to the glory hole that was farthest from the viewers' gallery. We made about sixty attempts, mostly on the early or late shifts where viewers could not watch our endless parade of failures.

Quite often, Arthur would call the factory or the Baron Steuben Hotel where I stayed to ask how *Excalibur* was progressing. Being always hopeful, I would answer, "Fine, we'll probably get it right tomorrow." We hadn't by the time I returned to New York City for the weekend, after more than a hundred tries. The breakthrough we needed refused to come. The waste glass barrels were full. Other gaffers, servitors, and stick ups, who often came to watch us, shook their heads and offered their best advice, but nothing worked.

Late one night on my next trip to Corning, I sat drinking black and bitter coffee from a waxy paper cup as I stared into the hellish heat of the glory hole. An old sweeper passed me, pushing his broom. This man, who had been a gaffer once, had taken mandatory retirement at sixty-five, but he liked to stick around. He paused and nodded to me. "You're never going to get that in and out of there the way you're trying to do it, son."

I watched the wax form like thin ice on the surface of my awful coffee, in no mood to take wild-eyed advice from the floor sweeper.

"You listen to me, sonny, I'll tell you something," he said. Then, bending on his broom, he whispered in my ear.

"I didn't get all that," I shouted over the roar of the furnaces.

He bent again and whispered once more, ending with the words, "Try that, my boy. I'll stay to see if you get it right."

What he had whispered to me was a method I would never have dreamed of trying, for it was so utterly different. When Parker returned, I told him. He shook his head, but nodded politely to the old guy. He, too, had little hope, but we decided to try it.

The method the old man suggested was in no way complicated. We were both shocked when it worked like magic the very first time we tried it. We looked around to congratulate him, but he had moved off, pushing his broom. We tried it three more times. It worked, worked, worked! We had it. Not everyone at Steuben was as delighted as I was, for this piece marked a watershed, the true beginning of a whole line of glass that came to be called "major ornamental."

We slightly altered the way of making this piece, but in essence the breakthrough had come from the idea of that old man. At our request, the parent company, Corning, suitably rewarded him for his innovative idea. It is still one of Steuben's two best sellers and its method one of our best-kept secrets.

Tapio Verkola, the famous glass designer for the company of Arabia in Finland, stated at an international glass conference that no one had ever imitated Steuben's penetration of the sword Excalibur into glass because it is simply an impossible feat. He and many other glassmakers had tried many times and failed. Now that sounded to me as though we were getting back to the ancient, magical legend of that first Excalibur.

Arthur had a passion for boxes. Once I conceived of the idea of adding a piece of gold or silver to Steuben glass, he said, "We're going to give these pieces a whole new category. We're going to call them major ornamentals, and since they sometimes separate into two pieces, glass and metal, as in the case of *Excalibur*, they are going to require a box. What kind of box should it be?" he asked me.

"I don't know," I told him. "I'll have to think about that."

Later, I was in Alanson Houghton's office in the Steuben Sales Department. He offered me a cigar from a very elaborate leather cigar box that his father, the CEO of Corning Glass, had given him.

I had stopped smoking and declined the cigar, but asked if I could borrow his green box with the delicate gold trim. I hurried up to Arthur's office and said, "Here's the new major ornamentals box."

"Just the thing," he said, opening it. "We'll have to change the inside. Velvet, I think, and they all should be red. Royal red."

That's the way it happened – with quite a bit of opposition from others in Steuben, for those boxes proved expensive. No going off to Mexico to have them made. In Steuben, we tried to have as many things as possible American-made, and these boxes, too, were homegrown, made by a small box factory in nearby New Jersey that curved the lids and did the elegant gold tooling exactly to our taste.

The best antique dealers explain that fine objects, collectors' items, (for example, an elegant, two-hundred-year-old pair of engraved dueling pistols), are much more valuable today if they are in their original leather case. A century from now, the same will apply to Steuben glass inside those handsome, velvet-lined, gold-clasped boxes.

17

A Red-Hot Iron

The pontil iron, with its end still red-hot, carried so casually across the blowing room floor, always caught my attention and made me watchful. Some glassmakers said it was a joke. Others whispered that it was a threat. If any gaffer was thought to work overtime during a break or at the end of a shift, the long, red-hot iron would come his way and someone carrying it might cause its glowing end to pass too close to the gaffer's hand. A serious burn to that hand might mean his skill in forming glass would be ruined forever. I discovered that the glassmakers had a long iron convincingly painted and glass-covered until it appeared red-hot and dangerous. What would the Eskimos have thought of a trick like that, I wondered. It would be like pointing a loaded rifle too close to someone and considering that a joke. It would never have happened.

Houston
1964

My friend, Leonard Parker, as a very highly skilled gaffer, believed that he deserved to earn a higher wage for his work. So did Steuben management. But, as in so many other union work situations, if the company raises one gaffer's wage because he is especially clever and energetic on the job, then every other gaffer, regardless of skill, must move up to his pay level, which may be altogether unwarranted. What to do?

Finally, we took Parker into management, where we could pay him what we wished. The only problem was that Parker was no longer allowed to be a gaffer and to work the glass himself. He could only advise the other gaffers, which he said didn't work at all – for them or for him.

Finally, he said he missed working with the glass so much he planned to quit. He did and worked on his own for a while making "art glass." Then he decided to return. "I'm going back, yeah," he told me, "back onto the blowing room floor with the rest of the guys to be a gaffer again. It's right for me." He did exactly that, almost until he died.

18

The Angel Project

"How much thought have you given to angels?" Houghton asked me. "I'd like to do a Steuben angel project."

I pondered that for a bit. "Not a lot. I've seen a good-looking painting of a Reubens Gabriel somewhere," I said, "probably in the Louvre."

"Was Gabriel high in the order of angels?" he asked.

"Well, sure, I suppose so. Most people have heard of him."

Houghton nodded. "What makes you so sure Gabriel is a him? Some say all angels are asexual. He could be a she."

"I don't know," I answered, hoping he would change the subject before it turned out to be one of those mornings comprised of his pre-thought-out questions and my dumb answers.

"Mortimer Adler's in town, came in from California last night. He's the Director of the new *Encyclopedia Britannica*. Mortimer knows a helluva lot about a lot of things. I'm taking him to lunch at the club. Come along, you can query him."

"I don't know all that much about angels," Mortimer admitted, "but I know the very man who does, Professor Gustav Davidson. And he lives right here in town. You'll like him."

"You phone him this afternoon," Houghton told me.

Mortimer duly introduced me to Professor Davidson, a white-haired, smiling, friendly man who asked me to join him and his wife for dinner at their apartment in the Village on Saturday evening. What a wonderful dinner we had as he made the hierarchy of angels unfold their wings and reveal their superhuman qualities to me. He was at work on his definitive book on the subject, *Dictionary of Angels*, and showed me a chart of the angels standing in ever-rising circles one order above the others. At the bottom were the angels, and just over them the archangels. Then, still higher, the angels called principalities, powers, virtues. Above them were dominions and over them thrones, then, surprisingly, cherubim and on top of all, the seraphim – described as having six wings in fire.

I had almost given up churchgoing during the war and I certainly knew almost nothing about angels. I didn't even know of seraphim, and here I was at home that night with my borrowed book that described the ancients seeing a seraph with six burning wings riding on a white horse along the cloudy slopes of heaven. I was hooked, as I told Arthur next day.

"What do the churches think of angels?" Arthur asked. "Why don't you have Bill Chase, the rector from St. James's Church, for lunch at the club and ask him what he thinks of angels?"

When I explained the angel project to Bill, an Episcopalian, he sighed, "Angels are very difficult, you know."

I didn't know.

"They stand outside, beyond the control of any popes, cardinals or archbishops, beyond the churches. Angels do whatever they like."

The church, I learned, does not choose to encourage angels,

usually avoids mentioning them, and much prefers saints. Saints are dead, their honors given by the popes, which makes them much more controllable. But angels are something else. What head of church wants to deal with those appearing and disappearing, uncontrollable presences, no matter how many of them can stand on the head of a pin or fly softly over battlefields.

I was excited about "The Angel Project" for Steuben. Arthur said he thought we would need twenty to twenty-four individual pieces to make an exhibition.

The question of whether angels would be saleable or not was never asked. The purpose was simply to determine whether angels would be a suitable theme to develop into a project that would perhaps lead to an exhibition and, Arthur hoped, as usual, a hardcover book on the subject.

I flew up to Corning to make angels. "Leonard, does it make you nervous performing in front of people in the gallery?" I asked Parker. "I mean, at nine in the morning, before we've had our second cup of coffee?"

"I must have had six cups already," Leonard Parker told me, taking a heavy drag on his cigarette. "I never pay any attention to those folks watching us make glass. What have you got in mind for us to make this morning?"

I unfolded my first drawing and laid it on the tool bench. Our whole shop gathered around to ponder this design, to purse their lips and frown or smile while they thought it over.

"How many wings does that angel have?" asked Parker, taking another deep, nervous drag on his cigarette.

"Six," answered Jimmy, the servitor. "I counted 'em, six!"

Parker turned around and looked through the screening at our eager, summer morning audience. The nearest ones were close enough to touch.

"Hell, we can't make that!" sighed Jimmy. "Hard enough to get two wings on an angel, right?"

I looked at Parker in silence.

"Jesus!" said someone in the shop. "Did you ever see or hear of an angel with six wings? I never heard that in our church."

"This angel," I told them, pointing at my drawings, "is a seraph, a chief, the boss. His name is Metatron, he's got six wings. He's described in the early Scriptures as having 'six wings in fire'!"

Parker lit another cigarette off the butt of his last and said, "We'll try it." He gave another nervous glance at me and then at our audience. More of them were filing in, men in wild, Harry Truman Hawaiian shirts, women in straw hats with golf tees in the band, kids jumping up and down in their seats in the amphitheater.

"What do you think?" Leonard asked me, just to be polite. "Your drawing's big. We ought to ask for six, maybe six and a half minutes of glass? Sticking on each wing, then reheating them is going to take a helluva lot of time. I can't hold onto a piece of glass that heavy for more than maybe thirty-five minutes. I'm not like Sammy Carlinio. That guy's all muscle."

"We'll have to work fast," I told him. I turned and looked at the guys in our shop and then at our audience, which was continuing to build – kids and parents, all summer folk from everywhere out touring.

This was to be a solid piece of glass, no blowing. It was carried in by the servitor, stuck now at its white-hot end to a large pontil iron.

Parker's iron held the huge, six-minute slug of hot glass on the wet cherry board, and with a soaked cherry paddle I used all my strength to try and give it shape. I felt as if my face and arms above my asbestos gloves would soon burst into flames. I could smell my eyebrows singeing. When the front was finished, Parker reheated the solid glass and we attached the angel's head.

When Parker started to shape the neck, separating the angel's head from its body, someone in the audience shouted through the wire, "What are you making?"

"An angel," I called back to them, smiling and nodding like someone about to do their first practice swing in a trapeze circus act, wishing to God I was still hiding behind the far furnace.

"Try to make a face on that angel," I called to Leonard over the fiery roar. "Houghton says he wants faces on any Steuben angels."

Parker gave me a weird look as he heaved the heavy cylinder of glass back into the glory hole and started turning the angel to prevent it from falling off while he reheated it.

"Arms now?" I asked.

He nodded to Jimmy, who handed him one arm and then another, each one eighteen seconds of glass. I chalk-marked the glass, and Parker pressed each arm firmly against one of the angel's sides.

"Looks good," yelled someone from the visitors' gallery. "Is it going to have wings?"

Jimmy, always a joyful showman, turned and spread five fingers on one hand, then held up another finger. "Six!" he bellowed.

"You're kidding!" came back through the screening from the gallery. "Who ever saw an angel with six wings?"

Parker gulped down half his paper cup of coffee, threw the rest away, and lit another cigarette during the fast turning reheat of the glass. The wings, we had decided earlier, would each weigh twelve seconds of glass, and would be attached behind the angel's body like multiple shoulder blades. I was delighted and could not help doing a little dance when I saw the first wing go on and stick, then get pulled out with the second iron.

"Make that wing hold air like a duck's wing landing," I told Parker, cupping my hand into what I hoped looked like a wing.

Several youngsters in the audience started crowing like roosters until their families stopped them.

Parker looked haggard as he thrust the heavy angel in the furnace to reheat it.

"Gimme another wing," Parker yelled.

When the angel came out with the second set of wings nicely cupped, the audience began to shout and applaud, and I did, too. Talk about angels and miracles – here was one before our eyes, a tour de force, the most difficult piece of offhand glass that I had ever dared imagine.

"Another wing!" shouted Parker, jamming the cigarette he was too busy to light behind his ear. He, too, was caught up in the magic of this huge, glowing angel. There was more shouting from the gallery, and many fingers gripped the screen. Most of the other shops had stopped making glass and gathered around us, helping to cheer us on or betting that we'd never get a piece that size safely into the kiln. In the final measuring process, my drawing caught on fire. This is not entirely unusual, but it did seem somehow prophetic at that moment.

The great angel genuflected softly to the right as we placed the fifth wing on the shoulder, got a firm stick, and Parker formed it perfectly.

"Hurry, for God's sake!" I shouted. "Get it in there. The stick up must be freezing." I knew that if it cooled too much at the base, it would simply fall off the iron.

Seraphim

Parker eased Metatron into the roaring red of the glory hole, but now I could tell that Parker was seriously tired, his arms were trembling. No wonder, holding such a weight for thirty-five minutes. Finally, he drew the angel out and held it upright. It was perfect. Our audience let out a roar of admiration.

"Give me the wing, the last wing!" Parker shouted.

I could see his hands were shaking as he held the iron.

He stuck the wing, then pulled it out and cupped it perfectly to match the other five. Now all aglow, the angel Metatron stood hugely, boldly, on the end of the iron. The audience shouted again.

"Get the halo," Parker grunted, sticking the angel inside the glory hole with tremendous care, fearing he might touch a wing tip on the round collar of the furnace.

I started to turn away, to watch the audience's reaction, to enjoy our triumph, when all of a sudden I saw a terrible expression appear on all their faces. Some let their mouths fall open. Some squinted, others closed their eyes. I whirled around and looked at Parker. He, too, had his eyes closed as he withdrew the empty iron from the glory hole. There was nothing on it. Metatron was gone.

All of us went together on the ten o'clock lunch break. Parker opened his lunch box and offered me the extra sandwich, which his wife, Marge, had been kind enough to make for me. But neither of us ate or spoke, and the other glassmakers eating near us didn't laugh or joke. They knew that our shop had been close to glory and that we had lost.

It was not unusual to try a difficult piece of glass and fail, then muster up and try once more. But we never ever tried to make that giant seraph again. Metatron's six wings in fire, as described in the ancient Scriptures, were just too much for us. I can close my eyes and imagine him again, standing tall and glorious, his halo glowing as in a drawing by William Blake.

19

The Big Opening

Arthur Houghton was on the Board of Lincoln Center, the grand arts complex containing an opera house, a ballet theater, and a concert hall. When it was nearing completion, he talked a lot about it, saying that the famous composer, Aaron Copeland, had written a new composition for the grand opening. I said that I'd like to go. It was a dumb thing for me to say, for I had limited interest in music. However, on the following day, Arthur announced that he had managed to get two extra tickets and would invite to dinner the very woman that I should take.

I got dressed up and arrived at Sutton Place on time. He introduced me before dinner to a woman whom I knew quite well. When we paired up to leave for Lincoln Center in the cars which drew up one by one, I looked at my concert partner in alarm, for she had donned not the elegant long black sable coat that she usually wore, but a Sherlock Holmes outfit. I could scarcely believe my eyes. A fore and aft peaked Sherlock Holmes hat and a hound's-tooth cape. Frankly, I was embarrassed. What the hell was she trying to pull off? Here I was with a fresh haircut and dressed like a serious New Yorker, and here she was making a joke of the whole thing!

The approach to Lincoln Center was like a moving caterpillar of women in luxurious furs or long black silk coats. The press was taking lots of pictures. I was embarrassed on my clueless partner's behalf, and I must confess that I tried to turn my head away.

"God," I said quietly to Houghton during intermission, "she's all right, but did you see the costume she was wearing?"

"Well," Arthur said, "she was an editor for *Vogue*, and I would guess she knows what she's doing."

Next morning, the papers carried a lot of pictures of her in her Sherlock Holmes costume, and Linda in our Design Department, who always knew everything worth knowing in fashion, said, "Doesn't she look super in that outfit?"

Well, I admit it does take a while to adjust!

20

Taxi Tricks

What about the whole business of being polite? New Yorkers don't seem polite because they're so outspoken. You live in New York City for a couple of years and you learn to join the crowd.

New York City has a population of eight million persons, and another sixteen million come crowding in to the city to work on weekdays. For pre-Christmas shopping, pre-Thanksgiving looking, and pre-4th of July fireworks, add another eight million. At those times, the tiny island contains more than the entire population of Canada, the second largest country in the world after Russia.

Now, living in Manhattan is some trick, and you have to develop special skills. For example, you stand on a corner of Park Avenue with your lady (a term applied to any female to whom you may or may not be married) and she has her arm up, too, and is probably better at flagging cabs than you are.

You stand a cab's length down from the corner to give the driver room to stop and leave pedestrians room to use the crosswalk when the light turns. Although you were there first, you find that two of these pedestrians have stopped in front of you, have their arms out, and are looking up the avenue for your cab.

You turn to tell your lady that these New Yorkers are a rude, wicked bunch of bastards, and when you look back, you see that another couple has jumped out in front of them. So now you're six and only third in line. No use complaining to them, suggesting that you were here first and they should find another corner. They won't move or answer, or they'll let off steam in a shouting match.

The thing to do is just go around in front of them and stand your ground. This is no guarantee that you'll get the next cab. The driver is usually going to size up the six of you and decide who he thinks will give him the largest tip.

During crowded holidays, New York cab drivers, if they speak English, or whatever language you speak, are eager to ask where you come from. The driver can easily tell if you are or are not a New Yorker as soon as you tell him where you want to go. It's not a question of regional accents. Lots of Texans and Canadians have lived in New York long enough to know it well.

What attracts the driver is if you fail to tell him exactly how to get where you want to go. As an out-of-towner, chances are you probably don't know exactly how to get where you want to go. He says, "Well, where you folks come from?" Be careful here. If you admit that you're from Iowa or Buttonville, Ontario, he says, "Must be nice and peaceful there. You folks probably don't know they're fixing Madison Avenue and it's a mess. You want me to take you round it so you won't get stuck in all that traffic?" He usually stretches his arms here and says, "I don't care. I'm driving this cab till midnight. I'll go any way you want."

You whisper to each other, then say, "Take us the best and quickest way."

Then you're off on a ride that's going to take you longer and cost you more than you'd believe.

Now, of course, there are some really kindly, friendly cab drivers in New York. But you're best off to deal with them in a quick, businesslike fashion, assuming they don't really give a damn who you are or where you're from.

A real New Yorker knows that the flow of traffic goes from south to north in the evening before the cocktail hour, so he goes and flags a cab going north. Once inside, he gives directions to go south – for example, to Chelsea. This may not thrill the cabbie, but it may get you to where you want to go on time.

Showdown

Charles Gimpel, an old friend of mine from the Arctic, where he practiced his skill as a successful photographer, was a notable international art dealer. The nephew of Lord Duveen, he had been born in Paris, lived in London, and became famous in the war as a resistance fighter. He told me a lot about himself and his part in the war, where he left London and dropped into France. But something happened to him there that caused him never to return to Paris. He had tattooed numbers on his arm from Buchenwald. I asked him how he ever managed to escape and he answered, "In almost the only way possible: relatives bought my way out of that camp." Try as he would, on dog sleds or jet planes, in igloos, or New York clubs, he rarely managed to escape the terrors of that war.

Charles was kind enough to introduce me to his friends, Alfred Barr, the Director of the Museum of Modern Art; Raymond Lowie, the designer; Philip Johnson, the architect; Larry Rivers and Jasper Johns, the artists; and others.

I was interested at that time in trying to do some more modern sculpture with Steuben. I formed a kind of exhibit on a long light box I had in my office. Charles brought Alfred Barr and Philip Johnson to see it. They instantly approved, calling it a wonderful new direction, a breakthrough for Steuben.

"Big Am," Amory Houghton, who was Chairman of the Board for all of Corning, came down and applauded the small show and went and told Arthur how much he liked it. So did Jack Gates. For a very brief time, even Arthur seemed impressed. He suggested I work with Paul Schulze, take over an office he had cleared, have it repainted a dark gray, and set up a pair of long light boxes for the walls. This we did with eagerness, receiving tucked away pieces formerly considered too modern for Steuben, especially from George Thompson, who was devoted to interior designs in solid glass forms, and Schulze, who taught classes at Parson's School of Design. When Don Pollard and Lloyd Atkins also contributed pieces, the little, very private show seemed about to bloom.

Alfred Barr came across from MOMA to lunch at the club and viewed it with me again. He said if we could successfully expand the number of pieces, that he would be pleased to arrange an exhibition of Steuben at the Museum of Modern Art. Then I received a message from *The New Yorker* magazine through Philip Hamburger, one of their "Talk of the Town" writers, saying that the magazine would like very much to do a story on these changes.

I hurried up to Arthur's office, certain that he would be delighted. He was not. He told me to say no to the Museum of Modern Art and no to *The New Yorker*. I heard this with utter disbelief. Wouldn't those two happenings be exactly what we were looking for, perfect acceptance on the highest level? Not for Arthur! I soon discovered that he liked little or nothing that was modern in the way of art. He intended to have Steuben continue to make its own path in the world.

Arthur retired from his position as President of Steuben at the age of sixty-five, which was then a corporate rule. But I, like some old Arctic survivor, continued on retainer. I have made 110 separate designs, with some in unlimited editions so that they have certainly been a profitable adventure for the company and for me.

22

Hokkaido in Winter

When I lived in Japan in 1958 and part of '59, I had two main purposes in mind. The first, of course, was to learn all I could about printmaking, so that I could take my knowledge back to the Inuit printmakers at the Cape Dorset Co-operative to set up an art market in Inuit prints. Fortunately, my time as an apprentice was well spent, and now Inuit prints are to be found all over the world.

My second purpose was to learn about the Ainu people living on the northernmost island of Hokkaido. These round-eyed Ainu, who tended toward baldness and beards, were generally believed to have entered Japan by the southern island of Kyushu, having come, perhaps, from India in ancient times. Their traces have been carefully followed northward through Japan. The theory is that they were pushed by the more warlike tribes living on Kyushu and Honshu, the two main islands, across the strait to Hokkaido and the Kurile Islands, which extend northward to Siberia.

I wanted very much to go to Hokkaido and asked some Japanese friends how I might undertake such a journey. They said I should simply buy railroad passage north from Tokyo, take a ferry across to Hakodate, then go by train north again to Sapporo. From there, they suggested a scholar, whom they knew, who would take me to visit several Ainu villages in the central mountainous country. Mingeikan, the folk art museum in Tokyo, sent me off with a letter of introduction to a young anthropologist, who, it was said, spoke Japanese, some Ainu, and English, and was friendly with the villagers. He was already in Hokkaido at the University of Sapporo, but they had written him and assured me he would be willing to accompany me to the Ainu villages.

I went north, traveling alone as I had so often done before, enchanted by the countryside of northern Honshu in the winter, with so many small, thatched farmhouses and snow lightly dusted across the fields. The ferry crossing to Hokkaido was cold and gray and uneventful – until I arrived in Hakodate on Hokkaido, where the Japanese were dressed for winter, some with huge red fox hats with tails hanging down and thickly padded clothing. Their faces turned and stared at me – not friendly or unfriendly – just hard, lined farm faces, wondering, I suppose, what I was doing there in my inadequate English trenchcoat, thin gloves, and packsack from which protruded a bundle of sketchbooks.

Hokkaido seemed like my kind of life again. Almost halfway round the world from Canada's Baffin Island were these similar-looking, short, hardy people in full winter dress. I looked forward to my time there making lots of sketches and learning all I could. I took the train north to Sapporo. The university there was, at that time, made of wood, and it seemed incredibly old and shabby. The students were vacationing. Showing my letter of introduction, I was led to the office of a professor whom the museum had said knew the young anthropologist and would tell me how to find him. The professor spoke no English and I spoke no Japanese, but someone came to interpret as best they could. When he finished reading the letter, the professor looked at me in alarm. He let me know that the man I sought had gone south the day before to take his winter holiday in Tokyo.

What to do? I was determined, having come this far, to see Tikabumi, an Ezo Ainu village that I had been told was within walking distance of Asahigawa. I left Sapporo that afternoon by train and traveled through the incredible winter landscape. Central Hokkaido looked to me like the mountains of the Laurentian Shield in southeastern and central Canada. It was a rugged, hilly country, white with snow, and had groves of maple trees instead of the elegant, unfamiliar bamboo on the southern islands of Japan. These northern people were truly dressed for winter. Seeing them made me long for my parka, but I felt totally at home.

It was pitch dark when the train stopped at Asahigawa. There were no streetlights then, and almost no other kind of lights, except faint glimmers from a few house windows. I spoke the words, "*Byoin nona*, hospital, where is it?" to an elderly couple I followed off the train. As they shouldered their bundles, they stared at me, then at each other, before the man pointed down what seemed to be the rough main road and repeated the word, *byoin*, hospital. They accompanied me in silence for a short distance, before saying, "*Sayonara*, good-bye," and turning off the road. I went on alone, full of uncertainty. It was very cold and dark, and I was tired.

A dog came out and barked in a hostile way at me, then sniffed my foreignness and ran away. I continued through the blackness until I saw a larger building. Only three faint lights showed beyond, then nothing. I went and knocked on what I hoped was the door of the small hospital. A young woman opened it. "*Byoin?*" I asked.

"*Hai, hairu,* yes, come in," she answered in a high, sweet voice. I stepped inside and removed my shoes. She led me into a dimly lighted room where half a dozen people squatted against the walls. I showed her my letter of introduction.

When she had read it, I said, "Houston-*san, Kanada Jin,*" and pointed to myself. She spoke to the others using that amazed tone, the way the Japanese women often do. I pocketed my priceless letter and fished out my small, thick Parrot's *Japanese-English Dictionary.* As you might guess, this painfully slow process was sometimes amusing to all of us!

Finally, half understanding me, the *kangofu,* nurse, sent someone scurrying outside. I stood there, awkwardly wishing there was something I could say. Then, remembering one of my few Japanese phrases, "*Ben-jo-no-nay?*" meaning, "Where is the toilet?" I spoke. She gestured and we smiled.

Another young nurse brought me a cup of tea. A long time passed before a worldly looking young man, taller than the rest, strode into the room and bowed slightly to all those present. All of us returned his bow. He wore military steel-rimmed glasses and looked like a university student.

"Awh, you speak English!" I cried gratefully to him.

"*Lie,* no," he answered, then read Colonel Yanazaua's kind letter of introduction.

He took a larger Japanese-English dictionary out of his padded jacket pocket and introduced himself as Toshi. We knelt together at the low, battered lacquer table, smiling at each other as we drank more tea, ate small, dried fish and rice, then with books tilted toward the light, we looked up word after word, each speaking in his turn – he in halting English, me in faltering Japanese. The nurses and all their patients who could walk gathered close around us.

Where was some of the usual saki – cold or hot – when we needed it most? To summarize the evening, our conversation went like this:

He: "You, Canada from, say she."

Me: "Yes, *Kanada, Jin* am, me."

He: "Why you?"

Me: "To meet scholar."

He: "Ohhh. Tokyo, gone now he. Too bad!"

Me: "Ainu, I see. Man speak Ainu want I."

He: "*Hai*, yes. Ainu there," he pointed northeast. "Tomorrow, you go. Somebody know I take you."

"Speak English he?" I asked hopefully.

"*Iie*, no," the young man shook his head, "but know he Ainu people."

"*Yoi*, good," I answered.

"*Neru*, I sleep, *koko*, here," he said.

The nurses removed the table and laid out two thick futon mats on the *tatami*. Everyone packed in very close around us. The student neatly slipped out of his clothes without my even noticing and was soon resting warm in his futon.

I took off my jacket, tie, shirt and undershirt, and undoing my belt, pulled off my trousers. I was rather shy in those days and hesitated, with all those strange young women watching me so intently, to take off my underwear. It was cold.

Toshi smiled and dug out his dictionary again. His message delivered very slowly was, "These people never see *Kanada Jin* with pants not on. They going to wait." He explained the problem to the women. They held their hands over their mouths and giggled, but kept on watching.

Finally, I took off my underwear. I heard what I thought was a sigh of disappointment as they politely said, "*Sayonara*," and shuffled off to bed giggling again as they, too, headed for night duty or their own futons.

Next day, the kindly student walked the snowy path with me to Tikabumi, the Ainu village not far away. He explained that there were three Ainu chieftains in the village and some other typical Ainu houses, perhaps retained to show visiting Japanese summer tourists from the southern islands. Without real translation, I had to rely on the account of the Venerable Canon Batchelor who had been an Anglican missionary among the Ainu. He had learned their language and their customs, and had written extensively on that subject.

The Ainu, like the Masai of east Africa and many other cultures, were camera-shy unless, perhaps, you offered them yen. But in Tikabumi, they did not mind my drawing them and were eager to see what I could do. They pointed out important cultural objects of theirs that they considered worth recording, like the moustache lifter used before drinking saki, and a small bear skull between candlelike wands with curly wood shavings. One of the old chiefs posed in his elaborately designed Ainu kimono, and two of the women donned their dance dresses and moved as though swayed by the wind. I knew from my reading that the Ainu had dozens of rituals that were vaguely similar to Inuit customs in Canada's eastern Arctic. I made many drawings and wished to stay much longer, but without a true interpreter, I felt helpless. Alas, that unique Ainu culture now seems to be fading as they melt into the Japanese population. Are Canadian Inuit and Indians destined to travel that same path?

Ainu dancers

23

Dr. Hamada Arrives

By good fortune, I had come to know Dr. Shoji Hamada, the great Japanese folk potter, during my five-month stay in Japan in 1958. I knew him mostly because of our connection through the Nippon Mingeikan Museum, but also he was kind enough to ask me to visit him at his collection of four ancient farmhouses at Machiko, his country estate. Outside his wonderful home sat his long, old-style pottery kilns that stretched like a caterpillar.

In Tokyo, we attended an exhibition together at Takasamayo, the large department store, which had reserved its top floor as a grand space in midtown to hold important art exhibitions. As a group of us passed through the ground floor of the store toward the elevators, Dr. Hamada stopped beside a large display of folk pottery, all close imitations of his own distinctive pots. He picked up several pieces and examined them.

Pottery kilns at Machiko

"Not bad," he said. "One of the specialties of folk pottery is that it must not be signed."

"Too bad so many other potters copy you," I said through Yasu Inoue, our interpreter.

"Not at all," he answered. "Much later, when someone looks at the best of these pieces, they will say, 'Yes, this is surely the work of Hamada-*san*.' And when they look at the worst of my own work, they will say, 'No, Hamada-*san* could not have made such a clumsy pot. It is the work of one of his imitators.'"

Later when Hamada came to New York, he was convinced that, as in Japan, a department store would be the best place to hold his exhibition. He chose Bonniers on Madison Avenue, a store famous for its Jensen fine silver, china, and modern, decorative art. Dr. Hamada had already visited Steuben and observed my works there, and we had renewed our friendship.

When I attended the opening where he showed some of his most wonderful works, I invited him to my place for tea next day. He brought with him a young girl who was doing his interpreting. He expressed delight that I had a large-sized black woodcut by Shiko

Munakata in the entrance hall with a Hamada pot beside it. He reminded me at tea that I had given him a very good Inuit stone carving in Machiko, and he said if I would come to Bonniers after work next day, he would be there and would present me with a gift.

When I arrived, he waved his hand around the gallery and he said, "Choose one."

I did so, with delight. Then he selected two more important pots and told the owner that I would be in at the end of the exhibition to take these gifts home.

Much later, Dr. Hamada died and my conscience said that I should give two of his wonderful pots to a museum, since I had no proper place to display them in my home. When I offered them to a museum and told them the details, they said, "Oh, so difficult to be certain they are really his work since Mingeikan potters never signed their pots. If you have the wooden boxes they were packed in, that would help."

"No," I admitted. "I believe Bonniers kept the boxes, perhaps at my request."

"A great pity," the appraiser said, "since the boxes are almost the only way we can authenticate it as his work."

That same comment has been made of earlier Inuit carvings and in both these cases it has posed a problem, since it was not in Mingeikan, the Japanese folk pottery tradition, or in the earlier Inuit tradition to sign their work.

24

The Great Blackout

Working a little late at the Steuben office after others had left had become a habit of mine. It offered some extra design time, especially when I planned to go directly out to dinner from the office. On that Tuesday night, November 9, 1965, well after five o'clock, the lights above my drawing table went out.

I got up and looked down the hall. Everything was wrapped in dark shadows. Peering out the windows, I could see the city to the west without a single light. The roar of midtown traffic had suddenly gone dead. Even the impatient honking of horns had almost stopped. The cross streets below me at 56th and 5th were gridlocked. Every traffic light was out. The New Yorkers themselves were still moving like dark streams of lemmings, or were huddled together along the silent streets gesturing, pointing, wondering what had happened – or worse, what was about to happen. They probably now felt trapped inside this greatest of all Cold War targets. The Americans had recently experienced the assassination of their President. The Vietnamese War was turning into a disaster. The Soviets had never seemed more dangerous. What was going on tonight? Had something vital been destroyed? Had an atomic bomb gone off somewhere? Theirs or ours? Would we at any moment feel the effects?

I felt my way along the hall and bumped into a girl named Kay, a cheery person whom I liked very much.

"What are we going to do?" she asked.

"We've got to find our way out of this building."

"I've tried, but the elevator on this floor isn't working. I wish we had a flashlight."

I thought for a moment and had a bright idea. "You know those tall white candles we put in the glass table candelabra in the front window? A bunch of them are stored in a closet just along this hall."

We fumbled our way forward in the dark, opened the closet, and found the candles. I took out my trusty Arctic Zippo lighter, and whirled its wheel with my thumb. It lit, but the candles totally failed us. It turned out they were made of wood, so they wouldn't melt in the window display and bend in the late afternoon sun.

We clutched each other and laughed helplessly at that, then crept slowly toward the emergency stairs. No red emergency light marked the exit, but we eventually found it. Pushing open the metal fire door, we clutched hands and the handrail. We started down into the utter darkness. Above us in the blackness, we could hear others cautiously descending, and soon encountered friends leaving the building.

What a relief it was to step out into the openness of the street! At our corner, I could make out a tall young man standing in the middle of the intersection directing traffic. The crazed honking of horns was over as New Yorkers like ourselves had come to realize how truly vulnerable we all were, at the heart of this great, blinded city.

We started wandering northward. Kay needed a taxi, but, of course, it was impossible to get one, and the subways were dead silent beneath our feet. I thought of the black winter nights of Baffin Island and how little anything like this would mean to Inuit in their self-sustained lives in the Arctic.

I had a bright idea. "I've got a friend, a surgeon, who lives on East 62nd Street. I'd planned to go to his place tonight. Let's go. He and his wife will welcome your company."

They did, with open arms.

"Come on in, for God's sake, and have a drink!" he said as I introduced Kay. "We're going to have a party here by candlelight. Let's call Arthur. Let's see if the phones are working."

They were working and there was a party going on at Arthur's house and he insisted that we come straight over. But, hell, how could we get there? Battery radio announcers were starting to talk about lawlessness and mugging in the streets. The whole dark world outside now seemed a dangerous, hostile place.

Quite a few drinks later, after nervously consuming hors d'oeuvres of olives, celery, cheese, and crackers, we started seeing the occasional taxi passing in the street. Kay's mother had failed to answer the phone, and Kay was anxious to go to her apartment. We said goodnight and walked to the corner to try and hail a cab. Finally, we got one.

I was overwhelmed by the new look of the utterly silent street. An almost full moon had appeared, giving each apartment building strange, boxlike shapes of light and dark. To my eyes, the blackened windows somehow gave them the appearance of moonlight on pitted ice that had been thrown up in a tidal barrier.

I remembered the words of an Inuit song:

Ayii, Ayii
I am afraid
When my eyes follow the moon
On its old trail.
I am afraid
When I hear the wind wailing
And the murmuring of snow.
I am afraid
When I watch the stars
Moving on their nightly trail.
I am afraid.

I stood there thinking of the Arctic, wishing I were there. What great tragedy, I wondered, had occurred somewhere far away? I wished I were back in the warm-hearted safety of the Arctic, where one would never dream of a nuclear cloud spreading on the night wind.

25

Harlem

I had been in Harlem in my army days. In 1941, I had an embarkation leave from Nova Scotia, and I went to New York in a kilt and had a helluva good time. I was swept up at '21' Club by a bunch of partying New Yorkers and taken to the Cotton Club and the Yellow Canary, where we danced and heard great jazz. The waitress picked her five-dollar folded tip off the table's edge without using her teeth or hands – some shocking trick. I knew I was out of Canada.

In 1964 or '5, when I was returning to New York by train from a weekend visit in New Haven, Connecticut, I was amazed to notice smoke rising from the city, and we could soon see and hear fire engines, ambulances, and police cars wailing through agitated crowds of people in the streets of Harlem. This was the very beginning of the Harlem riots, an event that turned into a tremendous problem for New York and was repeated in other major cities, with Watts in southern California being first.

As I followed the events in Harlem on television and in the newspapers, I told Arthur I wanted to do something to help. He suggested I go see Bill Chase, then the rector at St. James's, the Episcopalian church I sometimes attended. Bill recommended that I should contact a black minister in Harlem whom he knew, and he, in turn, referred me to "Harlem Youth in Action." This was a new organization recently formed and funded by the city, which was preparing itself to help teach Harlem's youths some useful skills. He said that he thought my twelve years of experience with the Inuit and their arts might be one of the types of help that they were looking for. Sure enough, I was soon given the address of a school on 125th Street and encouraged to make my way up there, introduce myself, and discuss how I might fit into their program.

I went home early and dressed myself like a schoolteacher in a tweed sports coat, corduroy trousers and a wooly necktie, and boarded the subway north. Although 125th Street was in high dudgeon that day, it was nothing compared with the action going on inside the school. The pupils, who were in their teens, were mostly boys, with a few girls.

I made a sign and hung it on an empty classroom door. It read, "Art Class." A small flood of laughing pupils entered the room, encouraged by a black teacher who followed them. "My name's Jim," he said, shaking hands. "I'm just called 'the Canadian' around here," he smiled.

"I'm a Canadian, and I'm a Jim as well," I told him.

"Well, I'm not really born there," he said, "but I went up to Muskoka, Canada, to the Lady Eaton Camp when I was a kid and, Jesus man, that was the best place in the world! You ever been there?"

"Not there, but close," I told him. I could tell from the first moment I met him that we were going to be friends.

"How often can you come up here?" he asked.

"I don't know," I told him, "one or two afternoons a week."

"Sounds good," he said. "Can you start tomorrow?"

"Sure," I answered.

"Our only problem is we've got no stuff, no art materials, nothing. I guess the people who are running Har You Act (is how he said it), they buy the stuff we need as soon as they can, but they say they need the money from City Hall. Jim, you make a list today of what you're going to need in art supplies and I'll make mine. I'll be teaching in the class next door. Tomorrow, I'm bringing some stuff I'll need, and I hope to God they'll give me back the money." Jim laughed. "You know, maybe sometime."

I told him, "I'll bring some supplies up with me." I went around and shook hands with the students in the room and wrote down all their names. They promised they'd be back tomorrow.

I liked the eager spirit that came bubbling out of these young black students. Every one of them turned up next day. I passed out large sheets of drawing paper that I had purchased at a discount from trusty old Empire Artists on Lexington Avenue, and said, "Draw whatever you want. Draw what you feel. Draw anything that you like best. Or worst."

I handed out the bristle brushes and opened the jars of colored paint. I was honestly astounded. Teachers can expect kids seven to eleven to be very bold and creative in their artwork. These students were at that most difficult age from twelve to sixteen that so commonly withers the art drive in our students. But these black kids seemed wonderfully able to express themselves in paint. While some chose uplifting subjects (doves flying over the Harlem streets' tenements), others chose dancing devils gleefully setting fire to everything.

At six o'clock when it was time to go, the students exuberantly showed me the only lockers that hadn't been broken, suggesting that I store the art materials. One of them placed his bicycle lock on the locker and gave me the key. I met Jim, the other teacher, who suggested that I phone Harlem Youth in Action and tell them we had classes going, but still had no art supplies. Could they tell us where we could pick some up?

There was no answer on the phone, so I bought more paint and paper and went north to Harlem again. To my dismay, I discovered that the locker door had been torn open and everything was gone.

"Goddamn it," said Jim. "That's a damn shame. These kids are ready and eager to learn something right now." We used up all the supplies I'd brought, but got some really exciting art out of the students.

When I next went up to Harlem carrying supplies, I had to take a taxi, for I was heavy laden with the necessary tools to begin teaching stencil and wood block, which had helped gain the Inuit millions of dollars for their finished art. I showed the kids examples of the Inuit work, and they were wildly keen to start.

Harlem sink

To my delight, an old, porcelain wall basin, which we used to wash our hands and clean up paint, had been decorated by the class. I don't mean just a little decorated. I mean it had turned into a burst of something that looked like peacock feathers done by the French painter, Henri Rousseau, using all our primary colors gorgeously and confidently edged in black. It had no lettering on it, but it did have, it seemed to me, the best elements of what later became spray can graffiti. You probably hate graffiti as much as I do. But this was so well done, I was overwhelmed. When I asked who did it, my students laughed and said, "Everybody!" I told Jim when he saw it that I would like to have it seen by others.

Next day, I asked Alfred Barr, Director of the Museum of Modern Art, to lunch at the 5th Avenue Club. When I explained what I was trying to do up in Harlem and the art that I had seen flowing upward from the washbasin in the school basement, Alfred immediately said that he wanted to come up with me and see it. I asked him if he could come to class next day where he could look at the wonderful washbasin, meet the students, and see the startling work that they were doing.

When we arrived and went downstairs, I could scarcely believe my eyes. The whole enamel washbasin had been torn out, brass taps, pipes and all. It was gone, as was the back wall and all its metal pipes. Only edges of their bright, original mural remained.

"They say they're going to fix this whole place up again," some of the students told us. "Remember that big, heavy guy among us? He stood up on the sink to do the really high painting. That sink sort of came off the wall. It started leaking water all over the floor. They had to take it out. They say they'll get a new one."

We searched around without success to find the painting from above the sink.

"I'd like to have taken that painting, sink and all, down to the museum and shown it as it was," said Alfred, after he stayed to watch the students paint, and was impressed.

Jim, the Canadian, was really mad when he saw that the sink was gone. We had to send students out to bring in pails of water. But the main thing was that our students were getting better at the work, and we were all coming to know and trust each other.

The New York Times next morning said that five million dollars had been appropriated by the city toward the Harlem Youth in Action program. But Jim and I were still buying our own paints and paper for our students, and he (wiser in these matters than I was) said he was beginning to lose hope.

Meanwhile, back at the office, Arthur was glad enough to have me take off the time from Steuben to help, but he didn't really seem interested in the fact that I was doing it. The excitement about the troubles in Harlem was dying down.

A few days later, it was announced in *The New York Times* that the money, five million dollars, had been released to Harlem Youth in Action, but the two leaders of the program could not be found for comments to the press. I was not really interested in that aspect. What I cared about was the astonishing originality and strength of the work done by the students and their eagerness to go further to develop their art. I thought that what they were doing with their painting could be equated with their music and their dance. It was loud and bombastic, yet somehow rhythmic, charged with their daring use of colors. There was always a lot of laughter and good feelings in those two classrooms.

The *Times* announced later that the two leaders and the five million dollars seemed to have left town, and no one was available to comment further on Harlem Youth in Action. I hoped that the mayor, John Lindsay, whom I knew fairly well, was doing all he could.

After class, I met Jim in the hall, surrounded as usual by admiring, friendly teenagers. "I don't like the sound of things," he told me. "Other parts of Harlem Youth in Action are closing down for lack of funds."

We walked together toward the main door that led out onto 125th Street with the kids still all around us. I caught the door first, pushed it open, and waved for Jim to go through. He smiled and motioned for me to go first, but I courteously held back. Finally, he gave up and stepped out the door.

Whack! What I remember next was a flash of breaking glass. Then I saw Jim go down. The kids ran outside yelling, trying to see or catch the person who, lying in wait at the arch above the door, had hit him with the vodka bottle. Jim was semi-conscious on the ground, his head bleeding badly.

"Get the cops. We need an ambulance," I yelled.

The kids didn't need to be told. A crowd was gathering when an ambulance arrived, and we went to the nearest Emergency Room. It took them seventeen – or was it twenty-seven – stitches to sew up Jim's head. I felt truly depressed as I made my way toward the subway that would take me back to midtown. The Arctic seemed such a warm, safe place, and I wished that night that I was back there among Inuit friends who tried to help each other.

I went up next day to visit Jim. He said he had a headache but was feeling better. He was eager to talk about the wonderful summer days he'd had in Canada.

I went back to the school at four o'clock. About half of the kids were there. I had brought nothing with me this time, and I wished I had. We talked, and when it came time to leave, they walked me through the dangerous main door.

I said to them, "That bottle yesterday was probably meant for me."

But they shook their heads and said, "Man, these days they don't care who they hit around here."

They insisted on walking me to the entrance of the subway and we just stared at each other. They said, "See ya!"

I answered, "Yeah, I'll see you."

But we never did. I'm ashamed to say that was more or less my last attempt to do good in the city, although I did continue to teach at a fully integrated summer camp at Wye Institute in Maryland.

I was baffled by what happened during the thirty years that followed. Even though people genuinely tried to improve race relations, it seems somehow to have made them worse. How the hell is this black-white problem in America ever going to be resolved?

26

The Pink Elephant

One of the most joyous aspects of working in the United States was the tarpon fishing in June at Boca Grande. It can be murderously hot in Florida at that time of year and I dislike that kind of heat, the kind that makes you feel like a well-basted turkey in an oven. But I'll put up with a lot for the chance to hook a hundred-pound tarpon, for they're all muscle and speed and jump.

One of the great blessings of this style of fishing is that tarpon, among the heroic fighting fish of this world, commonly weigh between eighty and one hundred pounds, but are just too bony and undesirable to eat. So the guide takes a scale from just behind the gill on the fish brought alongside, from which its weight can be worked out, and then lets the tarpon go. The trick is to try and catch a really big fish, but to eat only the smaller ones, like pompano or red snapper, that you buy at a good restaurant or a fish market on the way home. It means that good tarpon fishing in The Pass to the south of Gasparilla Island should with luck continue on forever.

Arthur had his own boat called *Bayou Maid* and a guide and boat captain named Francis Knight, a man famous for his fishing knowledge of the Boca Grande Pass. Arthur used to rent Knight's brother's boat for the fishing party, made up of good conversationalists who were also genuinely interested in tarpon fishing, and I felt truly fortunate to be part of such an illustrious group.

Mortimer Adler was one, a philosopher from the University of Chicago who was just finishing his job of editing the *Encyclopedia Britannica*. The others were: Russell Lynes, editor of *Harper's* magazine; Oz Elliott, editor of *Newsweek*; Bill Cahan, a New York surgeon; Ros Gilpatrick, Deputy Secretary of Defense; David Ogilvie, head of Ogilvie Benson Advertising, then the largest advertising agency in the world; Colonel H. Fitzroy, Professor Emeritus of American History, Virginia; and Jack Gates, like me, from Steuben. To this group he would always add Frank Oliver, an old China hand, who had retired to Boca Grande after a long career with the *Times* of London, and who knew how to make Mai Tais that would cause everyone to sing like canaries.

We took naps or swam in Arthur's pool. One morning, they found a twelve-foot alligator in the swimming pool, looking well fed. I was glad I wasn't there, for it would have spoiled the midnight swim. It was our habit never to go fishing before 5:00 p.m. We never had drinks aboard. Both boats would cruise The Pass and usually take a tarpon or two until 8:00, when it was growing dark, then rush in, each boat throwing up a huge, white spray, and tie up at the dock in front of the Pink Elephant. Arthur would count heads again – eight, yes, eight – then send one member of the party up to the bar to order from Miss Ernestine sixteen double martinis. Then we would go up and seat ourselves around two tables forced together and joyfully eat crab and oysters, shrimp and pompano.

The Pink Elephant was always a noisy place in June, crowded with fishermen like ourselves from all over the country. You would have to shout to be heard, but none of us seemed to wish that we were anyplace else in the world.

After dinner, only one of our two boats would go back out to fish in the Pass again with those who had not yet taken a fish. I loved night fishing and it was often the best. There were two fishing chairs riveted to the back deck where two of us would take up staunch rods baited with crabs. Two others would sit in chairs behind, waiting for their turn. It seemed to me that out there at night, with huge thunderheads and sometimes lightning flashing over Cuba, and a million stars above, we would have some of the best conversations I've ever known. Everyone was a specialist in some field or other, and it was a great chance to learn in a wide variety of ways that few experienced at school. We would talk about tarpon or philosophy or politics, or watch for satellites that seemed to favor a course over nearby Cape Canaveral. Satellites were new at that time, a source of wonderment as they moved like slow, shooting stars across the firmament.

One evening, President Lyndon Johnson gave us fair warning, then dropped in to visit our party in a helicopter, landing more or less on Houghton's lawn. I remember that his bodyguards carried a corked bottle of Cutty Sark whisky for the President. Whether for protection or just because it was his favorite brand, I'll never know. That visit was during a hot time in the Vietnam War. Arthur Houghton had a lot more to do with government than almost any of us knew at the time, and probably that was just as well.

Boca Grande is an island famous for its pirate, Gasparilla, and there are endless rumors of buried treasure. There are more modern legends, too. The island has a toll bridge where they then charged seventy-five cents per passenger in any vehicle. On a famous occasion, Francis Knight, who helped Arthur with the boat, was driving off-island one night on a solemn mission and stopped to pay his toll.

"That will be a dollar fifty," the toll man said.

"Why?" asked Francis.

"Because you're not alone in that car, Francis. I'm charging you for the corpse you're carrying in that casket in the back."

Francis started yelling and refused to pay the extra toll. All hell broke loose on Boca Grande. Some folks were on one side, some the other. I never heard how it was finally settled, though there was plenty about it in the *Boca Beacon*, and no doubt the story, like the tarpon fishing and the Pink Elephant, is still going strong.

27

Double Shock

Jack Gates, my Steuben pal, had been unlucky and had not yet on this trip had a strike. Although others in our fishing party had various reasons that caused them to leave, I remained with Jack to keep him company while he took one more try on our last day. We broke our habit and went out in the late morning. We fished until almost noon, when Jack got a good, strong strike. It was a heavy, very active fish that performed many aerial acrobatics. Jack was not anxious to take in the fish too quickly, and as a result, our guide, Francis, unwillingly followed it out into deeper and deeper water.

"He's slowing down now," said Jack, and tried to reel the big fish in closer and closer to the boat.

I stood up to watch. As I did, I saw a monstrous gray shadow rising, lunging at the tarpon, driving it half out of the water. The huge jaws of the shark, with teeth and red gums exposed, sheared the big tarpon almost in half, taking a large chunk, before it turned swiftly away with part of its victim in its mouth.

The tarpon now tried desperately to escape from the widening swirl of blood, but in a moment the shark was back, taking two more fierce bites, and leaving Jack with only the tarpon's head.

We were awestruck.

"Oh, God," Jack said, shakily, "did you ever in your life see anything as wild as that?"

"No, never," I told him, for the awful swiftness and power of that
shark had unnerved both of us.

"It must have been twenty feet long," Jack said.

"Bigger than that," said Francis.

"I'm finished for the day," Jack said. "Let's go in and have a
couple of drinks then lunch at 'The Pink.'"

We went back to the house, took a swim in the pool (no ocean
swimming for us that day), then packed and were driven to the
Sarasota Airport. On the plane, I tried to read and so did Jack, but
I couldn't get the image of that rising shark out of my head. It really
was like something out of a nightmare.

About halfway to New York, the hostess came and asked if I was
Mr. Houston. She informed me that the pilot of the plane had
received a message from my sister asking me to phone her in
Beaverton, Ontario, just as soon as we landed.

My hand shook as I dialed the pay phone, knowing something
bad had happened. "It's Mother," my sister, Barbara, sobbed. "She
died suddenly this morning."

"You just try to take it easy, Barb," I told her. "I'll inquire about
flights and be up there as soon as I can. I'll phone you from
Toronto."

Jack Gates kept me company at the airport in New York as I
bought a ticket for the next flight, which was at nine o'clock that
night. That gave me time to go into town, change clothes, grab
extra money. Imagine two such very separate, never-to-be-forgotten
events in one day. I wept on the way into town, but tried to turn
my head away.

"She was seventy," I said, "and wasn't sick a day."

"I know just how you feel," Gates said. "I lost my mother, too."

When I arrived at Beaverton next morning, my mother was
already laid out in her open coffin in the center of her large, familiar drawing room, her face powdered and peaceful, looking somehow like a piece of marble sculpture. There were banks of garden
flowers all around her, ready for the neighbors' visits that I knew

would soon happen in the style of that warm-hearted Ontario town beside Lake Simcoe.

After the church service, half a dozen cars followed the hearse to the quiet, country graveyard where our mother was buried beside our father and among many of our other Scottish ancestors. Barb agreed to stay on and keep the house, and in a few days I returned to New York and found my mailbox full of kind letters from all my fishing friends and so many others in town. I sat staring out into the back garden and the three graceful hawthorn trees planted there. This apartment and New York really were beginning to seem like home to me. With both my parents gone and my two sons at school in Europe, I thanked God I had a sister as dear to me as Barb.

28

Explorers Club

Some American climbers in Alaska took a rest and found themselves watching a pair of Arctic wolves, wondering what they would be doing at such an elevation where their kind of food was scarce. They saw the wolves stop and start tearing at something, eating it in the snow. The climbers became curious and approached the wolves, who slunk off reluctantly, leaving their meal.

What the climbers found were the upturned, gnawed legs of wild ponies. What would they be doing up here? Their best guess was that the ponies, now long extinct, had fallen into a crevasse and been quick frozen into the glacier, thus preserving their flesh, which had drawn in the wolves. With the help of others in the expedition, they dug out the two ponies and shipped them, still frozen, south to the American Museum of Natural History in New York City.

I was a regular visitor behind the scenes at the museum because I was interested in the new installation of Inuit artifacts.

"Have some lunch with us," said Dr. Junius Bird, one of the curators, a friend of mine. "You'll like this stew we've been eating this week," he said. "Warms you up on a winter's day."

They seemed reluctant to talk about Eskimo artifacts. They seemed more interested in watching me eat my stew.

"What do you think of it?" they asked. "Does that meat taste fresh to you?"

"Sure, it's damn good!" I answered politely, though I imagined their stews came out of a tin can.

"We were just wondering," they smiled. "The meat in your bowl is between fifteen and twenty thousand years old."

I laughed in disbelief, until they told me about the ponies. They were carefully preserving the skeletons, they said, and had taken hide and hair samples, but the flesh absolutely would not keep. They had tested it in every way they could before – now that they had no further use for it – they decided to serve it for lunch.

"There's lots more in the freezer," they said. "What would you do with it?"

"I'd serve it," I said, "at the annual dinner of the Explorers Club. I'm on their committee."

Over the years, they had seen everything, including famous Arctic explorers at white-tie dinners engage in violent fisticuffs with other famous Arctic explorers when medals had been involved. After all, our member, Dr. Kane, had been jailed for refuting the claim of fellow member, Admiral Peary, as to who had been first to have reached the North Pole. Ten-thousand-year-old stew would be nothing to our club.

"Yes, that's it," I said. "We'll serve the rest at this year's Explorers Club Dinner." At that time, it was a black-tie affair at the Waldorf, where only one woman, the club secretary, was allowed, and she was hidden at a small table in a private box. I know, it seems amazing now.

We employed a famous Swedish chef who turned that ancient, frozen, pony meat into the best meatballs that anyone had ever tasted. Mind you, at that same dinner, they served other meats such as grizzly bear, zebra, caribou, African locusts, snake, fried bees, and dozens of other delicious specialties. But the club members said that the ancient pony meatballs were by far the most popular. Well, no wonder. It's an old club with lots of illustrious, well-aged members as well as newer ones such as Peter Freuchen, who once said, "It takes balls to be an explorer."

29

Nantucket and Tikta'liktak

Fritz Eichenberg, a world famous wood block engraver, directed the printmaking studio at Pratt Institute's extension in lower Manhattan. He published a magazine entitled *Artist's Proof.* Fritz wrote me when I was in the Arctic, saying he had been impressed by the first Inuit/Eskimo print exhibition in New York and asking if I would write an article about their work. I did my best, though writing was not at all a part of my life at that time. I was untrained and was nervous about trying to do it. I had never asked the government for a typewriter because I did not know how to use one. Later, when I reached New York, I saw the article neatly edited and presented with Inuit prints. I thought, well, writing that wasn't all that difficult, and anyway, I was probably safe since in art magazines like this, people often fail to read the text, looking only at the pictures and the captions. But I certainly never thought of myself as a writer.

At the height of summer in 1964 when it was so blistering hot in Manhattan that no Inuit would have even tried to function, I met Fritz again and he asked me to come out to visit him on Nantucket Island for a long weekend. I jumped at the chance, for I knew that place had been part of the inspiration for Herman Melville, one of my great literary heroes.

Nantucket was as charming as I hoped it would be, with long, sandy beaches at Quidnet beside Fritz's house. We walked, picking up stones and interesting bits of driftwood, and talked of the old

New England whalers who had lived here. We visited the small museum. A wonderful collection of scrimshaw was on display, most of it sailors' engravings scratched into ivory sperm whale teeth. (That early contact was no doubt one of the reasons why thirty years later I wrote *The Ice Master*, a novel about Arctic whaling.)

When we returned to his house, he told me an ancient German fairytale and, in return, I told him the Inuit legend of Tikta'liktak. He liked it very much and said, "I'll have someone visit us for tea tomorrow. You'll have to tell her that story." And next day, I did. The visitor, a delightful woman named Margaret McElderry, seemed thrilled by that legend, and somehow, almost magically, we all remained lifelong friends.

When I returned to Steuben in New York next day, Margaret McElderry was already in New York. She phoned the office and said, "What's the name of that Tik-ta-lik . . .? Anyway, you should make a book of it. I'm sure we'd like to publish it."

Margaret McElderry, I soon learned, was one of the two most highly regarded children's book editors in North America. But I was determined to put a stop to this writing idea. "Sorry to tell you, I can't write books," I told her, "but I'll be glad to tell someone the story and then I'll illustrate it."

"You're going to write and illustrate that story," she said, laughing in her wonderful way. "You start thinking about it. I'd like to see it on next year's autumn list here at Harcourt, Brace and World."

Now what kind of a marvelous miracle is that for a Canadian who has just come stumbling into the U.S. out of the frozen North? I thought about it all right! It had long been in my mind, an Inuit legend, for years as well known there in the eastern Arctic as, say, *Robin Hood* or *Treasure Island* is in English-speaking homes. By the end of the week, retelling the story to myself as I walked to work, I knew it by heart.

On Friday evening after work, I started writing in my apartment, drawing the draperies tight so I would not be tempted to look out at the real live soap opera occurring in the neighboring windows. It was boiling, sickening hot outside, and I was writing about the icy North. I turned the air conditioner on high. I worked until midnight, always planning ahead with small sketches of the action in the story. I wrote all day Saturday and went for a walk that evening. It was still dripping hot. I was at it again early Sunday morning, and by the ringing of the Hungarian church bells at eleven, I was finished.

I knew a kindhearted girl in town who, when I told her of my plan, offered to type the story for me. She suggested double-spaced typing to allow room for corrections. She was right. Margaret had to edit quite a lot. But toward the end of that week, Margaret phoned and said she thought it was going to work. She sent over by bicycle messenger two hard-covered dummy books, both blank, of a size and number of pages we thought might fit the text. I added lots of illustrations – only black and white, of course. Color was still quite rare and expensive in those days – reserved, I guess, for well-known authors and illustrators.

On the way home on that second weekend, I stopped at the Doubleday store across the street and bought two children's books that appealed to me in style. I liked the way that the text was cleverly punctuated by many full-page and half-page drawings. I was such a beginner I even had to write out what went on at the start of a book, noting how they had used a blank page, a half title page, and a full title page, then a card of necessary information with copyright stuff, the publisher, date, etc. It was all new to me.

I had decided to do my illustrations with black crayon pencil on a Minnesota Mining type of transparent photo paper. (Don't waste time looking for it, it's gone!) It was grainy and broke into all kinds of light grays to dead black. These halftones, I had been told, could be reproduced for exactly the same price as ordinary type.

I had a wonderful time all weekend and took all the drawings with me to work on Monday. I had lunch with Margaret that day and was delighted that she liked all of them, save one or two, which I gladly re-drew. I spent quite a bit of time on a dust jacket, drawing the illustration for it, then worrying about the location of the title and style of the lettering. I still worry as much about these now, after thirty books, as I did then.

Margaret sent me proofs. Only when I saw them did I start to worry about Canada. Since this was a book about Arctic Canada, and by a Canadian, surely sales would be much better there. Perhaps, I thought, that was the only place this book would sell, even though the U.S. population is ten times larger than Canada's. I asked my next-door neighbor, a graduate of the Yale Law School, to look at the contract and tell me what to do. Next day, he advised me to make two separate contracts, the second one dealing with Canada alone.

That book, *Tikta'liktak*, won all kinds of important prizes, went into many different editions, and was translated into a surprising number of languages. I thought perhaps writing every book would be as easy, but I would learn my lesson in due course.

30
The White Dawn

In 1968, I had lunch with two editors from Harcourt, Brace and World: one, my children's book editor, Margaret K. McElderry, and the other, Julian Muller, the senior editor of adult books. Julian was a precise old Navy guy, very experienced in the publishing world, and Margaret had me tell him the story of three American whalers who had lived and died among the Eskimos. I had learned about the story from Pitseolak and other elders around Cape Dorset.

"Why don't you write that as an adult book?" they both suggested.

Margaret, being fully occupied with children's books, said she had never edited an adult novel before, but she was characteristically kind enough to take it on. We were supported by Julian Muller.

I agreed to try it, although I had never dreamed of undertaking such a task. But, then, I had never dreamed of writing children's books either, and that had proved possible.

But first, if I was actually going to write a book about the Arctic people of Baffin Island, I was going to need to get serious, and clear the decks for action in my New York apartment. Intending to use my dining room table near the sliding glass doors that led out to the garden, I drew the draperies and removed the pictures from the near white walls to avoid any distractions.

The local stationery store sold me a ream of lined white foolscap paper and a new fountain pen with a large bottle of black ink. I didn't know how to type, and personal computers were not yet available. But the fountain pen was a great leap forward from the wild goose quill pen that I had used in the Arctic to draw and some-times to write with.

I did not need to set an alarm, for I had kept the habit of early rising established in my army days. When I awoke, I would lie in bed and plan the first paragraph I hoped to write, then jump up, make coffee, put on a kimono and slippers, and immediately start to work. Numbering ten pages in advance and writing double-spaced for easy correcting – my manuscripts needed lots of that – I would write from 6:00 to 8:30 a.m., then walk the eighteen blocks to work as quickly as I could to try to be at Steuben by 9:00. This walk allowed me to think of what had happened and what was about to happen in the manuscript to come.

In those early morning hours, I would sometimes lose my nerve at all the work ahead of me. Then I would have to take the three children's books that I had previously written, hold them together, and say to myself, "These are just as thick as any adult novel." Could that be the reason that all my early adult books were broken into three separate parts?

The White Dawn was a book that I had been carrying, churning inside me, ever since I had heard parts of the Eskimo legend and realized that I knew more than other writers about the White/Inuit misunderstandings that explained the events. I was eager to tell it, but that did not happen in one great rush. The manuscript took five drafts.

The White Dawn: An Eskimo Saga was a hardcover book of 275 pages which sold in 1971 for $6.95. That book really launched my writing career, especially when it was chosen as a main selection of the Book-of-the-Month Club. This was during those last great days when nearly everyone bought and read books. Today, I find our intellectual friends are more likely to discuss foreign films or media-driven scandals in Washington.

I was thrilled, bowled over by the book's immediate success. It was purchased by many European book clubs and it went into thirty-one editions worldwide. The Pulitzer and National Book Award people even contacted me to ask if I was an American, and, alas, I had to admit I was not. The phone enquiries came within an hour of each other when I was in my hotel room in the Baron Steuben.

Because I lived and worked in the heart of Manhattan, there was easy access for those in the business of purchasing movies to phone me and ask if I owned the film rights. When I said yes, they invited me to lunch – not just once, but every day. Producers and directors told me exactly how they planned to make *The White Dawn* as a film. One suggested we do it on his golf club's 18th hole where in winter no background could be seen, just plain snow seeming to disappear to the horizon. Another suggested, during a plane ride to L.A., that the three whalers speak Finnish, a language known by few, and that the Eskimo characters speak English – one of the problems with this ingenious scheme being that the Eskimos who would be involved did not speak English.

Small film companies based in New York and Los Angeles want to discover and buy what, in their opinion, is a filmable property. If you're lucky, they'll also pay you to do a film treatment – about twelve pages outlining how you would change your book into a film – and then they may ask you to do the screenplay. (It is well known that movie producers do not pause to read books.) That gives you a real chance to have some influence on the eventual film.

31

Hollywood North

There are few thrills in this world that can match for me the excitement of creating characters – devising locations and events that first come to life in a book which expand into real, living, breathing persons in my mind and the minds of readers – then developing those characters for the screen. It is an overwhelming thrill for an author to have the ideas he has created appear – with much help from actors and others – and come running, laughing, crying, fighting, singing, dancing into life.

So I was excited and intrigued when I was asked about the purchase of *The White Dawn* as a film. I didn't have an agent and didn't get one for a while. When the bidding started to sound serious, I asked Julian Muller and Margaret what to do. They said, "Why not turn the selling problem over to Harcourt, Brace? Our publishing company has someone to advise you. Movie contracts and lawyers can be tricky."

The offer from Filmways was the one we first pursued. As it turned out, their New York office was almost across the street from Steuben, near the St. Regis Hotel on East 55th.

Marty Ransohoff, the producer, looked young to me, and he was built like a football player. Other film people liked Marty or they didn't. No one was in between. He had made a number of successful films like *The Americanization of Emily* with Julie Andrews, *Catch-22*, *The Cincinnati Kid*, and *The Sandpiper*, with Richard Burton and Elizabeth Taylor. I favored doing *The White Dawn* with Marty partly because he asked me to do the screenplay, and partly because we both like fishing – he deep sea for marlin, and me wading and fly fishing for trout and salmon.

On my signing of a six-figure contract, Marty and Filmways took on the unknown chore of shooting a major film with the whole background location on Baffin Island. They then sold this to Paramount

Pictures, and since no one from Hollywood seemed to want the job, I was asked to be the associate producer on location, a job I feel I never would have been given in a warmer climate.

I had learned how to write books. But how the hell did you write a screenplay, and for a huge Hollywood studio, too? One way or another, I acquired four existing screenplays. They were the first that I had ever seen, and I was intrigued to learn that they are usually 120 pages long, one page a minute for a standard-length, two-hour movie; unlike a book, a screenplay has large white spaces between character names and dialogue. Screenplays will usually take far less time to write than a book, which is great; but on the other hand, almost everyone in the world finds that they can read your screenplay in less than an hour. And because they've been to lots of movies, they're certain that they can change scenes, alter the development of your characters, make it a lot better, and certainly change the ending.

I guess this has been happening to screenplays from the very beginning, since producers and directors with much more experience and more clout are determined to have their way. God knows there are enough jokes about that, and plenty of horror stories of writers finding their work made unrecognizable, until it is tempting, in the end, to sort of give up, take the money, and run (a terrible admission). Twenty-five years after *The White Dawn* was produced, I'm pleased to say that I am, to this day, on good terms with Marty, the producer, and Philip Kaufman, the director, and the actors.

There is really only a two- to three-month frame of time when a film crew can satisfactorily carry out their work in the Arctic. Real winter is too cold and violent, a time of bitter winds and darkness. Even the usual equipment will not work, and in the three months when it turns somewhat summerish, the Arctic loses much of its natural covering. What remains of the snow turns gray-brown, and the inland looks like a satellite shot of Mars. In spring the sun returns, the weather softens, but it still looks like the dead of winter, and it is often well below zero. We never used to count wind chill into our weather factoring, but, believe me, there can often be a tremendous amount of wind chill in the Arctic.

I journeyed with Phil Kaufman, the director, and Don Guest (like me, an associate producer), into Frobisher Bay (now known as Iqaluit) to scout locations and audition Inuit people we might wish to cast in the film.

Frobisher was an exciting place for the Inuit during World War II and during that long post-war period when SAC (Strategic Air Command) had a base there for the purpose of refueling, in the air, the huge B-29s carrying atomic missiles. Those planes remained airborne, flying to the North Pole where they could see their opponents, the huge Russian aircraft called Bears, patrolling for the USSR, each ready to strike, all airborne and on instant alert. I used to play poker with the fighter pilots on that base, and it seemed to me that every time I got a good hand, the scramble alarm would sound. Those pilots, dressed for flight, with their oxygen masks hanging on their chests, would fling down their inferior cards and rush for the hidden bunkers where their already warmed-up fighter aircraft were ready to leap into the night sky and bring down the enemy who never came, perhaps because of them.

For our movie we decided to have everyone we needed in the cast from the Baffin area, plus three imported actors to play the lost whalers. The three from Hollywood were Timothy Bottoms, Warren Oates, and Louis Gossett, Jr. Marty had arranged to hire the abandoned air force hangar and a number of long huts that had been military sleeping quarters, forlorn-looking buildings covered with wind-torn tarpaper.

We asked the local Inuit to come to the hangar so we could select some extras. I had grave misgivings about this, saying Inuit in general spoke no English and would probably not understand or be interested in taking part in the filming. The power and fame of films had not yet reached them. However, on a wintry Saturday, we sent word around to Inuit living on Apex Hill near the almost abandoned airbase, that tomorrow we were asking them to gather in the hangar where we would select extras and pay them well for the first big movie ever made on Baffin Island.

"I'm not so sure anyone will come," I told Philip and Don Guest. "What do they know or care about this movie?"

"Hell, they'll turn up, all right, a lot more of them than we can use. We did this same thing last year on a Sunday afternoon in a town in New Mexico for a cowboy film we were making, and everyone in the place turned out. It looked like a goddamned fire sale!"

When we went over to the hall on Sunday, it was empty. No one was there. Only one teenager came in later because he saw the lights on and said he thought there might be a bingo game.

"I've never seen anything like this!" said Don in amazement. "Everyone likes to be in the movies. Before the shooting in Newport, Rhode Island, of *The Great Gatsby*, F. Scott Fitzgerald's story, the producers practically had to beat away the socialites, so many were eager to act as extras."

"Well, this is a different world," I told them. "Half of everything you hoped for is going to be much easier and better than you'd expected, and the other half will be much worse. You'll soon find out."

"We'll get a stronger message out to all of them tomorrow."

Ravens in snow

As we started to walk home in the failing evening light, the wind increased and blew the snow, curling like smoke off every drift. Before us on the side of the buried road, three large black ravens hopped in through the foglike whiteness, pecking at something half hidden in the snow. *God*, I thought, *what a helluva first impression these Hollywood guys must be getting.* I had told Marty and the producers and others that in spring the Arctic, particularly Baffin Island, would be a dream of a place to make a film, and now we were in a place where no extras even wanted an interesting job. And the whiteout was getting so bloody thick we couldn't see a damn thing but three hungry ravens, vanishing into the coming blizzard as they pecked at God knows what.

It got better. I flew over to Cape Dorset. I started to persuade my Inuit friends who would make appropriate characters that this was going to be an interesting event. I persuaded Simeonie to play the role of the leader, Sarkak, which he did wonderfully well – with one major misunderstanding that I'll describe later. Ann Meekitjuk Hanson agreed to play the female lead. It made her famous, especially in the whole of the Inuit world. Ikaluk, now Joanasie Salomonie, played the Inuit male lead. (The names of those actors have all changed now. They used to have but one name. unfortunately, that confused the government of Canada, so they were encouraged to take a second name to help the bureau-crats identify them.) Soon the whole process of making the movie fascinated the local people, and they supplied many rich details for the legend that they all knew, since the events had affected their own great-grandparents.

Filming on Baffin Island produced special problems. But the one plane daily out to Montreal solved the problem in getting "rushes" – rough footage – out and back to see if retakes were necessary. Helping in the production of the very first full-length movie to be filmed in the Canadian Arctic, or probably any other country's Arctic, provided special pleasures, too. The pleasures did not, however, include getting the dogs.

32

Going to the Dogs

Sled dogs were desperately needed for our film, but they were impossible to find in Iqaluit. We needed dog teams totaling maybe fifty good, strong dogs, and I had forgotten that the people around there had given up on dogs as quickly as we had abandoned horse and cart, and had rapidly changed to snowmobiles. In this they were urged on by all their military money and by the bonanza of discarded army equipment, including thousands upon thousands of drums of aging aviation fuel.

I contacted several Canadian bush pilots I knew who were in the business of flying north or south or west and chartered them to take me north to Igloolik, an island just west of Baffin Island, seven hundred miles away. I had called the settlement to confirm that the people there still lived in a more traditional way and so had many dogs, enough to spare us what we needed. But they were seven hundred miles (one thousand kilometers) away.

We took off in the early morning, the horizon already aglow with the strong, yellow Arctic light reflecting off the snow. We headed up across the Baffin inland to Nettilling Lake, then on toward the newly discovered Prince Charles Island (much larger than the State of Rhode Island), then on to Igloolik, where they had put out blackened coal sacks to mark the smoothest landing surface on the snow-covered sea ice. Years before, on an Eastern Arctic Patrol flight into Igloolik, we had been thrown, tipped sideways, and had cracked a wing. It had taken more than a week for repairs to be completed. That's how I had come to know the *Igloolimmiut* and respect them as good hunters with big dog teams.

Dogs to Inuit are like our horses to us – some are slender and sleek for racing, others big like draft horses built to pull heavy loads. Igloolik is famous for its walrus herds, and their hunters needed big dogs to haul home the heavy kill.

I shook hands with everyone assembled on the ice as we left the plane.

"Don't take too long here," the pilot said. "That's a nasty-looking cloud bank out to the west."

Evaluardjuk, an old friend, was standing, smiling broadly, and beside him was the dog team driver, Peter Arnatsiak, who looked critically at the Otter. "Dogs, a lot have we," he said in Inuktitut. "Too many for your little plane."

"Trips two make we," I answered. "Dogs – I'll go with the first half, you come with the rest when the plane returns."

We started pushing dogs, running them up a loading ramp and inside the cabin of the plane. We managed fourteen, with barely room for me. It's rude to go into an Inuit community and leave so quickly, but hunters and their families understand that when the hunt is on, move fast. And that's the way I felt about all the problems related to making the film, the first in the Arctic since Robert Flaherty's famous documentary, *Nanook of the North*.

I waved out the window as the Otter turned, preparing for its takeoff run. I could tell that the dogs hated the turning. They stood heads down, legs far apart, eyes wide.

"You okay back there?" the co-pilot shouted, aware that I was in a confined space with fourteen big huskies, all so wild that they would turn on a stranger unlucky enough to stumble and fall beside them. I nodded and he slammed the small door between us.

As the plane gathered speed, bumping over the hard snowdrifts, I could hear some dogs howl with anguish and saw others already throwing up. The smell was ghastly. Then at the moment we were airborne and started to do the usual turn, the dogs began to fight. I don't mean just the usual bit of fighting. These dogs had come from two different working teams because I'd asked for big, good-looking dogs, and now sick, dizzy, and frightened half to death, they expressed their fright by tearing into each other. I mean, fighting right beside me, half on me. Lord Jesus, I was scared to death!

I hammered on the little door and the co-pilot opened it a crack. His eyes widened. "Quick, let me in!" I bellowed. "Open up! I'm coming in!"

He half opened the door and I lunged through. There was absolutely no room for me up there. The pilot squeezed sideways as the co-pilot slammed the door, shutting out the snarling, screaming mass of outraged huskies.

"What a fuckin' smell! What a mess back there," the pilot gasped.

I drew my knees up under my chin as all three of us shared the noisiest, worst ride back to Frobisher that even now I hate to remember.

The fighting, which had finally died down, erupted again the moment we banked the plane to land in the strip. We three staggered out the side doors, while some brave Inuit opened the Otter's freight door and got the dogs out. While I shook my legs, trying to get some feeling back into them, the big Igloolik dogs lay on the snow, recovering from their dizziness and licking the wounds of other dogs that lay near them. Huskies, even after a fight, have the habit of helping each other, just like their masters must if they're going to survive.

"Okay," the pilot said, "you ready to go back and round up the other half?"

"No, thanks," I answered, hoping he wouldn't see how I was shaking. "I've got work to do on the set. There's a driver up there waiting for you with more dogs. He'll take care of them on the way down."

"I'll bet it turns out to be another three-man ride up front," said the co-pilot gloomily. "I wish to God I'd taken that other job flying fuckin' bananas out of Jamaica."

"Come on," said the pilot, "we need the money. You can clean up the back of this bloody aircraft soon as we get back."

33

Camp Boss

"Simeonie, where the hell's Simeonie?" Philip called to me. "This is his big morning and it's snowing right on cue. Where is he?"

"I don't know," I said. "He's always been on time." I looked at Joanasie, the younger lead Inuk actor.

"Oh, he went home yesterday, it being Sunday," Joanasie told me. "He got a ride on the police plane, I heard."

"Good God," I gasped, "right in the middle of a movie, he just leaves?"

"Yes, I guess so," said Joanasie, giving me that familiar little smile of his, meaning, "We're our own people, Uncle. We do what we want to."

Philip was bewildered. "But he's Sarkak, the camp boss, the most important actor in all this. And he's gone?"

I rushed to investigate. Thousands of Paramount dollars were ticking away every hour on the set and we needed Simeonie.

"You find him yet?" Assistant Director Jon Anderson called to me on his bullhorn. "We're ready to roll. Somebody find him."

"I'll go check his quarters," I told Philip, the director, "but the word is he went back to Dorset yesterday."

"How far is that?" Philip asked, his face turning red.

"Not so far," I lied. "I'll get a plane and go over and get him. You'd probably do best to put off that scene for a day or so."

"Holy Christ!" gasped Kaufman. "This is one goddamned expensive playpen we're fuckin' around in here. Yeah, go and get him soon as you can. I don't know what the hell I'll say today when Marty calls from L.A."

I jumped into the old military jeep we'd rented and tore over to the place where Simeonie lived.

"Yes, he's gone," his niece said, "gone to visit his family. He'll be back next time he can catch a free ride with the police plane."

I jumped back into the jeep and drove over to the airstrip. The bush pilots, I was told, were over at the bunkhouse having coffee.

"Can any of you come right now?" I asked them as I went in the door. "I've got to get to Dorset fast and I'll come straight back with you."

"Sure!" one pilot said. "Harry, you phone and make some kind of goddamned excuse as to why we can't go to Pangnirtung today. Tell them we'll go tomorrow if this good weather holds out."

"They'll love that," Harry, his co-pilot, yelled. "Why do you always give me the dirty work?"

We hurried out of the bunkhouse to the plane. It was in the hangar and didn't need to warm up, though the weather was still cold. I explained what had happened during our two-hour flight.

"You must be mad as hell at that character," laughed the pilot. "Just skipping out on you like that, and him with a major part in the movie. Simeonie's a real camp boss and he's playing camp boss, isn't he?"

"Yeah, that's right, but I'm not mad at him. He thinks we're just fooling around here, not doing something serious like hunting. He really doesn't care about – or maybe even truly understand – the money he's making, the most ever paid in the Arctic. He's an honest-to-God nomad doing what hunters do. He wanted to see his family, so he just went home to see them."

When we landed on the ice at Dorset in the fiord in front of Kingait Mountain, I crawled out of the Otter and trotted up to the collection of winter tents between the Hudson's Bay trading post and what had been my old house.

"*Kanuiipisiit*," I said to Latcholassie, the first man I saw. "Simeonie, have you seen Simeonie around here?"

"*Ayii*, he got back yesterday. A bunch of us ate some meat with him. He told us all about you and those *ajjinguat* you're making. He says the food's awful, but you're feeding them fair and square. He likes playing he's Sarkak well enough, but he thought he'd come home for a visit, maybe get some spring hunting in to feed his family."

"Sweet Jesus," I said, "which tent's he sleeping in?"

"That's his tent down there at the end. He may already be out hunting. No wind. Saomik, Left-Handed, good to see you again."

"Glad to see you, too," I called back as I hurried through the rough barrier ice up toward the tent.

Two little kids were out in front watching me. They ducked back in through the low tent door and in a moment, Simeonie's wife appeared.

"*Itiriit*, enter," she welcomed me, all smiles. "He's still in the bed having a cup of tea. He's been telling all about the games you've all been playing together at Iqaluit."

I ducked inside the low door. The large tent had a warm, friendly glow of spring light filtering through the old, worn canvas.

"*Ayii*, Saomik, decided to come over hunting, too, did you? It's the right time for it. Seals are up on the ice in this good weather. I saw them from the police plane."

"Listen, Simeonie, listen to me. The whole bunch of people that came up from the South, the *Americamiuts*, the *Canadamiuts*, and all Inuit who are helping over at Iqaluit . . . they're all, every one of them, waiting for you to come back . . . with me . . . right now!" I looked at my watch.

"It's important," I said. "I told all those people, even the ones in the South you've never seen, that you were the best man to play these games, that you were wise, and that you would stay until the very end of the movie . . . um . . . the playing."

"Well, I will," said Simeonie as he put down his tea and started to get out of their bed that stretched across the whole width of the tent.

"You know that food?" (I sure did. We had rented the old air base dining hall and kitchen and brought in a chef from Mont Tremblant Village who provided what I honestly believe was the best food ever served in the Arctic, and the communal eating with Inuit actors and the crew made a joyous relationship.) "Well, I just wanted to see the family and get some real red meat to eat, not cooked all brown the way *kallunaat* like it. I mean real red meat." He passed me a knife. "You take what you want, Left-Handed. The boys got that seal yesterday, not long before I got here."

"You can take all the meat you want back in the plane with you," I said, taking a delicious slice of raw seal. "It's empty, just you and me and the pilots."

Simeonie was busy getting dressed.

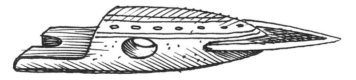

Harpoon head

"You two going hunting today?" Simeonie's wife asked us.

"No, not today," I told her. "I flew over here just to get your husband and take him back to play until that movie's finished. He's kind of the main part, the big player. He's the camp boss there and we've got to get back right now while the weather's good and start playing again."

"We're going now," Simeonie said to his wife as he gathered his rifle, his hunting bag, and an extra pair of skin boots. "Saomik, are you sure you don't want another cup of tea?"

"No, thanks. Let's go. *Tavvauvusi ilunnasi*, good-bye."

In some strange and unexpected ways, it wasn't easy helping to make a big movie when you knew as little as I did about the process. But my years of close friendship with Inuit living in the camps on south and west Baffin had made it possible for me to do some things that would have been difficult for Hollywood to do. The Inuit immensely enjoyed working with the expert technical people from the South and so did I. The three imported actors were good human beings, and I believe we all had an educational experience that none of us will ever forget.

34

Bad, Bad to Kill that Boy

If you ever see *The White Dawn*, which is available on video, and shows up now and then on television, you may notice that there are very few children in the scenes. Early in the filming, we used to ask mothers who were extras in the film to bring their young children with them, but it never really worked out after the first day or two. First, because when most women came on the set, some distance from Iqaluit, they would have lunch there with all the rest of us and would have no way to get home until after 5:00 or 6:00 p.m., when the day's shooting was over. Their babies grew restless in the hood and would start to cry, oblivious to all the shouts of, "Quiet on the set!" The sound men would wave their hands in the air, then have a fit, begging at first, then cursing and demanding that the mothers and their crying children be sent away. Because of this, no infants in the hood or young children appeared on the set, but remained safely at home with their aunt or grandmother. During the highly pressured twelve weeks of shooting time, we never really found any good solution.

Inuit used to have a general habit of silence and a natural economy of movement, when outside their dwellings. I believe this was because of the animals they hunted. Children quite quickly learned to act like adults and knew not to jump around too much and frighten away the food they depended on. Our schooling habits, however, taught Inuit children an opposite view – to run and shout, to play noisy, mindless games like Leap Frog and Jack-in-the-Box and to jump in the air. This style was fine, perhaps, for southern educational systems, but all wrong in the Arctic.

I believe this one single great difference in human deportment began to drive a serious wedge between Inuit young and their parents and especially their grandparents who lived in their dwellings with them and had done more than a little to educate them before the government day schools took over.

Inuit have a subtle sense of humor, which was not easily apparent. When everything had been prepared for the acting, the photography, and the sound recording, the assistant director, Jon Anderson, would order the clapper board closed and call out, "Roll it!" That meant absolute silence on everyone's part, a new thing to Inuit who were watching.

"What does 'roll it' mean?" Joanasie asked me.

"It means the camera wheel is going to unroll and hundreds, maybe thousands of small pictures will be taken with the words and sounds."

Joanasie, who was not in that scene, hurried over to explain that to the local Inuit audience.

Next scene, perhaps an hour later, the whole of the audience was on their knees like American Air Force crapshooters. And when Anderson again called "Roll it!," all of the watching Inuit shook their right fists vigorously, then opened their hands and rolled out two square-shaped stones.

This was the cause of much local mirth. Inuit had invented an ancient game where they rolled ivory walrus teeth carved into birds to determine the direction they would take to hunt next day. So this was just their play on the English language. They were rolling it, all right. But they covered their mouths so their laughter at this joke of theirs could not be heard.

There were other, less humorous, rewarding times during the filming as I saw the whole impact of their legend returning to them. At the most dramatic moment of the film, a young white sailor has unknowingly run to a cliff's edge to escape Inuit who plan to kill him. Joanasie made his wonderfully impassioned speech in Inuktitut as the executioner rose from among other hunters and, drawing his bow, aimed at the young sailor.

"Bad! Bad to kill that boy!" screamed the grandmothers who were watching. And many other men and women joined in the shouting, forgetting that this was only playing, perhaps even believing that the arrow, which traveled along an invisible length of piano wire, had actually pierced deep into Timothy Bottoms' chest. The whole scene had to be reshot several times, which was not at all unusual in the film business.

Each time the bowman released his arrow, before it appeared to bury itself in the good guy's chest, the screaming and shouting of the old women started again. "Bad, bad to kill Timothee!"

When I got into bed that night, I stared at the ceiling and thought about the attitude Inuit possess. Long ago, three shipwrecked sailors had come into their community and ruined their carefully balanced, isolated lives. And now, here were the elders cheering for us, the outsiders, and admonishing their own relatives for trying to set things right again. Today when recalling that scene, I wonder if their reaction would now be the same. Has our education, our way of doing things vastly changed the way they think of us? And, more importantly perhaps, how much has it changed us? Will they come to try, like the Indians, to stand angrily apart from us? Or will Inuit just throw up their hands, as we have, turn on the TV satellite dishes that we've supplied for them, and join us?

Some of the crew had interesting stories of their own. One told me that he was fresh out of jail in Hawaii. When I asked him what he'd done, he laughed.

"I had only about six months more to serve," he said, "when word came to that jailhouse that a film director was looking for me to help make this picture. They took me over to the courthouse there among the flowers and the palm trees and the judge looked up my case and said, 'Hell, man, we'll be glad to see you off our rolls. Go, for God's sake, a good job like that in the Arctic sounds like it's just made for you. Go ahead, freeze your ass off, clear your muddled head. Get married, man, and stay up there forever. These islands can make out fine without you.'

"The hell they can." The crewman pulled up his parka hood and laughed. "Screw him! I'll be back in Hawaii soon as this picture's over. But I will try to stay out of the can."

35

A Sleeping Dictionary

My son, John, and his younger brother, Sam, managed to live their childhoods in the Arctic without really having to resort to the English language, except when being taught from the Calvert correspondence course by their mother. When John and Sam went with their mother and grandmother to attend school in England, they quickly lost their ability to speak Inuktitut. I discovered that this is not uncommon for children brought up in foreign countries where other children and local nannies had helped them absorb their language.

Later, Sam went to Fettes College in Edinburgh, Scotland, and John to Yale in Connecticut. While John was there at college, we saw him often on the farm where we lived, which was only seventy miles away. It was during his sophomore year that the screenplay for *The White Dawn* was completed, and when, after several additional trips to California, everything was finally in order to go north and begin the shoot. Then John asked me very earnestly if he could come into the Arctic and be a part of the filming crew, working, doing anything. I called Marty Ransohoff, the producer, in Los Angeles, and he said, "Sure, your kid can go up – as coffee boy, but not much salary." That sounded like my early Arctic trips and I gratefully accepted. John was delighted at even the mere thought of going back.

Preliminary plans were completed in Toronto. Marty had hired a crew – one half of them American imports and the others Canadians from Montreal and Toronto, plus lots of Inuit snowmobile drivers, boatmen, and igloo builders. First shooting of the film was to begin just as the Yale term ended, and John flew up north to start his job. That journey, he says, changed his life.

Because John was always cheerful and eager to be of help, he was asked by Philip Kaufman, the director, to stay by him some days to watch what was going on and see from Philip's point of view why things were important. Mike Chapman, the English film photographer, asked John to be his second assistant some days, allowing John to understand that aspect of the picture. Eventually, almost everyone on the film allowed John to work with them.

He went about his work totally absorbed in the phenomenon of filmmaking. I saw him only occasionally, always dragging coffee around in a large, aluminum urn and dispensing it cup by cup to the cast and crew, often along with oatmeal cookies.

John discovered, however, that in his twelve years of absence from Baffin Island, he had totally lost his ability to speak or understand Inuktitut, the language of Inuit in the Canadian Arctic. Inuit were particularly interested in this, scarcely able to believe that he could no longer speak their language, though he had spoken nothing else to them when they had last seen him.

"Jonasikudluk, your son, Little John, he's rude," several older women told me. "I used to have long conversations with him when he was small about just everything, and now that he's grown, he won't even speak to me," one woman added.

The Inuit interested him greatly, but there was this communication problem. Except for Joanasie Salomonie, who rightly considered himself John's uncle, and Ann Meekitjuk Hanson, who was like John's older sister, both of whom spoke English, the other Inuit spoke Inuktitut exclusively.

There was nothing anyone could do about that situation, I believed, but I was wrong. There was a little actress with a small speaking part in the movie. She was down from the north – was it Pangnirtung or Clyde River? – and as delicate and beautiful as a talented young geisha from Japan. John, I noticed, used to offer her more cookies than seemed strictly necessary, and tried hard to communicate with her. How he did that with his lost language, I'm not sure. But several mornings when I went to the place where he slept to ask him if he wanted to share breakfast with me, he was gone.

About six weeks later, when the film was drawing to a close, the weather had warmed considerably, and we were going back to retake a shot of some big ice that had grounded on a small rock island out in the bay. Mannumie Shaqu, playing Sowniapik, sat up in the bow of the whaleboat while I stood in the stern. It was a real double-ended, twenty-two-foot chase boat left by the last of the Scottish whalers – called Dundeemen by Inuit.

A cold northwest wind was blowing across the open water, and the half dozen people with us had their hoods drawn up and their heads turned away from the wind. Suddenly, Mannumie yelled my name, then called out something back to me in Inuktitut. I swept back my hood to hear him better. Before Mannumie had the chance to call out again, John piped up from the center of the boat, "He says, 'Go left, it's too shallow.' He can see rocks under the water ahead."

We turned to port, entering deeper water, before I called to John, "How do you know what he said? It was all in Inuktitut."

"*Kaujimangilanga*. I don't know." John laughed. "But today I understood him."

"You've been using a sleeping dictionary," I said to him – that being an expression the old Hudson's Bay Company traders aimed at their men who spoke the language well, thanks to female instruction.

When the filming was completed, we had a wonderful wrap-up party, and I could see that the coffee boy was usually among a crowd of Inuit, laughing and talking.

When John's graduation party from Yale was done, we – a group including myself, Sam, and John's mother, Allie – sat down together and John asked, "What do you think I ought to do?"

"Why don't you get a Master's, then a Ph.D. in Anthropology?

"No, I'm finished with schooling," said John, who had done remarkably well.

I told him, "Our family owes a lot to Inuit. Why don't you go up to a different place, not Cape Dorset, which is doing so well, but to, say, Igloolik or Pangnirtung and help to start a printmaking program there."

"Great!" said John. "That's exactly what I'd love to do."

He went straight north to Pangnirtung and stayed there for four years. I went in to see him and Inuit in Pangnirtung several times. Their prints were splendid, done by masters like Lipa Pitsiulak, Thomasie Alikatuktuk, and Solomonie Karpik, John's hunting companion. Best of all, perhaps, was the fact that John had totally regained his childhood mastery of the language and much more – a wealth of Inuit Arctic knowledge.

He was asked to join Carroll Ballard in the filming of Farley Mowat's book, *Never Cry Wolf*, which was successfully shot in the Yukon and Alaska. Later, John worked on the Disney film *From Time to Time*, which was based on Jules Verne's book and that took him not eighty days but eight months around the world, then *Kabloona*, shot by a Parisian production company in Siberia with Canadian Inuit actors. He also worked on *Fly Away Home* and took a Turner picture, *Glory & Honor*, north to Iqaluit. His early understanding of the North and his ability to speak French and the Inuit language have blossomed into a successful film career.

36

Back in the North

During the dark month of November 1986, I returned to Baffin Island to give readings for Children's Book Week.

To my delight, I found Inuit school children reading many of the books, both myths and legends, that I had written years before. I never imagined Arctic children reading English – let alone my books – or that my works would stay in print so long! When I was asked to give a talk, I spoke of *Kiviok's Magic Journey*, a myth, and *Tikta'liktak* and *The White Archer*, two legends that the students knew very well. They especially liked *Frozen Fire*, a young adult novel in which I recounted the story of an Inuk boy who was lost on moving ice, and how he survived. I combined that with a second story, with a core of truth, about a boy who had come north with his father who searched for precious metals using a helicopter. *Frozen Fire* has been by far my most popular children's book; with *Black Diamonds* and *Ice Swords*, it is part of a trilogy.

I believe that having a direct living experience with the culture about which one is writing is invaluable, perhaps even essential. This has long been my method of relating northern stories, and I believe it would apply to other cultures around the world. Only after twenty years of living part of every year close to the Haida Indians will I now consider writing about them.

Taping or copying down some oral legend directly from the mouth of a native narrator and guiding it verbatim into print is the task of an anthropologist, but scientific papers rarely make exciting children's reading. A story must first be a good, understandable story, whether it is part of a children's book or an adult novel, and an author must not be tempted to let too many facts clog the way. Authors of children's books, therefore, have the challenge of combining fact and fiction in stories, which are both interesting and informative.

Authors working with other cultures have imaginative work to do. I feel you should listen carefully to what individuals say about their lives, hear what they value or perhaps disdain, and try to understand their traditions and customs and, indeed, their myths and legends. Finally, you may hear a core of truth, something that excited them and has the same effect on you. As William Blake has written, "One thought fills immensity."

None of the far northern people used the written word to convey the delights or fears of their astonishing and sometimes magical world. Instead, they used the age-old art of storytelling, using their myths and legends. This extraordinary art involved the breathtaking excitement of the human voice mixed with animal sounds and shouts, and was usually accompanied by dancing and the rhythm of the drum or the howling Arctic winds outside the snowhouse that had been made large for dancing and feasting. Sometimes the storyteller's helper clicked a goose quill against his teeth to help build excitement and suspense. Meanwhile, the storyteller revealed through many means the agility and cunning of the bear, the huge, fearless bulk of the walrus, the beauty of a flight of geese, the tenderness of a woman to a child, or perhaps the mystical gaze of the moon looking down upon you gathered inside a winter snowhouse or a summer tent.

Originally, in almost all native concepts, the world was flat. Older Eskimos usually described its edges as being hidden in ice fog. It was said that travelers could and sometimes did fall off the earth. The sky, meanwhile, was held up by four huge, carved, wooden posts. Television and schooling have spoiled all that for Inuit. Now the children see classroom globes, and adults see our round world spinning on TV during the introduction to the news.

An anthropologist recently asked an old storyteller, "Whatever happened to that flat world of yours?"

"Well, it was certainly flat when you and I were young," the Eskimo answered, "but then you people blew it up with that great bang and the spreading cloud. We've seen it on the TV. You curled up the world like a ball of dried seaweed. I don't know how we northerners are ever going to get it flat again."

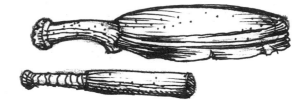

Drum and stick

37

Short-Wave Radio

I was very surprised to find myself a published writer, and maybe some of my former schoolmates were even more surprised! But looking back, I realized that one of the training courses that assisted me most in writing occurred in the Arctic toward the end of my work there as the civil administrator of west Baffin Island. Occasionally, I was required to send and answer messages via the Hudson's Bay Company short-wave radio. This represented our only contact with the outside world, except for the once a year "shiptime" when official and personal mail could be sent out and received by ship. The open radio line was carefully listened to at 8:00 p.m. by every English-speaking person in the Canadian eastern and central Arctic. Although it was the only daily contact, it made it possible for a person to come to know very well the character and personal triumphs and disasters over many years of someone a thousand miles away without ever seeing or knowing them.

When sending and receiving conditions were bad, and that was often, these messages were of necessity passed using Morse Code, a system of dot-dash spelling. But a good post manager's wife could "read" the key while having a conversation with someone and washing dishes at the same time and know all the news of the few *kallunaat* who occupied thousands and thousands of miles of frozen white coastline.

Knowing this, since I was doing government work and sometimes dealing with sensitive information, I quite often sent coded messages that could not be understood by anyone. It was widely known that I was using a *Slater's Code Book*, but since the keys to understanding changed weekly, it was a mammoth task for an amateur to decode it. Still, the Arctic contained exactly that kind of individual, people who, having nothing particular to do for, say, the months of December and January when it was permanently dark and cold outside, would deal with your message like a chess game or a super clever crossword puzzle. Even I, hearing a coded message passed from some other remote Arctic station would sometimes try and sometimes succeed in breaking it, but only because of the code user's ignorance. Here is a tip from an old code-breaker. It is imperative in sending code never to repeat a simple word such as "and" or "they," for that can unlock the whole complex code.

The messages we sent out on the Hudson's Bay Company radio were broken into ten words, fifty words, one hundred words, and so on, which established their charge rate. I, being a Scot dealing with Scottish traders, prided myself at staying within the charge limits. First, I would write out the required message containing all the necessary information. Then I would cross out all the words that were not absolutely necessary to maintain a clear understanding of my meaning. I usually found that I could reduce my message by half and still convey the information.

When I moved south and began to work on children's books with Margaret McElderry, she mentioned this with delight, saying that brevity is so important in good children's books and, for that matter, in adult books as well. I maintained that gift of brevity for perhaps twenty-five years, but now I'm afraid I've gone and lost it, probably as a result of living where everybody now uses hundreds of words where a few selected ones would do.

38

Airsick Bags

In the early days of my coming to New York, the word "briefcase" was not even in my vocabulary. I'd stuff some designs into a brown manila envelope, taxi out to La Guardia Airport, and take off for Corning in the company plane or a commercial plane. I was just getting used to the idea of seatbelts as a safety precaution, which we never used in the Arctic in those days. I was astonished by the notion that Mohawk Airlines would provide you with their company's monthly magazine, and most interesting of all to me was a pure white vomit bag, now more properly called an air sickness bag. I had discovered, like many others, that flying offers the purest kind of relaxation, as well as freedom from all the cares of the world. While most passengers sat fully absorbed in the morning newspaper, I was busy developing the plots and illustrations for various children's books, and most of my adult novels as well. There is something inspiring about flying through the air, but the ideas must be recorded. I rarely brought spare paper, but I always had a pen. So taking out the vomit bag, I'd let down the food tray and start to organize my thoughts.

1. What is this story about?
2. How will this story begin?
3. Who are the main characters?
4. What happens in the middle of the story?
5. What happens at the climax?
6. How does this story end?
7. Title?

Of course, plans made on the vomit bag will change, but they all potentially turn into books. It goes without saying that this bag, 4½ × 10 inches, two sides, demands brevity of word and thought.

You'll find yourself landing long before you're ready to fold the airsick bag inside your pocket and unfasten your seatbelt.

39

Inuit Storytelling

Pure storytelling by Inuit (or their close observers) is usually an attempt to convey the meaning of an event. The storyteller may drift into legends like *King Arthur* or into myths like *Aladdin's Lamp*, but to retain the listener's interest, an Inuit story will deal with exciting, thought-provoking, scandalous, courageous, loving, or murderous themes. Yet, Inuit stories are usually almost incomprehensible to those using other languages. They do not begin the way our stories do. They have no need to end as our stories do. The storytellers make no concessions to foreign listeners. They assume we, the foreigners, must know all about their highly specialized lives, and so they never explain where a shaman hides his magic tools or how a snow shovel must be stood up like a man or it will run away and hide all winter beneath the snow.

Imagine the changes that have occurred in the Arctic in the fifty years since I first traveled there by chance. To give one example, Arctic settlements are now decorated by satellite dishes receiving color television programs from all over the world. In the eastern and central regions, where very few adults understand English or French, Inuit turn off the sound, which means that real events on the evening news cannot be separated from fictitious soap operas, hospital dramas, police car chases, and shoot-'em-ups, murder mysteries, and war movies. All our truths, myths, legends, wars, and violence are mixed together without any interpretation. No wonder so few Inuit are willing to come down to Toronto or New York or Los Angeles and risk their lives in the South among us!

I would like every North American to consider the fact that people have come to this continent during four separate periods.

As we now understand our history, Indians walked over a land bridge from Asia into America about sixteen thousand years ago. Inuit/Eskimos probably walked across or paddled around the ice about five thousand years ago. Vikings sailed to Canada a thousand years ago. We latecomers began to arrive over the last five hundred years. I believe we should all be welcome to write about ourselves. No literary restrictions here, please. The main fact is we are all North Americans, sharing a huge and wonderful continent together.

When today's great Inuit and Indian carvers and storytellers disappear, will their children carry on the culture? I believe they will, because of the inherited traditions and the innate talents of the young people. North American natives have never been so threatened by the juggernaut of civilization as they are today. But remember, we are dealing with Inuit, some of the world's hardiest survivors and, in many ways, the continent's most creative thinkers.

Hear this:

Ayii, Ayii, Ayii,
I wish to see the musk ox run again.
It is not enough for me
To sing of the dear beasts.
Sitting here in the igloo,
My songs fade away,
My words melt away,
Like hills in fog.
Ayii, Ayii, Ayii.

40

Nothing on Paper

Someone I had been introduced to at a party telephoned me and said he had a wonderful idea that he thought would be perfect for Corning. He said he wanted to come to the office and show it to me. When I told Jack Gates, he said, "You be damned careful of anything like that. If I were you, I wouldn't even look at it."

"Why?" I asked.

"Because we may have new projects being developed at Corning that neither of us knows anything about. If someone comes and shows you some design that is similar to one that Corning is already making, there could be trouble, especially since the man could easily have made his similar design with somebody's inside help. He need only wait until Corning brings out the product, then sue the hell out of the company for stealing his carefully copied and pre-dated idea that he has managed to show to you, and says you stole for the company."

I had trouble with this sort of thing in another way in New York. A man I knew and trusted said he thought I was creative or inventive, and one day as we descended in an elevator from lunch, he offered to pay me 15 percent of anything he earned if I would merely present him with a good, usable idea.

I stopped him in the lobby below and said, "This might be the kind of idea you're looking for." And I described at some length how an Arctic wind mixed with a snow-reflected sunburn was really hard on the face. So I had found it best not to shave with ordinary shaving cream after a long dog-team trip, but to use a small quantity of seal oil. I would imagine some company could build that quality into a shaving cream.

He said, "Yes, that's just the kind of idea I'm talking about. Thanks."

Unlike other New Yorkers, he made no attempt to draw up a contract with me, and thereafter, when I saw him at cocktail parties and dinners, he was always deep in conversation, then disappeared. Less than a year later, the finished product appeared, a new salve-like shaving cream to be used by active, outdoor men and women who suffered from chapped, wind-burned faces. It was a product of the very company with which he had connections, but, believe me, I saw no percentage of any kind.

When I phoned to confront this man about our verbal arrangement, he answered, "Yes, I'm in on that. It was just an idea I had." Then he said he had another call and hung up.

I began to realize that my Eskimo trust in others would have to be packed away. When I mentioned to Arthur what had happened, he said, "Let that be a warning to you, Houston. I have a wonderful lawyer. Feel free to ask him for advice if you need help."

I did once ask that wise lawyer about a book contract a publisher was urging me to sign.

"Do you need the money now?" he asked me.

"No," I answered.

"Then," he said, "don't sign."

41

Garden Apartment

Dick Flender, my friendly landlord on East 69th Street, was a native-born New Yorker. They are somewhat rare. After Yale and the University of Virginia Law School, Dick had gone into banking at Morgan Guaranty and invested in a handsomely refurbished brownstone house. I heard through the grapevine from a girl who lived next door that the Flenders' garden floor tenant was leaving. I went right away and saw this apartment and took it. Thankfully in 1963 the price was one-tenth the price it would be today. I signed a two-year lease and continued to sign ongoing leases for the remaining time I lived in the city. I came to know and admire Dick Flender and my beautiful landlady, the concert pianist, Norma Flender, and eventually became godfather to their son and daughter.

After my time in the Arctic, I greatly valued the privacy of my paved patio, about thirty feet by forty feet, in the rear of the apartment. It had three feathery hawthorn trees and earth below in which to plant flowers and grow a garden. I had never gardened in my life and did not plan to start one. But I treasured my patch of outdoor privacy and used to leave two comfortable chairs out there next to a marble-top table. In the garden I would read, or, better still, have a private conversation with friends.

My landlord was not at all like this. On a Saturday or Sunday afternoon, in good weather, Dick liked to sit on the wide front stoop to his five-story brownstone that we shared. He enjoyed watching people flow by on our street. This smacked to me of some kind of old, tenant-style living in New York, when folks did sit on their front steps to enjoy the neighbors. By contrast, most Canadians prefer to hide behind their house in secrecy, as I do, and quietly drink their whiskies or, for the more conservative ones, a cup of tea.

Finally, at Dick's urging, I worked up my nerve and sat with him out front sometimes and said hello to our neighbors or commented on the dogs led past and watched them sniff and pee against the indestructible New York ginkgo trees. That was in the days before the city discovered the even tougher, better looking, flowering pear tree. The Arctic retreat of our private back garden made Dick feel lonely, even though hundreds of high windows looked down upon it.

One night, on my way home to host a small cocktail party I saw some fake plastic tulips, bought eighteen of them, and planted them artfully in my back garden. Some guests arrived and we had drinks in the living room, then moved out into the garden to view that marvelous city glow when the stars are just beginning to appear. The light was dim, and my planted plastic flowers glowed yellow, red, and ghostly white against the shadows of the wall.

"How do you manage to keep such a lovely garden here in the middle of this city?" one guest asked, as other compliments flowed.

I was suitably modest. But I think that one event did twist me into sympathy toward my future wife's real gardening. Now I'm hooked, as well.

42

Big Abe

Norma and Dick Flender had a truly memorable dog named Abraham, a gray Irish wolfhound of gigantic proportions. I had never in my life seen such an enormous dog. Like some human giants, Big Abe was somewhat awkward in the vastness of his size. When that dog decided to lie down on the floor above me, I could hear him go down awkwardly in two sections, like someone dropping two heavy sacks of musk ox bones.

When the Flenders went away on weekends, and if I planned to remain in New York, they would ask me to take Big Abe out for a walk on Saturday and Sunday. Of course, I would always appear to welcome this request, but in truth I suffered fear and trepidation. Big Abe, I felt, was mentally a little out of touch. Even though we had had contact hundreds of times, he had never really come to recognize me, as almost all dogs would.

On Saturday near noon, I would grasp the Flenders' key and mount their front stone steps. "Good morning, Abraham," I would call.

Dead silence inside.

I would turn the key in the heavy, steel-faced door. "Good morning, Abe, Old Boy," I'd call again in a voice usually reserved for very pretty girls.

This time, I'd hear the heavy humping and thumping as Abraham struggled to his feet and came ominously to the inside of the door. He sniffed, then gave a half groan or growl. I was used to big dogs; I had known intimately a team of huskies, but in Inuit style, we never tried to socialize with them.

Calling Abe's name in my friendliest voice, I would struggle to unlock the door, then swing it very gently open, ready to slam it quick and run. Abraham would stare at me, his black eyes almost hidden by his shaggy eyebrows.

"I'm coming in, Abe," I'd tell him. "I've got to get your leash."

When I had it, he would half turn around and seem unaware that I had snapped it on his mighty collar. But seeing the open door in front of him, Big Abe would amble out and awkwardly make his way down the stairs.

As we started along East 69th Street, I noticed again that his rough-haired gray back was as high as my elbow. Many people in the street, at first glance, thought I was walking some hairy type of pony. It made me nervous at first, then gave me kind of a sense of power as I saw people coming toward me realize that Abe was some kind of monstrous dog and cross the street to get out of his way.

When Abe awkwardly cocked his ungainly leg to soak one of our street's ginkgo trees, it was like a garden hose. Even though Abe and I made many walks together and met dog lovers who would call to Abe by name, I noticed that even they would usually not come close to him. I never did develop a true friendship with Abraham. Perhaps some kennel had overbred him to achieve his immense size.

In the North, Inuit/Eskimos do not practice any form of dog breeding. During their nomadic lives, they traveled widely by dog team, and that allowed a healthy, natural mixing. But it is said that in the central Arctic they used to stake a bitch in heat out in an area where wolves were known to be hunting caribou. This, they say, would often introduce a whole new strain of wolves into the dog family. Wolves have broad feet that are good on snow, and they are able to go for a week or more without food, but they lack the extraordinary spirit of the husky dog to work, to pull. Thus, the first generation from that wild wolf breeding was not thought by them to be much good, but for many generations after, the Inuit/Eskimos believed the wolf strain helped to produce the best of all sled dogs.

43

Stopping Smoking

A year after I first arrived in New York, I read a small piece on the front page of *The New York Times* that quoted *The Journal of the American Medical Association*. It read: "Smoking is bad for your health and is a known cause of cancer."

I thought, well, that's it. I'm going to quit. Just stop cold turkey. I went out and threw my pack of cigarettes in a trashcan, where I could not retrieve them. I had smoked two packs a day for years. Smoking had always seemed such a comfort when traveling by dog team in the Arctic that even newcomers who had never smoked would take a cigarette – if you offered to roll one for them, their hands being far too cold for that. They would smoke that down until it burned their mitt, then beg for another.

Now those days were over for me, to hell with smoking, forget it. But to my surprise, I found it just about impossible to concentrate on work. Oh, how I longed for a cigarette. But I held out in agony for almost a week, until the night of a party. As I showered and dressed for dinner, I thought, the first thing I'm going to do when I get to this party is to beg a cigarette off the first person I see, get a dry martini, and start living again.

I got the martini and just as I was about to light the cigarette, my landlady, Norma Flender, who knew that I had stopped smoking, rushed over, took my unlit cigarette, and flung it into their fireplace. She kept her eye on me for the rest of the evening. I was afraid to smoke.

Next morning I did not buy cigarettes as I had planned to do. But when the craving became awful, I bought and smoked a really terrible five-cent cigar. That cured me for the rest of the day. On many of the following days, I'd have to leave my drawing board to go out and trot around the block at Steuben and sometimes puff on fake menthol cigarette tubes. After a couple of torturous months gnawing a shopping bag full of chewing gum, my addiction had more or less eased.

When I went north as co-producer for Paramount Pictures to help make *The White Dawn*, we had a week of unusual warm weather for April, and the large snow dance house that we had built as part of a set collapsed. Phil Kaufman, the director, and I were in a fit.

"What's to be done?" I asked my friends, as I have always done when there was an Arctic problem.

"Are you going to take pictures inside the igloo?" they asked.

"No, only on the outside, but actors have got to be able to go in and out of the snowhouse."

"We'll show you how to do that," they said. "We'll build an igloo of solid snow that won't cave in.

They cut a deep hole inside the entrance, just deep enough for an actor or two to squat inside after entering or before leaving.

"Wonderful," said Kaufman when I showed him. "Look at all the other snowhouses that have melted. Can you have them reconstruct the village tonight for tomorrow's shoot?"

"Maybe," I answered.

It was 7:00 p.m. The night cold was arriving. Half a dozen Inuit pitched in and so did I. About 11:00 p.m., one of them offered me a cigarette and I took it, and smoked it with a cup of coffee from the thermos. It tasted awful, but I smoked another at 3:00 a.m. It tasted better, and the third at 7:00 was manna from heaven. And we were finished.

"No, thanks," I said when they offered me another cigarette next day. I had been hooked hard when I was a teenager, and I was going to make certain that it never happened to me again.

44

Rocketing Monte Carlo

After my Arctic days aboard a rugged, thirty-five-foot Eskimo boat, built at Peterhead in Scotland to withstand the winter storms of the North Sea, I was not at all prepared for the elegance of the chartered yacht, *Marala*, which plied the gentle, ice-free waters of the Mediterranean. With a British crew of twenty-four, and a splendid French chef, we embarked with Arthur Houghton's party of ten on our two-week cruise.

Most days, we anchored after breakfast off some port on the Italian Riviera, went ashore, and shopped. This process amazed me. The small port shops would have clothing of the latest Italian and French styles. When articles were about to be purchased and confusion set in about the difference between the Italian lira and the American or Canadian dollar, the shop keepers would smile graciously and shake their heads – no cash, no travelers' checks, no credit cards, nothing was required at that time. They would simply find out your address, and have the purchase delivered to you in North America on trust. The length of the privately hired yacht anchored in their port and its daily charter rate was guarantee enough for them of later payment.

We would almost invariably have lunch seated around a long, outdoor table in the best restaurant in the port. Good as the food and wine were, meals prepared by our French chef aboard were better. I sometimes worried about him sitting out aboard, doing nothing.

We would return to the *Marala* about three, perhaps have a nap, then swim off the side, have high tea in the fading sun, and start thinking about the evening. Would we ten, who knew and liked each other very much, all stay aboard for dinner and whoop it up by ourselves, or would we sally forth once more, dine ashore, and find a cafe for disco dancing? Whatever we chose, we would dress that night for dinner and enjoy life.

Men in dinner jackets, white or black, have solved their costume for years, but for women, it was an entirely different matter. Pucci was a huge fashion hit in those days of bold, riotous patchwork colors, which seemed a perfect reflection of Italy. The ladies on our cruise had planned carefully and intended to appear in a different gown each evening. But this plan was not allowed to interfere with impulsive buying of gowns for future New York parties.

Marala would make her move during the night and we would wake up in another port. Looking out at Monte Carlo, I leaned on the rail in the warm Mediterranean breeze and wondered if the Arctic char would be crowding into the fish weirs on Baffin Island, the men throwing the biggest fish out for their women and older daughters to catch.

Our captain aboard *Marala* was British, of course, and as handsome as Noel Coward in his younger days. He joined us on the back deck during a long and enthusiastic cocktail party as we prepared to go ashore to attend the big Monte Carlo ball of the year. Two ladies in our party, one of whom had been raised partly in Italy and spoke flawless Italian, asked the captain what he would do in case of a dire emergency aboard *Marala*. I heard him start to explain before a better idea occurred to him. He set down his empty glass and, excusing himself, marched determinedly toward the main bridge. A few moments later, we saw two, then another two, then two more rockets go ripping like shooting stars up over the town of Monte Carlo through the velvet blackness of the sky. Holy smoke, I thought. That should be enough to alert every ship in the Mediterranean.

In no time at all, we saw an official car screech up to *Marala* and two men dressed in white dinner jackets with medals jangling came leaping up our gangway. "Where's the captain?" the head of the harbor police yelled in Italian.

"*Scusa, scusa.* I'm so sorry," our beautiful Italian linguist said to him as she and her friend crowded in on the harbormaster and the police chief. "Our captain speaks no Italian. Could we be of help? Let us get you a martini. You must have had a wearisome day, what with the ball and all. We'll be looking forward to a dance. We hope we'll see you there."

The two officials quickly became very agreeable. Finishing their double martinis, they prepared to leave. "No more bad tricks, *senora*," called the harbormaster. "See you at the ball."

All smiles, they left. The captain rejoined us for another drink, then hurried away. To our horror, we saw another great salvo of six rockets go arching off *Marala's* bridge out over Monte Carlo.

Up on the main road, we could see the harbormaster's car whirl around. This time, the two officials seemed to fly aboard. "*Porca miseria!* Where is your goddamn captain? We're gonna throw him into the jail and we're impounding this goddamn ship. You hear?"

It took more time and feminine charm to settle with them this time, and the discussion among ourselves about the whole event caused us to find the captain and give him hell for shooting off his emergency rockets. Although he didn't need it, we plied him with another martini or two and somehow didn't manage to make it to the famous annual Monte Carlo ball that night, nor did we leave port until the following day, and then very quietly.

Well, hell, we'd had fairly rowdy Arctic shipboard parties most years aboard the Canadian government icebreaker that came into Cape Dorset to deliver the annual mail and supplies before it disappeared, battering its way through the incoming tidal ice. And it was not unknown for captains to take a drink or two.

But our captain was on his very best behavior the day King Constantine of Greece, on a very blustery summer's day, came aboard the private yacht that Houghton had chartered. We watched the king leave a small cluster of people on shore, and with two sailors in a smallish boat come bouncing out to join us for a visit.

"Where's his wife?" the ladies aboard asked each other, their voices full of disappointment.

The ship's companionway unfolded and our captain stood smartly at attention and saluted the king as he boarded.

One of our party was a famous New York surgeon who was ready at an instant's notice to leap in and handle any medical or social emergency that might occur. After the introductions and the serving of drinks and hors d'oeuvres, we stood in a small knot at the starboard rail around the king. He kept peering anxiously toward his shore party at the jetty.

"My wife regrets she could not come out with me today because of the strength of the waves," the king announced to us.

"Oh, we understand," said the surgeon, always eager to set a king at ease. "It is because of your forthcoming child that your wife wishes to avoid the waves."

"No, no," said the king. "This will be our third coming child."

45

Alice

Corning's chairman, Amory Houghton, the former American Ambassador to France, was widely known as Big Am. When he and his cheerful wife, Laura, gave a cocktail party at their apartment in New York, I managed to arrive on time, and was overwhelmed by their great collection of beautifully displayed glass paperweights.

At the height of the party, the Ambassador came and greeted me. "What are you doing this evening?" he asked. Before I could answer, he said, "I have two seats for *Man of La Mancha*."

I knew it had become so popular that it was all but impossible to purchase tickets, so I eagerly accepted.

"The one catch is," he said, "you'll have to take a girl we know named Alice. Come on, we'll find her. There she is."

I saw this tall, lithe, blue-eyed blonde. "Alice Watson, this is Jim Houston. Would you consider going with him to the theater tonight?"

"Sure," she smiled. "It's said to have such wonderful music."

We stood and talked and ate more smoked salmon than we normally would, thanks to the Houghton family devotion to fishing on Quebec's Moisie River. We went from the party to the theater and talked all the way about Alice's early schooling in Montreal when she had been there with her family. Her father, a physicist and Yale professor, had been part of the Manhattan Project and had worked in Canada on the atomic energy program at Chalk River. Alice was a keen skier and had stayed with the Houghtons at Rougement in Switzerland when traveling with a classmate after Smith College.

Man of La Mancha was great, and I enjoyed it to the full, perhaps because of the new-found person sitting next to me. We had an after-theater dinner at Sardi's, an exciting place for newcomers in New York. Alice had just taken a new job at American Heritage Publishing Company as a photo editor, American history and preservation being her keen interest.

Suddenly, the whole city – hell, the whole country and all its wonderful possibilities – seemed to open up to me. We went out a lot together after that. I met Alice's family at the Yale Club and was invited to spend a weekend at their home in New Haven. We scarcely knew it, but we were both on the road to a whole new life, which goes on with as much love and enthusiasm now as it did then.

As for *Man of La Mancha*, we bought the New York newspapers when we left the theater and read the reviews. What we both thought had been a marvelous, never-to-be-forgotten musical, they panned like hell, saying it was awful, not worth seeing. Thirty-five years later, it's still playing around the summer circuits and in foreign countries round the world. Like, I suppose, Alice and me, as we continue to pursue our strange zigzag life.

46

Vietnam Saturday

When I remained in town over a winterish weekend, I often went in to Steuben on a Saturday morning. This was a rare thing for anyone in design to do and one had to have special keys to accomplish it. In the quiet of the building, I found it the best time and place to create designs. No telephones, no bustle.

About eleven o'clock, Houghton would quite often call down and ask me if I was there, what I was thinking about, then suggest that I visit him in his office on the floor above. He was always in a good mood on these occasions. He wanted to see in advance any design ideas that I might have.

Neither of us ate or drank coffee during our Saturday meetings and we never went out to lunch, but we would often have a discussion about books or people we both knew. We rarely spoke of politics, no matter what was going on. And in the spring of '68, a helluva lot was going on. On my way to work that Saturday, I had walked past streets lined with unmarked buses. These were full of police sitting dead still and alert, rigged out in their riot gear, and seemingly ready for anything.

When I mentioned the numbers of police vans on East 60th and 61st near 5th Avenue, Arthur frowned at me for bringing up political affairs and said that if I read the *Times*, I would know that some hooligans were going to try a march up 5th about noon. "You'll see them right here beneath the office windows."

He stood up, looking like the air force colonel he had been, and glared north up 5th Avenue. There was very little traffic.

"The radio said it's going to be a peaceful march," I muttered.

"Yes? Well, look at the barriers they're putting up at the cross streets," he said angrily.

"Just veterans disapproving of the war. And probably their sons."

"Things like you're about to see in the street can get out of hand," he warned me. "Remember what happened on that day at the Bastille in France? Just a relatively few excited workers heard some rumors and started yelling around the Bastille. First, a damned weak-kneed governor who never should have been in charge let them inside the outer wall without resistance. The crowd increased. They drew in a pair of cannons and suddenly the Bastille and the King of France's authority and his rule had collapsed. Paris was run by a mob and in no time the guillotines were set up with their blades sharpened."

He was really rolling. I said, "The radio says this parade has been licensed by the police. It's legal."

Houghton snorted, "Do you think people like Abbie Hoffman and Jerry Rubin are in any way concerned with legal? They and others like them will snatch this country unless we stop them soon."

By this time, we could hear drumming and voices greatly amplified on loud speakers, then maybe twenty or thirty young men and women ganged together passed the Plaza Hotel, then F. A. O. Schwartz and Tiffany's. They went shouting and singing right through the red traffic light at our corner of 56th and 5th.

"Goddamn them!" Houghton shouted. "I hate them! They've no business to be doing that."

We could see many more coming up behind them, waving banners and placards.

"The radio says they have the Mayor's permission and a constitutional right to march," I said.

"Do they have marches like this in Canada?" Houghton demanded.

"No, they have no war going on."

"So, Houston, you approve of this? You've always been a kind of nihilist. You'd hate this if you saw it happening in Canada."

The police were out of the vans now, truncheons in hand, walking watchfully along 5th Avenue beside the marchers.

"I don't like it," I admitted, "but they've got a license and there's police right with them."

Houghton gave me another murderous look and sat down behind his desk and started shuffling papers. He did not speak or look up at me again. I quietly left the office and went down into the street to watch the marchers at close range, hearing more clearly the slogans they were shouting. It all ended without major incident. But in spite of that, Houghton did not speak to me for more than a month.

Arthur, with his links to all areas of the American Establishment, including the CIA, was a man who took political events very seriously. You could not cast him as a hard, right-wing Republican because he had admitted he'd voted for a Democratic president when he could not stand the Republican candidate. Once, in the middle of the Vietnam disaster, the sitting President, Lyndon

Johnson, phoned him and announced that he was coming from Washington to Arthur's place at Wye Plantation, on the eastern shore of Maryland, to visit on the weekend.

"Come right ahead," Arthur told him.

But when he hung up the telephone, he said to his wife, Betty, and to me, "We're not going to be here. I think we'll go to London. Holly [his teenaged daughter] can stay here and entertain them." And she did just that.

47

Psalm Warnings

Arthur had an unnerving story that for a period he was very fond of telling. It was about a poor English minister's daughter who found it necessary to emigrate to America to find work. Her old father had nothing to give her save a small antique book he had purchased earlier in a country sale. He thought of it as a Bible, for it had been printed in Cambridge, as stated on the title page, and was about three hundred years old. The minister had taken it to a nearby town and had had it appraised.

"Bibles don't bring much, Reverend," the appraiser had told him, "but if I were you, I'd ask for thirty, perhaps forty pounds."

With this Bible and a small trunk, the minister's daughter left on a ship for America. She found employment doing housework for a woman in Manhattan, and after some time, she showed her the small Bible.

"I have no idea what such a book is worth," the employer told the girl, "but I do know of an antiquarian book man who buys and sells books. I'll write him on your behalf and give you his address."

On her afternoon off, the girl went to see the bookseller and showed him her small book. "This is quite a book," he said.

"That's what my father and I were told."

"What do you want for it?" he asked her.

"I've been advised to ask forty pounds for it."

The dealer read the title page again and leafed through the pages. The condition was good and all the pages were in place. He opened his cash box and carefully counted out her full request in American money.

The girl and her father had been misinformed. The small Bible had not been printed in Cambridge, England, but in the Cambridge of the Massachusetts Bay Colony by Reverend Cotton Mather. In fact, it was the first book ever printed in America and was considered one of the rarest books in the world, *The Bay Psalm Book.*

Bay Psalm Book

"Now what's the right and wrong of that?" Houghton asked me.

"What would that book be worth today?" I asked him.

"I don't know," said Arthur. "There are probably fewer than a dozen in the whole world. Most are probably all in major libraries or museums, the others were lost or fell to pieces long ago from overuse. At least fifty thousand dollars."

I was astounded. "That was bloody awful of that dealer to have cheated the poor girl."

"He didn't cheat her," Houghton said. "She made the mistake of stating exactly how much she wanted for that book, and he gave her exactly the amount requested. You be warned by that and learn, Houston!" He frowned at me. "Always ask a person how much they will offer you for any item before you ever tell them the price you want."

48
Bidding for the Met

A number of old, ivory, Eskimo objects – more properly called Dorset and Thule artifacts – the first roughly fifteen hundred years old, the latter seven hundred years old – came up for auction at Sotheby's, New York, in the late sixties. I was asked by the Metropolitan Museum to bid on a pre-selected number of these objects. It was yet another zigzag, and an exciting moment in my New York life. I mention this because at that time an expert at the museum gave me some important advice about bidding at auction which, I believe, might help as a useful approach to anyone buying at an auction.

1. Pre-decide and write down the high bid you will enter.
2. Try to make the opening bid, but keep it reasonably low.
3. When a higher bid is made, follow immediately with your slightly higher bid.
4. When your bid is topped again, quickly make another bid. Make opposing bidders in the room aware of your aggressiveness.
5. Keep the action moving fast, as though there is no end to your bidding power.
6. Carefully keep in mind your limit, but never set this limit at an obvious ending bid like $5,000.00. Always go just beyond such a well-rounded number and bid $5,200.00. That alone should discourage other bidders.

I was successful that day and grateful for the lesson.

49
Canada's Scarlet Maples

The Canadian Centennial Ball was a huge, formal event held in 1967 at the Waldorf Astoria on Park Avenue. I was asked to volunteer to create the table decorations. What to do? Live beavers, one at every table, had been suggested, as well as loons and polar bears or Canada geese! I thought maple leaves were the answer and were available. But, dammit, the ball was in the spring with the leaves still green as grass.

Nevertheless, I kept on thinking maple leaves and developed a color cure in my mind. Alice and I took a train to New Haven to pick maple leaves in her family garden because only ginkgo trees survived in New York City streets, and stealing leaves in Central Park was out of the question. When we had each stuffed a large Bloomingdale's bag full of green maple leaves, we took them back to New York. I went out into my garden and sprayed one with some watercolor paint left over from some animation films I'd made for NBC. It worked. A shot of yellow and a dash of scarlet and those leaves advanced their colors into glorious autumn. We sprayed hundreds of them, three for every guest's place, and decorated the tables in the ballroom.

Maple leaves and glass

We saw Canada's second century in with a minimum of speech-making. There was a great deal of bagpiping, singing in French, and dancing with Scots' kilts flying. I attribute the large amount of champagne and of scotch consumed that night to the madness of the pipers. Peter Jennings, who was to be an usher in our wedding at Yale, was at our table. It turned out to be an early tribute to Canada's new flag.

50

New York Short Cuts

Felix was an Italian barber working in New York. When he started to cut my hair, he was not too crazy about his partner, a much older Italian who owned the business on West 56th Street. He discreetly asked me to pass the shop if he were busy and not to let the old man cut my hair. I never did. During my era of haircuts with Felix, he flew three times to Italy to be with his mother when the priest summoned, but his visits cheered his mother so that she continued not to die. Felix's English was very poor. Some thought it didn't exist.

He indicated to me that he wanted to read my book, but could read no English. When the rights to my book, *The White Dawn*, were sold to an Italian publisher and translated, I received three copies. With pride, I hurried over to my friend, Felix, though I didn't really need a haircut. (Felix's prices, after his move to the St. Regis Hotel from the old man's smaller shop, had soared from $4.00 to $25.00 plus tip.) When I proudly handed him the book, he was overwhelmed and got another barber to interpret his profuse thanks.

Although I continued to use Felix for my barber, he never said another word about the book. I thought he hadn't liked it. Only later did I discover that he didn't read Italian, either.

Next door to the Felix and partner barbershop was a diamond merchant, who was very old and bent, with bad eyes. I used to ask him questions about gold for my Steuben work. One time, I told him that my sister, Barbara, in Florida, was giving me a diamond brooch from our family because I had told her I planned to get married again and stop running around the streets of New York. After I received the pin, I told him it was in an antique Victorian setting.

"Bring it in," he said, and next time, before my haircut, I did.

As I entered his shop and the bell began to ring, I opened the small box with the diamond brooch. I was still five to seven feet away when he cried out, "Nice, very nice, good size, but big flaw right down the middle of the stone."

Later, when I double-checked, I discovered that he was exactly right. Not bad at that distance for a very old guy with poor sight on a diamond that was not all that big!

51

Getting Married

After more than five years of bachelorhood and a wonderful time in New York, I remarried in 1967. In *Confessions of an Igloo Dweller*, I wrote that there was nothing simple about getting married in the Inuit world. That was referring to earlier days, before the Anglican and Oblate missionaries began ruling the Arctic roost and before Christian marriages had become the style. Parents were all-important in the nuptial agreements of their children, many of whom were promised in marriage before they were even born.

It was decided that Alice and I would be married in Dwight Chapel of Yale University. I asked Arthur to be my best man. He readily agreed, so long as I promised not to have the ceremony performed by Bill Coffin, the politically outspoken, left-wing, anti-Vietnam War, Yale chaplain. This condition caused a bit of a stir in the Watson family, but soon it was resolved and an old friend whom the family referred to as Uncle Sid, the retired Yale chaplain, was asked and agreed to perform the ceremony.

I was given a riotous bachelor's dinner in New York, then went up to New Haven for a bridal dinner and luncheon.

As the actual time approached, Arthur and I found ourselves alone in a small side room off the chapel. I remember that the windows had leaded, diamond-shaped glass. As we heard the organ start to play, Arthur went to the window. He stepped up onto a wall bench and swung it open. "Houston," he said, "I'm not joking. I know about such things." (He was married four times.) "This is your one last chance. We could both jump out of this window right now. It's only a short drop into the ivy. There's my car, waiting for us in the street. In two hours, you could be safely back in New York or even on your way to a nice, safe holiday in the Arctic."

I laughed and said, "No, thanks. I'm more than eager to go through with this marriage."

"Well, good luck," he said, as one of the ushers opened the door and beckoned us toward the crowded pews.

Later, with a Highland piper playing a regimental tune and the wedding party dancing wildly, everything seemed completely perfect. And that's the way it's turned out to be. I'm glad I didn't jump!

52

Sam

My son, Sam Houston, was always a different kind of cat. After my first wife, Allie, and I separated, we agreed to send him off to school at Fettes College in Edinburgh, Scotland, partly because he loved horses and so did his Scottish uncle who kept some prize hunters and made Sam a member of the Berwick Hunt. That, in part, must have contributed to the differences between Sam and his beloved brother, John, who spent his school years at Pickering College before heading off to Yale.

When they were in Ottawa, Sam's mother had encouraged the boys to work on Saturdays at CAP, Canadian Arctic Producers, an excellent organization that she had started. It maintained very favorable prices for the carvers and printmakers with broad distribution of Inuit art not only in Canada, but around the world.

Sam returned home to Canada after Scotland and went to Dalhousie University in Nova Scotia, but he was restless and eager to leap into the business world. Before his official time at Dalhousie was over, he left to begin work in Vancouver at several prominent art galleries.

When Alice and I were passing through Vancouver on our way north to spend some time writing and fishing at our cottage on the Queen Charlotte Islands, Sam phoned me at the Hotel Vancouver. He sounded wildly anxious to show me something – I thought perhaps a super Inuit carving. He asked that we meet him at the hotel's south entrance in five minutes. When Sam pulled up in the warm spring sunshine, he was driving the longest, lowest, jazziest purple sports car that I had ever seen.

"Isn't she a beauty, Dad?" Sam yelled. "Don't you love it, Alice?"

Three teenage girls stopped and gasped at the unbelievable car, then looked at each other before smiling affectionately at Sam.

"Sorry, Alice, only room for one other passenger. Get in, Dad. I'll take you for a spin. This baby's called the purple ladybug. God only knows how fast she'll go. I haven't had a chance to test her."

"Well, no speed tests today, my boy," I said in my most somber voice. "Where the hell's the door handle?"

"Oh!" Sam laughed. "No door handles needed on a special car like this. It doesn't have a roof either. You just step over the door and settle yourself right down in that soft leather seat. Careful, Dad, it's kind of low."

A special car

Sam idled the engine and his dream machine moved out into the sparse traffic. We waved good-bye to Alice, who called out, "Come up north and fish with us, Sam."

"I don't need to know how fast this thing will go," I told Sam, "and neither do you."

"Oh, we won't go fast today, Dad, not in this lovely weather. We'll just take a turn up around the university and back."

True to his word, Sam did not drive fast as we headed south over the Burrard Street bridge, with its view west to Georgia Strait. He seemed to prefer cruising along through the glorious scenery, talking about how much he liked Vancouver, how his career as an art dealer was developing and that he was already representing Tony Onley, one of Canada's best painters, and was contracted to represent the American artist, Robert Rauschenberg, in Japan and Europe, and was planning with an English artist to wrap up an Alberta ranch — barn, house, fences and more, Christo-style – wrap it all in thousands of meters of multicolored cloth.

When I heard Sam say things like that, I thought of them as youthful pipe dreams. But remembering them after all these years, I realize that he did complete almost every one of those ambitious projects he planned. Nowadays, Sam works in real estate and is busy building a number of movie complexes between Aspen, New Mexico, and Huwaii.

As we reached the University of British Columbia campus on Point Grey, little wandering churches of students stopped to admire the purple doorless, roofless wonder as it very slowly passed them. The girls waved, and Sam waved back at them with great enthusiasm.

"A wonderful town, Dad," he said. "I loved Edinburgh, but . . ." he interrupted himself to wave at some female friend again, "just look at all those girls, with the mountains out beyond them across English Bay."

A blonde girl with a packsack of books on her back called out, "Sam! Sam!"

He waved and said, "See what I mean, Dad? These are really friendly people out here. Back east, they call these folks lotus-eaters and accuse them of having too much fun, but, hell, don't you believe it, Dad." Sam worked the floor shift. "This is the place and the car for me."

"Where the hell did you get this car?" I asked.

"Oh, I just borrow it now and then from an art collector friend of mine. It's good seeing you again, Dad."

53

Checkin' d'Lights

One dark and rainy Saturday night in Manhattan, having been recently married, Alice and I were luxuriating around the apartment, feeling its warmth and admiring our new pictures and other decorations. We heard a hard and violent knocking at our door. God, who could that be at 7:00 p.m. on such a wet, miserable night? We were certainly not expecting anyone, but with Canadians you never know.

I brushed my hair, straightened my tie, and went cautiously to our steel-sheathed front door reinforced by the heavy iron outer grille that I knew was locked. This time the bell rang harshly. I unlocked the door, opened it a crack, and yelled, "Yes, who is it?"

"Checkin' d'lights" was the rough, soaking wet reply.

"What?" I asked again.

"Checkin' d'lights."

"Our lights don't need checking. They're working fine."

I slammed and relocked the door. Even the most naive newcomers to a big city have heard of this one. Some thief posing as a plumber or an electrician cons his way into your apartment, then he robs you, or worse! Living here, I didn't need my Arctic thin-ice knowledge. Now I needed brand-new city smarts.

I went back to the living room and told Alice what all the noise was about. We poured another glass of wine and settled down. The bell rang violently again. "Persistent devil," I said to her. "I'll tell him off."

I returned to the front door and opened it more guardedly this time.

"Checkin' d'lights," came a desperate shout through my thick, iron grille.

"Beat it, will you? Our lights are fine. One more ring out of you and I'll call the cops!" I could see the silver rain pouring down beyond the crack in my door. I heard a disgusted grunt and then wet boots trudging away from our entrance.

"Some town," I said. "You can't be too damn careful here." After a long pause, the telephone rang. I picked it up. It was Norma, our landlady upstairs.

"Did anyone ring your doorbell down there?"

"Yeah, but I outfoxed him. He said he was checking the lights."

"That's right, he was – CHICKEN DELIGHT. We called them for a delivery. It hasn't arrived. We're hungry!"

"I'll send him up if he comes back here, dear," I mumbled as I hung up the phone.

54

Pedestrian Power

Some streets in Canada, like Winnipeg's Portage Avenue, to take one example, are just as wide as Park Avenue, but without Park Avenue's central island of flower beds. Believe me, when one of those Canadian stoplights goes on, the citizenry stand patiently waiting, though no car is in sight, until the light turns green and they begin their long journey across the avenue.

"I prefer New York," I told my friend, Paul Schulze, as we walked in Manhattan one day. "New Yorkers don't give a damn about the stoplights. They watch for a narrow opening in the traffic, then skip across and go about their business."

"Yeah," said Schulze. "Well, some of these cab drivers are a goddamn disgrace. They'll cut right in as though they're trying to kill you."

"I know, but everyone here is in a hurry," I admitted. "There's nothing you can do about them."

"I can!" said Schulze. And when a yellow cab cut close, he reached out and slapped its rear bumper as hard as he could with the flat of his hand, then crippled up, half kneeling on the street.

The cab stopped instantly and the cabbie jumped out, eyes wide with alarm at the prospect of a personal injury lawsuit. He tried to help Schulze upright, muttering apologies.

"You son-of-a-bitch!" screamed Paul. "You try to cut in on a decent citizen like me again and I'll slash your tires."

The cabbie leapt back into his taxi and drove off.

"There," said Paul, examining the redness of his palm. "That guy probably saw you hesitating, holding back just because the light was red, and thought, *This character must be from Canada or Uzbekistan or someplace foreign. I'll give him a scare.* He then sped at you. Don't put up with it. This is your wild and crazy city just as much as it is his."

55

Finding the Farm

At home in our Manhattan apartment, Alice and I had an important conversation. "Let's buy an old colonial farmhouse somewhere in southern New England. Not so far away that we can't easily drive to and from town," she suggested.

"If you can find a good place like that," I told her, "I'm more than game to try it. But you've never spent much time on a farm."

"True," Alice admitted. "When I was growing up, we never even had a cat or dog. That's why I'd love to live on a farm with lots of animals."

We bought one of those small, gently rounded Volvos, circa 1965, in a periwinkle blue, which was Alice's favorite color. We kept it in her family's garage in New Haven because it cost like hell to house a car in New York City. Alice had given up her day-by-day job as an editor at American Heritage and was now free to search for a suitable weekend house in the country. After weeks of roaming the back roads in Connecticut, Rhode Island, and Massachusetts, and my going out to look at a few of her more promising finds on weekends, Alice finally discovered a place that she thought perfect, an eighteenth-century farmhouse hidden in the woods.

Returning from one of my frequent trips to Canada and into the Arctic, I took the train to New Haven, paying a return fare that then cost $4.30. Alice met me with our Volvo, and I nervously practiced my driving on Interstate-95, heading northeast toward Rhode Island. I had more or less forgotten how to drive during the war years between 1940 and 1945 when I had been elsewhere in the army, then in Paris studying, and then in the Arctic. Dog teams, yes; Volvos, no. Alice looked nervous, but spoke words of encouragement, confident that I'd eventually get the hang of driving again.

"Oh, I believe you're going to like this farm," she said excitedly as we turned onto the narrow country lane. "Careful, slow down. You're going to turn again, we're almost there. This place is called Escoheag."

At a red farm gate almost buried in gold and yellow autumn leaves, I turned again and drove another quarter of a mile.

"All this road will be ours, I think," said Alice. "We could be on our place right now."

At that moment, a pair of ruffed grouse ran ahead of the Volvo and burst into flight along the laneway toward the as-yet-unseen house.

I stopped the car and looked at Alice. "How many acres did you say?"

"One hundred twenty-five," she answered, "with a chance to buy more."

We peered into the growth of pines and maples growing among a sea of laurel.

"This looks like wonderful partridge country to me," I said, squinting through the sun's rays filtered by the scarlet leaves. "This looks right."

Ruffed grouse

We drove slowly forward again between the rugged, old stone walls, until I caught the flash of water in a stream, then beyond that an open sheep field, and crowning it, the farmhouse. It was a classic colonial clapboard, with a huge, central chimney and a weathered roof. Each window had twenty-four small panes of glass. The house was painted a muted New England red, and not far from it there was a grand old barn with a mighty oak tree flanking it. This was the Crandall Grant. The house had been built in the 1750s, with a keeping room, a fireplace in each of the seven rooms, a well inside the summer kitchen in the ell, and an old carriage and smithing shop behind. Judge Robert Crandall had been buried on the property in the high field south of the house with all his family. Outside the low stone walls around their graves, there were a dozen erected stones that presumably marked the slaves' and servants' graves.

In New York, we had learned that almost every purchase has a lower price, but the Yankee owner of this property would not reduce the price by a single penny. Furthermore, he would only give us a tentative option to buy. We stayed on pins and needles for half a year before receiving final consent to complete the deal. When everything was signed, the former owner told us we had got such a good price because few women who had viewed the farm felt as intrepid as Alice. Wives who came here with their husbands would take one look at the quarter-mile of lonely lane, edged with impenetrable laurel bushes and dark, overgrown pine forest behind, and say, "I'll tell you one thing, I'm not living in a place like this alone, no, sir, not for one damned minute!"

We used the advance from my novel, *The White Dawn*, a work then in process, as a down payment and took out a mortgage on the farm. Our feelings from the first night onward were those of excitement. The beauty of the house and land was exactly what we had been looking for.

The wagon road that had once passed less than a stone's throw from our new, very old front door had all but disappeared a century earlier. But you could still trace it through our woods, for the trees, because of the road's long use as an Indian trail and then a road for horses, did not fully fill in that well-trodden path.

It was also easy to follow the old road because of the fieldstones that had been pushed aside to clear the wagon trail and form the bordering walls. These walls were not well built, but they represented a tremendous amount of hard, backbreaking work by long deceased humans and their oxen drawing stone boats to the edge of the fields. In fact, the forest and fields on our farm were properly called a glacial moraine. The gray stones, now rounded smooth with lichen, were so numerous that many had just been piled together in the center of some fields, like cannonballs, and never made it to the edge. The rocky land was poor, eventually suitable only for sheep farming. That fact, in part, had caused the great American movement west, when families in the 1800s left their almost barren farms, packed up, and headed out in search of more fertile lands that they heard were there for the taking in Ohio and farther west. This caused them to leave behind some spectacular eighteenth-century colonial houses and strong barns – ghostly silent, perfect places to draw and paint, write books, and once again enjoy a gentler, rural life.

Long ago, our old Rhode Island farmhouse had been an isolated homestead. Many women would have dreaded the place in those days, too, for this had been Indian country and they would remember King Philip's War, which had already occurred not long before this farm was formed fairly close to the Great Swamp. King Philip was a powerful Wampanoag chief and had been killed in the final

battle of a bitter war between his people and the New England settlers. They carried his head out of the swamp on a long pike pole.

That war was a bitter exception. So many places in New
England retain their old Indian names because very early relationships with the Indians were good, and the new settlers were sometimes saved from starvation by the openhanded generosity of the
eastern woodland tribes. The name changes came when settlers
farther west were attacked with greater frequency as the Indians
realized that they were losing their tribal hunting lands to the
whites. The history of those now all-but-forgotten troubles is
recorded in our books but also on our early maps, where old Indian
places were renamed using Anglo-Saxon, French, or Spanish
words. These changes are especially noticeable from Ohio west
where there are fewer and fewer Uncasvilles or Chitougwas. The
names were changed to McCloud, Whisky Creek, and Tombstone,
then Los Angeles and San Francisco, as Spanish traders and missionaries closed in from the southwest.

Owl

Our farmhouse in Escoheag was so deeply buried in the wild woods
that it was difficult to find. Sometimes we would ask guests to luncheon on the weekend. They would journey from New York,
Washington, or Boston, and instead of arriving at noon, they would
come up the drive at 2:00 or 3:00 p.m., half mad from doubling and
redoubling the route, always just missing the entrance sign to our
laneway. They apologized and moaned at first, but a double martini
or two would set them straight on their weekend course again!

It was a wonderful privilege for me to live on Letfern Farm, as
we called it, after an earlier Scottish family farm. This was a great

change after a busy New York City life, in spite of how satisfying that had been. It gave me much more time to write, draw, do watercolors, and enjoy nature around us. Of course, we didn't leave the city altogether. We kept a very small apartment on East 62nd Street and drove in almost every week to spend a night or two.

Being in the country gave us a chance to go antiquing and to try and find authentic, eighteenth-century furnishings. That pursuit was much more rewarding then, and far less costly than it is today, especially at country antique fairs. New England is a treasure house of antiques, long squirreled away in barns and attics. The rugs and carpets we found at fairs or shops were slightly or even considerably worn, but they were semi-antique Kazak, Bokhara, Hamadan, and more, brought back in great rolls by New England's sea captains who, while sailing around the world, laid plans for newer, larger houses at home.

Sometimes Alice and I would set our alarm for 3:30 in the morning. Carrying a bun and a thermos of coffee, we would drive to some distant, outdoor fair, arriving just at dawn when the dealers were setting up their tables and hadn't had a chance to run around and ask each other how much every item was worth. This kind of hunting, to my mind, took the place of the excitement of Arctic hunting for food, or fly fishing for salmon. No animals were killed in this pursuit, and yet the thrill of finding something you thought essential for your own house was more than equal. On weekends at the Norton, Massachusetts, Flea Market, held in a very large, open field in the middle of nowhere, there were usually more than one hundred dealers. One could find things to buy from a dollar to five thousand dollars and more. This market was not well known and had not been picked over as much as others such as Brimfield. Still, you'd have to be there before five o'clock in the morning with a flashlight, and in the back of your car carry books on the antiques that interested you the most, and have straps to carry furniture home on your car's roof. Our first question to a dealer was, "What's your very best price on that?"

Our house was a good, typical size for that period, and when we bought it, it was stripped of furniture, except for some things given us by Alice's family from their New Haven house and some things my sister, Barbara, had sent down to me from Beaverton, Ontario after our mother died.

There were hundreds of aspects about that farm at Escoheag that pleased both of us. There was lots of studio space in the summer kitchen in the ell attached to the back of the house, and a large old barn that smelled of hay and very faintly of animals long gone, and soon the rich smell of the increasing flock of Southdown sheep. Near the house, there were a few open fields called the deer field, the blueberry field, and the large cemetery field, where the Crandall family lay, perhaps still dreaming of much earlier days.

56

Ghostly Houses

Lester and Barbara Lewis were our farming neighbors and that was truly fortunate for us. They were likable and sociable, a wellspring of local knowledge, especially information about farming. Without the help of Lester and Barbara, we would have remained two outsiders who had bought a nonfunctioning farm as a place to write, paint, and entertain weekend guests.

Lester encouraged us to trek with him through terrible tangles of laurel, scrub trees, brush, and generally unkempt forest, climbing over old, stone boundary walls hidden in the undergrowth, trying to understand the area of our farm. Suddenly, on its edges, we would come face to face with an ancient, unpainted, eighteenth-century house with a sagging gambrel roof, most of its windows broken out, and all its paneled doors removed. Inside, among the cobwebs and ghostly shadows, were fireplaces, some of them large enough to walk into standing upright, and off the central chimney, perhaps half a dozen other fireplaces – three on the main floor and three on the floor above. You had to be very careful climbing the stairs, if they still existed.

Old abandoned houses such as these, Lester told us, had been left to rot and fall, with trees grown up sometimes right through them.

All this had once been cleared land producing crops and providing pastures. Lester judged that a dozen such houses had been hidden not far beyond our woods. For a while, Alice and I talked of trying to buy and collect them, taking them apart, and having them hauled over to our farm, then rebuilt there, selling each with about five to ten acres of forested land. We never had a chance, but probably could have gathered the money to make that dream come true. But one day, Lester told us bad boys had set one of the houses farther away ablaze, and if there had been wind that night, we could have lost our house in a major forest fire. So the state, without further warning, sent fire crews in to conduct a controlled burning of the rest of the old houses, and all that history was gone forever. What an opportunity missed, and what a shame those eighteenth-century houses, now rare in North America, had to go up in smoke!

57

The World's Best Cat

Neither Alice nor I cared anything about cats. But we found a very small, lost tabby kitten mewing hungrily behind a highway vegetable stand where we were buying fresh corn. Determined to find its rightful owners, we brought the kitten home and fed it milk. But we were very busy for the next few days, and by the time we could arrange the kitten's return, we couldn't bear to part with him. So we gave him the Inuit name of Pingwa ("plaything" in Inuktitut) and Pingwa became a ten-year family member, essential to the farm.

Pingwa was gray, with a tigerish striped appearance. But, of course, to us Pingwa became like no other cat that had ever walked the earth. I must tell you that Pingwa had a high intellect and developed a mind entirely of his own. He was reasonably affectionate most of the time, and liked to stretch out and lie across my knees when I was writing. But if we went away for a few days to New York or elsewhere, upon our return Pingwa would act as though he'd never known us and treat us with absolute disdain. We'd have to wait for him to allow us to rejoin the family, with the privilege of rubbing behind his ears. Only then would he slowly condescend to sit anywhere near us after our desertion.

Pingwa

Pingwa had become a house cat, a barn cat, and a wild cat. He became, by instinct, a serious hunter. Many chipmunks that had enjoyed living in our old stone walls around the house began to disappear. Mice no longer scampered freely through our house or barn. Birds survived at our feeder because they could fly up into the dogwood tree and crack open seeds while perched on a thin limb. However, in spring, I'm sure Pingwa cut down on our families of ruffed grouse. I should never have allowed that quick, lovable hunter to roam the woods, for I am very fond of all wild birds. I was on the Board of the Rhode Island Audubon Society, and when our blue jays failed to return to the farm one year, I telephoned our headquarters in Providence to ask what had happened, secretly worried that Pingwa might be responsible. "Don't worry," the director of the Audubon told me, "they're all safe and sound in North Carolina. We don't know why, but they've just decided not to stay up here with us this winter."

Pingwa, once on the farm, never left the place to go on walks with Shulu and me. But one time, to show off perhaps, he decided to horn in and trot along behind our young springer spaniel (whom he held in deep contempt). We made our way toward the old schoolhouse along the farm's gravel road. A cat's footpads are silky soft, not made for such rough travel, so in the end I had to drape the cat around my neck and carry him home. This was much to Pingwa's taste, but made Shulu mad as hell.

I often inquired of friends who owned dogs and cats as pets how they got along together. The answer was almost always, "Fine." This was anything but true of ours. Pingwa, who was first on the farm, always resented the arrival of the springer pup. Later, we acquired a second cat, a beautiful but very dumb white Persian named Mitko ("needles" in Inuktitut). That cat liked to sit inside the sunny front window and look as decorative as an orchid. Pingwa never truly tolerated either of them on the farm – until the last day of his life. In the morning, I saw Pingwa go up and rub affectionately against our dog's hip. Right at that moment, I knew, as did Shulu, that something was terribly wrong with Pingwa. Both Shulu and Mitko watched him, perhaps in sympathy, until our best cat, Pingwa, stretched out and died in the last golden rays of the afternoon sun.

58

At Home on the Farm

On late spring nights, we were blessed – or some of our houseguests might say cursed – by the Letfern chorus. I never seemed to notice it until I lay down and turned out the light to sleep.

Alice would say, "Listen, almost everyone in the orchestra is tuning up tonight."

We were both authorities on this wild symphony. The main body of music makers was made up of the peepers, some near, some off on the other side of the pond. To the south, down beside the spring, there was some ratchet-voiced creature warming up with some other smaller denizens of the wetlands around the pond. Then a young lamb would bleat from the north pasture and the ratcheter would answer. Surprised, perhaps, they would both pause to listen. Through the darkness would come the lonely hoot of an owl sitting in the dark pine stand, and later the high squeal of a rabbit. Altogether they gave the feeling of a great, modern orchestra, tuning up out there in the dogwood-scented blackness of the night.

A frog – female, I think, for she had a light, contralto voice that rose above the others – called saying, "Here I am, here I am." Soon the bullfrogs, all three of them, would lend their bass voices to the orchestra, making many wisecracks and maybe other sounds. I was glad they all lived around our farm's pond, and we would sometimes swim naked beside them. Of course, it really was their farm pond much more than it was ours. So many generations of their families had lived there for at least 250 years, and probably much longer.

Frogs

One of the great pleasures of living on the farm was to lie awake on summer nights and listen to the whippoorwills calling to each other across the fields, then receiving their answers from the edge of the maple grove. Sometimes I used to count their calls. One famous whippoorwill – I wish I could give her a name – called 117 times straight, surely a breathtaking world's record as far as I was concerned. About six or seven calls in sequence are usually about average for a whippoorwill.

I tried to imagine in my mind's eye how all the players looked out there in the light of the moon, with the nighthawks hunting insects up above them. As the symphony practiced for the major summer concerts yet to come, Alice and I would sigh contentedly and fall asleep.

We had a gurgling, running brook but only one deep well for water on the farm, and that was inside the house. It produced clear, cold water, delicious to taste, and during our thirteen years there, it never ran dry. There was an old-fashioned, wooden rig with ropes above the well to draw buckets of water, but by our time the water was electrically pumped into the household system. Oh, yes, we had flush toilets, too, and other modern conveniences. We were locally considered as New Yorkers, but with some kind of a weird Yale and Alaskan twist, thanks to Alice's father being a professor, my time in the Arctic, and our constant autumns in Scotland or summers on Canada's northwest coast.

I'm going to tell you something very private about that old house. It has a small, secret room built inside of it. We have had Canadian SIDs and British MI5s, CIAs and FBIs, and God knows what other Secret Service types to stay on weekends in that house and have challenged them to search and find the room, but none of them could ever find it. We would certainly never have found it, either, if the former owner, after the sale, had not told us where to look for it and the incredible trick of how to enter. It gave us an entirely new perspective concerning the history of that early Crandall Grant and of Judge Crandall who had built the secret room inside that house. Was it a place to hide women and children from roving bands of Indians, or was it somewhere to hide the family treasures?

59

Yikes, Snakes!

I used to lie on my back in bed on very early mornings at the farm and examine the crack in the plaster that zigzagged across our ceiling above me. I'd plan the main thrust of my day's writing, then, driven by a kind of new excitement, I'd rise from our bed about 5:00 a.m. – no alarm – and make coffee, drink some juice, then go out behind the house to what we called the writing room, where the Inuit carvings could watch me from their shelves. Shulu, our springer spaniel, would always come with me. Before we went inside, we'd stand together and wet the stone wall. Inside, he'd lie peacefully beside me on the floor while I wrote following my bed plans. At exactly seven o'clock, Shulu would demand that we both begin our ten-minute walk to the one-room schoolhouse. When we arrived, we'd sit together inside at one of the larger double desks, imagining all those children who had sat there before us. I'd look out the wavy glass windows to the east at the sun rising like a glowing orange between the trees. As the light increased, we'd hike back to the house to have our real breakfast with Alice. Afterward, I'd return to my writing room and work until almost noon. I'd nap an hour after lunch, then go and draw in the woods or play in the workshop trying to repair or remove paint from some country antiques, or just generally enjoy life in any way I chose that day.

I've always been unreasonably fond of my dozen years of Arctic life, but I must say living on Letfern Farm proved to be a pleasure that was hard to match. The isolation was exactly what we both liked about the place. Oh, we readily admitted that if you wanted to have a dinner party on a Friday or Saturday night, you would have to be prepared to import your guests from Canada or New York or Boston and load them into the spare bedrooms. But doing that gave us some of the very best weekend parties of our lives, including the one I will always associate with snakes.

I don't particularly like snakes. And, indeed, I never associated them with old New England country houses. Yet one early summer's day, when I looked out at our stone wall behind the house, I saw a thick, black snake as long as your arm comfortably sunning itself. As I went toward it carrying a hoe, it slithered away into the thickness of the old wall. I saw another big one about a week later. It was crossing the lawn of our small front terrace. The snake disappeared, which meant it could only have crawled inside our house.

There is a season when snakes shed their almost transparent skins, and apparently they often do this between two stones which help them pull the old skin off. When I went down to our cellar to get a bottle of wine, I saw a big skin hanging out of the wall. To my alarm, when I looked more closely, there wasn't just one of them, there were seven skins of various sizes. I could scarcely imagine so many secretive black snakes wintering over in our house with us. I didn't want to frighten Alice with this news. But that was not the end of it.

One busy weekend in summer, we were having a crowd of guests from New York who couldn't have driven home after the party and had been asked to sleep over. That would take up every bed. I hurried up to our third floor – the attic really – which had three spare bedrooms arranged around the large central chimney. I started opening the bureau drawers to check that they were empty so the guests would have some space. The last drawer I pulled out gave me an awful shock. There before me, filling the drawer, was a huge, coiled snakeskin.

Oh, my God, I thought, *how the hell did a snake that size get inside that drawer?* I loathingly lifted the skin out of the drawer and hid it behind the chimney, counting myself lucky that I had found it instead of Alice – or worse, much worse, one of the guests!

The weekend went off splendidly with nothing but good weather and the usual skinny-dipping in the pond. On Monday when the last guests had safely departed, Alice called down to me, "Did you take my snakeskin or did one of the guests?"

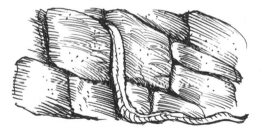

Snakeskin

"My God! Did you put that thing in the drawer?" I asked her.

"Sure," she said, "it was a beauty. I wanted to show it to my mother."

When we came to sell the house thirteen years later, I told Alice, "Don't you say a single word about those damned snakes!"

After the farm had been purchased from us and Peter, his wife, and two children were settling into it, we dropped in and asked them how everything was going.

"Oh, fine," said Peter, "we love it. But where are the snakes?"

"Well, I don't know," I said. "Have you seen any?"

"Not a one," he answered, "and Oliver, my six-year-old, is very disappointed. His main interest in our buying this house from you was that he'd heard there were a lot of really big black snakes crawling around."

60

The Big Fight

Lester assured us that there had been sheep raised on our farm long ago. Alice, the professor's daughter, was wild to learn about animal husbandry and wanted to try and raise one or two. Lester gave her such a look! Our first nervous acquisition was a pair of lambs from a farm girl who had named them Sassy and Spooky. They brought pure joy to Alice's heart. But these two sheep seemed lonely and unbred, so we bought Big Virgil, a Southdown ram of powerful size, obviously well equipped for any such job. He had been named by a young farmboy we knew who planned to be a classical scholar. Big Virgil had virility to spare. When I would come into the barn at 5:30 in the morning to water and feed everybody there, he would start battering at his separate pen door, making a great rumpus, demanding attention, determined to be fed before his ewes. Big Virgil had this mighty look to him, especially in springtime before he and his ewes were sheared by a wooly, bearded man we hired to come onto the farm and do the shearing.

Because it wasn't right to breed a third generation of sheep to the same ram, we bought – instead of renting – a new, young Southdown ram named Buckeye, and by September, Big Virgil was roaring awful warnings to Buckeye, demanding the return of his ewes. And Buckeye answered by rubbing violently against the fence, like a soldier eager to show his strength fighting or loving, whichever came first.

"I'm going to move Big Virgil two fields away," Lester, our wise farmer, told us. "We don't want those two getting at each other."

"If that happens and you aren't here," Alice sighed, "what could we do?"

"I've heard," said Lester, "that if two rams are about to fight, you can try to grab one of them by the wool on his back, straddle him, and dig your heels in. A ram doesn't show his strength until he gets up steam during his charge. They say if you've got ahold of one, the other won't attack."

Three days later, Alice let out a shriek. Big Virgil had broken through both fences and was in the same field with Buckeye and the ewes. I had seen Lester drive his truck off the farm an hour earlier.

"Nothing we can do except let the best man win," I told her, showing that prudent Canadian stolidness that has shaped our country.

Alice, being American, was out the door in a flash, climbed the fence, and ran across the field to the place where Big Virgil stood tensely facing Buckeye. His head was down, and he was snorting and pawing the ground with less than a stone's toss between them. Anyone could tell that in a moment, all hell was going to break loose. Alice dashed up behind Big Virgil, got his girth between her knees, and grabbed the thick wool on his back.

To my surprise and gratitude, Virgil gave up without a fight, and so did Buckeye.

"James, come and get in front of Virgil. Help me chase him back to his field," Alice called, still clinging to his wool.

Buckeye, too, had lost interest in the fight, but he still guarded his ewes as we eased Big Virgil back to his lonely pasture.

Anyone could see that Alice had the heart to be a farmer! She joined the Southdown Breeders Association. Blue ribbons from the county fairs for vegetables and flowers soon hung in the barn as she joyfully enlarged the flock.

We had a stenographer on the farm, a friendly country girl named Judy Poston, who used to come and type for us sometimes. One day when I was trying to shape a design for Steuben, she came and called to me.

"The sheep are in the cow garden."

That garden hadn't held cows to milk for perhaps a hundred years.

"They're eating Mrs. Houston's phlox, the best ones."

"Oh," I said, "don't bother yourself. She'll be back soon."

"I'll get them out of the cow garden and I'll close the gate," called Judy.

I waited to hear the screen door slam, but there was nothing, only silence. Finally, I went to the front door and could see that the sheep were in the lane, but Judy lay on the grass between the stone wall and the gate. Big Virgil was strutting back and forth in front of her, proud as a peacock.

Judy sat up slowly as I went to help her, both of us keeping an eye on Big Virgil who snorted and looked excitedly at me. "I'm all right," said Judy. "One of those sheep must have butted me from behind."

I led her up the stone steps to the house. When I looked back, Big Virgil had turned away and was back to munching on Alice's phlox. Had he mistaken Judy for one of his soft-eyed ewes?

61

Britannia

During our time on the farm, we received a surprise invitation to visit the Royal Yacht *Britannia* in Boston harbor during Her Majesty's visit in July 1976.

"This means we've got to go into New York," said Alice. "I'm going to buy a new dress and you need a haircut and a new suit."

When we returned home with far too many fancy-looking boxes, we agonized over the best Inuit carving to present. Finally, we chose an Osuitok musk ox with gleaming horns, a dark green serpentine beauty of heavy stone.

"We've got a Steuben box that will fit that carving perfectly," Alice told me. "We'll wrap it in that regal-looking gold and purple French paper you've been saving."

Both the carving and its wrappings looked absolutely splendid when we finally tied it with a strong golden cord.

"We've got enough gasoline to get to Boston," I told Alice, "but who knows whether we'll be able to buy enough to get back home."

Cars stood in long lines at the gas pumps that year. This was the height of the Arab oil crisis, and we had a larger, splendid, somewhat old-fashioned car, a gift from my sister, Barbara. It guzzled gas like a thirsty camel.

When we reached *Britannia*'s wharf beside *Old Ironsides*, we parked the car and scurried over to join the line – me carrying the heavy, handsomely wrapped treasure and Alice fingering our invitation in her new black purse and flashing her matching shoes. In the line in front and gathering behind us, we could see familiar faces known to everyone from seeing them on television: John Kenneth Galbraith, Senator Ted Kennedy, the president of Harvard, and the mayor of Boston. But there were some understandable security concerns; some parts of Boston contained IRA supporters and, historically speaking, not all tea parties in Boston Harbor had turned out well for the British monarchy.

We were making progress in the slowly moving line of husbands and wives being presented to the Queen up on *Britannia*'s deck above us when two trim-looking men in business suits approached us. One of them said, "Sir, may I ask what you are carrying in that box?"

"Sure," I said, "it's an Eskimo carving, a really good one."

"I'll hold it for you," said the other man.

Somewhat reluctantly, I handed over the box, warning him to be careful not to drop it.

"Heavy!" he said, looking at his companion, and then at me. "Can we open it?"

"No!" said Alice. "You've no idea how carefully we wrapped that box."

"I'm afraid we must open it, ma'am, or drive it away immediately," said the one with the English accent.

"Okay, open it," I said, not looking at Alice.

I won't say that they ripped the wrappings open, but they did appear to be in a hurry. Those nearest us in the line seemed to back away and crouch a little, concerned for their own safety perhaps, but madly curious to see what fiendish device was hidden in the box.

The FBI man held the tattered packaging while the Scotland Yard man eased the stone carving out of its box. "Crikey!" he said. "It's smooth and cold and heavy as lead."

"Well, as you see, it's an Eskimo carving," I said.

"Sure." The American narrowed his eyes. "But what's inside this heavy piece of stone?"

Alice looked up, I thought, to ask God for help, when I heard her call out, "Martin, can you help us? We're in a terrible fix."

Sir Martin Charteris, the Queen's First Secretary, was leaning over *Britannia*'s railing.

"Oh, these are the Houstons. We know them," he called down to the security men. "Let them come aboard. We know about that package."

Tattered box

Together, we tried to rearrange ourselves and mount the gangway. An equerry placed me first, then Alice behind, in the proper British fashion. I quickly passed the heavy, troublesome, now torn and tattered package back to Alice as I, standing military straight, prepared to meet Her Majesty. My bow was, I'm sure, much more elegant than Alice's, for she still held the clumsy, awful-looking box.

The Queen looked past me and smiled sympathetically at Alice and her burden, then nodded to an aide to take it from her. After that was over, the whole event, like the weather, turned fine. We had a perfectly splendid day. And we managed to horn in on a Massachusetts gas lineup and buy gasoline enough to get us home just in time to put on overalls and rubber boots, then go and feed the sheep.

62

Farm Fare

Imagine suddenly having a garden, after living in the Arctic where nothing save a few ground berries grew out on the land, and one kind of seaweed was the closest thing to a vegetable. It was a glorious shock to both of us. Alice had come from an academic family who knew nothing of farms, agriculture, or domestic animals.

Lester, our friend and farm advisor, brought Alice seed packages of peas, beans, carrots, and beets and showed her how to plant them. When they became edible, Alice served them like new-found treasures, and from then on became a totally different person. Sheep and gardening – vegetables or flowers – can hit some women hard emotionally.

The good-sized brook that ran through the farm on the south side of the house had soil that was particularly rich and black, dampened and enriched by the stream. Alice, with Lester's help, planted beds of asparagus, thinned out an old raspberry patch, and raised corn, tomatoes, zucchini, cucumbers, Brussels sprouts, Jerusalem artichokes, pumpkins, and God-knows-what-else, often separated by rows of annuals, all bordered by sunflowers that finally towered above our heads. Inside the vegetable garden looked like an English paradise. We grew far too many zucchini and cucumbers, which Alice couldn't give away to other gardening friends, for they had far too many of their own! But New York City was an entirely different place. Friends at Steuben Glass couldn't get enough of our fresh country produce. They loved zucchini, cucumbers, and tomatoes. One enthusiastic calligrapher even asked us why we didn't start to keep hens and bring fresh eggs in every week.

After a long, hard winter ending with the flowing of maple sap, Canada geese could be seen flying overhead. The farm began to bloom into spring. Snowdrops, daffodils, tulips, and iris appeared. Fiddlehead ferns began uncurling all along our country lane. We would see wild lady slippers here and Jack-in-the-pulpits there. The mountain laurel that had been on the farm for several centuries bloomed in June, spreading a thick haze of pink and white over all those unkempt parts of our property. Then tiger lilies bloomed in wild profusion along all our old stone walls. We'd hear crows calling, woodpeckers hammering, and blue jays swearing at Pingwa, the cat. It was hard to imagine why we had ever lived anywhere else in the world.

63

The Schoolhouse

Our springer spaniel, Shulu, was very insistent about forcing me out on a walk with him during all our years together on the farm. Shulu, like other dogs, had a handy clock built inside his head, so he would tell exactly when it was 7:00 a.m. or 5:30 p.m. and start thrusting his head into my lap and giving me that look of his that meant, "Come on, old boy, let's go. I want to flush a grouse this morning or chase some squirrels." Shulu was a country dog who felt incensed at any thought of a leash around his neck, though he was frighteningly careless about cars.

We made our usual walk down our farm road through the woods, then onto Woody Hill Road that led to the one-room schoolhouse in the district. This schoolhouse had been built in 1854 by the Escoheag farm community. I mean, they collectively cut the large stones used for the foundation, squared the timbers, milled the lumber for the clapboards, and cut shingles for the roof, then put up the building with their own hands. They hired a girl from elsewhere in Rhode Island to serve as teacher and paid for her board at the nearest farm. Most of these young teachers got married to young local farmers and produced lots of children who, in turn, were sent off to this same one-room school.

The school had two separate doors, both facing toward Woody Hill Road. One door was to be entered only by the girls, who were charged with gathering fresh water from the stream just behind the school and covering it with a clean cloth over the pail beside the drinking ladle. The other door was strictly for the boys, their task being to split dried hardwood for the stove and light it early on cold mornings.

Axe

The teacher had a small alcove for her desk, and the students, some in double desks of various sizes, faced the double entrance doors with their backs toward the blackboard. What was written in chalk on the black-painted board were lessons aimed at only one part of the student body, because the age level in that one-room school ranged from five years to sixteen years old, and they were learning at different grades. Some of the oldest boys were confident enough to propose marriage to a young teacher, an idea, they said, that was sometimes accepted.

Out behind the schoolhouse stood two neatly painted outhouses, one for boys and one for girls. The school's maintenance was done by local school board volunteers. The raising of the flag each day was the prerogative of the teacher or more likely some eager farm boy whom she favored.

The students of Woody Hill School had always walked to and from their homes, though the distances for some seem formidable today. During World War II, the concept of a schoolbus was accepted, and transportation was offered for the distant students. After the war, the state built a larger, new school, miles away. The Woody Hill School was closed and slowly sank into disrepair.

When we first knew it, the old school had developed a large hole in its shingled roof. One door had been torn off, and there was a litter of square-hewn beams around it almost hidden by brambles. Old Mr. Barbour, who had a long white beard, had bought the building as part of a piece of property where for some time he had run a small sawmill. When we asked if Mr. Barbour might sell the schoolhouse, the postmistress, Laura Durfee, laughed. "He wouldn't sell anything to anybody," she said. "Others have tried for that property. But, no, he'd never sell it."

Alice loves American history, state or national. She used to see Mr. Barbour at the post office, sitting in Mrs. Durfee's front room, a place just big enough for two, with a counter and a dozen pigeon holes for neighbors' mail. Mr. Barbour came once a week on Fridays and Alice would try to draw him into conversation, searching for historical tidbits from earlier times.

"I'm afraid to ask him about letting us buy the schoolhouse," Alice told me, "for if he turns us down, I'll never be able to ask again."

"Why not write him a short letter and have it in next Friday's mail, asking him to sell the school to us and to name his own price?"

The week after, Alice received a phone call from old Mr. Barbour's sister, stating his willingness to sell the whole property to Alice for a price that we thought fair. On Friday, Alice attempted to close the deal. "All right, you go ahead," he said, as he hobbled out through the post office door. "You and your lawyer draw up the proper papers, Mrs., and I'll sign 'em."

Alice did, and the schoolhouse was ours. It was a season when Lester Lewis was not too busy on his own farm or ours, and we hired him with his friend, Everett Roberts, to repair, then put new shingles on the roof and clapboards on the outside walls where necessary. We all worked together to scrape and repaint the inside and outside of the schoolhouse white, as it had usually been, then oil the floors and search the countryside to find antique double desks to replace the ones that were missing. And believe it or not, we found some of the original schoolhouse desks, all saved in a barn on the nearby Woodmansee farm. Mrs. Woodmansee had come to the school as a young teacher and married within that Woody Hill community, and she and her husband now owned the large farm across the road.

Both Lester Lewis and Lephe Smith, who helped us on our farm, had been students in this one-room school and another. They both remembered them with great fondness. Once the school was restored, Lester sent out invitations to all the former students who had been taught there and now were scattered across the country, some living as far away as California. Those who went to the Woody Hill School seemed to me to have turned into a particularly honest, straightforward lot of people – swamp Yankees, they called themselves – keen observers of nature, with love of flag and an abiding interest in local and national politics.

We enjoyed our daily walks to that gentle, one-room schoolhouse for about six years. Then we gave both school and property, bounded by the road and brook, to the town of Exeter. Lester still cuts the grass there in summer and a few visitors come and sign their names and addresses on the blackboard. Lephe Smith used to come and wash the blackboard clean once a year. She swore just doing that at age seventy made her feel like a giddy, young schoolgirl again.

64

Disaster

Many animals and other visitors were welcome on our farm, but the gypsy moth was not among them. What a plague! Most years, these pests in the caterpillar stage have little effect on our vegetation. But one year, around 1980, they burst out in armies, causing murderous devastation on the farm.

One night when the moon was hiding behind a blanket of humid, summer clouds, I lay in our bed and listened. Outside the window, I could hear a strange and unfamiliar sound like nothing I had ever heard before. I woke Alice. "Listen," I said.

Out in the pitch darkness, we could hear the sound of munching caterpillars in the hundreds of thousands, desperately hurrying to consume all the oak leaves on our two largest trees that stood outside our bedroom windows. The other sound we heard was the rain of their excrement falling, bouncing off the oak leaves.

"It's terrifying!" Alice said. "There must be a million of them, all eating, killing our best trees!"

We were both up at the first morning light and outside to view the damage. I could scarcely believe my eyes. Both of the big oaks that had been fully leafed for summer now stood totally stripped, without a leaf. The caterpillars were still there, fat and sassy, parading up and down the strong oak trunks. Many hung on long threads from the branches like spiders swaying in the rising, morning breeze.

Lester came and stood beside us.

"Will that kill these oaks?" I asked.

"Probably not, if these caterpillars disappear and don't come back next year. But a second or third year as bad as this would surely kill these oaks."

"I hope they keep away from that big blue spruce in front of the house. That's my favorite tree," said Alice.

"You better enjoy it while you can," Lester added. "They like oak leaves best, but after that they'll go for the next best food that they can find."

He was right. They started on the blue spruce that evening, and in the morning it, too, had been stripped bare.

"Do you want me to cut that spruce down right now?" Lester asked. "It's never coming back, and just looking at it that way will make us all feel bad."

"You're sure it won't come back?"

"Yes, sure," said Lester, and he cut away the house-tall skeleton that had shortly before been our farm's most beautiful tree.

The presence of caterpillars in the district was a disaster, leaving all our woods and those around us stripped of leaves. We heard on the radio that the main area of devastation had not been wider than a dozen square miles, with our farm almost at the center. We remained late in British Columbia that year, in no hurry to return to the farm and view the glorious fall colors of the leaves, for there were no fall colors that year.

65

Winter

On moonlit autumn nights, Pingwa would call up pleadingly to Alice in our bedroom, complaining that there was a new chill in the air and that he wished to sleep on his favorite, padded, dining room chair. Pingwa had long since given up his calls to me, but he knew that the warm-hearted Alice would usually rise and let him in. If she didn't, Pingwa would trot silently down the laneway to the barn, check the place for mice, then nestle in the soft, sweet-smelling straw where his favorite lambs had lain.

Winter came, frequently with snow. We put off driving to New York. As the days began to lengthen, the weather began to strengthen. On stormy days, the sheep stayed in their large pen under the barn. By the end of February, the sun rose blearily through the haze behind the sugar maples. Alice and I would sometimes sit in winter parkas on the wide front steps of the farm and have breakfast, often sharing coffee with Lester. We would watch a red fox cross the thinly iced pond and talk about which maple trees we planned to tap, and how we would boil sap on the ancient, outdoor fire pit, using first dry, then the greenest wood that we could find. Such are the romantic plans that part-time farmers thrill to make as they, too, feel the spring sap rising in their bones.

Sap buckets

When we actually got down to the reality of cutting the firewood, carrying the sap buckets, and one of us up tending the fire all night, the overwhelming enthusiasm for our own homemade maple syrup lasted only three years. The whole project ended early one morning when I lugged our last large cauldron of almost-rendered sap into Alice's kitchen and put it on two burners of our stove. I planned to sit and watch it slowly bubble, smelling divine as it reduced itself into thick, rich syrup. But I got an unusual idea about the chapter I was writing and went to my desk to jot it down on paper. Suddenly, I could smell maple syrup – not sweet, but scorching. Running to the kitchen like the Sorcerer's Apprentice, I found the syrup foaming, boiling up out of the pot and running over Alice's stove, down the oven, and across the floor. Both cats and our dog sat looking at me in disgust! They wanted out of there before Alice came down – and, believe me, so did I!

66

The Ice Storm

Many eastern Canadians and U.S. readers will be all too familiar with the deviltry caused by ice storms in 1998. The worst storm that I have ever witnessed this side of the Arctic came to us one winter's night and spread itself across the farm. It started first with big, wet white flakes falling so thickly we could not see the barn or the old road just in front of our house. Then, sometime after midnight, it turned to freezing rain.

When I rose at five and made my way to the bathroom in the dark, I thought, *Dammit, another bulb has burned out.* But we had lost all power. Raising the window shade, I saw outside that the laneway in both directions and as far as I could see had turned into a glistening white and silver fairyland. *How beautiful*, I thought, *I must draw this. Alice must photograph this rare sight of the trees bending so gracefully like weeping willows along the Wood River.*

As I stood staring in wonder at this sight, I heard a loud crack. What was that? And then another and another, and I saw a swaying motion among the trees toward the deer field. Oh, my God, those were branches breaking, trees splitting from the still-gathering weight of ice as a mistlike rain continued to fall and freeze onto the thick coating of ice that covered every branch and shrub. I stumbled through the dark to our front window. The snow on the sheep field down by the pond glimmered icy as a skating rink.

"Alice, get up and look at this," I called to her, and when she did, I heard a wail of wonder that turned into horror.

"Your favorite oak tree by the barn, it's torn to pieces," she cried, "split down the middle to the ground!"

Now we could hear many other branches breaking off the maples overburdened with their glorious-looking silver loads of ice. We flung on our clothes, stamped into our boots, and rushed outside, slipping on the front stone step, for everything was covered with a sheet of ice. Fortunately, or perhaps unfortunately, there was not a breath of wind, just the continued falling of a light freezing rain that clung and added to the weight of every tree.

Alice tried other lights. "The power's off," she said. "All the lines must be down."

"The crews are probably out fixing them now," I said hopefully.

The oil heat was off. Our electric blanket was off. The stove remained cold. Nothing worked. Fortunately, our ancient, eighteenth-century house had seven good-sized working fireplaces, and we had a lot of cut, dried wood.

I lit three of the fireplaces and set the others ready in case the power did not come on soon. We each took a ski pole to steady ourselves as we crept down to the barn, carrying pails of water hand drawn from the well. The sheep were bleating in the darkness, and Big Virgil was battering at his pen.

"We've got a Swedish Primus stove to cook on, but, dammit, it's in the British Columbia house. I'll try cooking in the fireplace," Alice said. "Farm women must have done that here for a couple of centuries."

After carrying lots of wood and missing Lester terribly, we found that a shot of rum was just the thing to warm our hearts. Alice built up the keeping room fire to get a bed of glowing embers. The house was now gray and bleak and cold inside. We both put on thick socks, heavy woolen trousers, sweaters, parkas, and hats. Alice hung an iron kettle on the fireplace crane and made hot onion soup. Not long after that, we heard the whine of a chainsaw as it started up at the bottom of our lane.

"That must be Lester," we agreed.

Ski poles in hand, I made my way cautiously down through the shining trees that were bent and iced together like magic wedding bowers, except that every now and then one or several of the heaviest ice-laden branches would break and come crashing down.

It was Lester, trying to clear the lower lane with his saw, but there was just too much down already with more crashing over the road from both sides of the lane. "I've never seen anything like this," said Lester. "Neither has my dad. You're going to lose a lot of trees."

As he spoke, a large maple split straight down the center, bending outwards, crashing down in two directions, sending out a shower of shattered ice that went spinning across the heavily ice-crusted forest floor.

Shulu, who hated to miss anything, had terrible trouble making the slightly uphill journey back to the house. He scrambled then fell, scarcely able to claw his way over the crust. Pingwa sat sphinx-like in the window watching our dog's awkward actions with scarcely hidden delight as Shulu slipped and slithered completely out of control.

The telephone lines were down, and our general power remained cut off from our farm for six days and nights. We burned more cords of wood than we would have in an entire winter. But still the house remained cold, lit only by small pools of candlelight. Fortunately, we had some months before found a huge bargain sale of candles and had bought enough, we had hoped, to last us for years. The smallish library, which I used as a writing room sometimes, had a square, stone fireplace with no damper. Once you got it really heated from daylong and nightlong fires, its stones continued to give off heat and truly warm the library if you closed the room's three doors and kept the indoor Indian shutters tightly shut.

We were well off for food. Even though our freezer had ceased to function, the temperature outside was around freezing. We took out an Arctic char that we'd been saving, and Alice laid it on some tin foil, buttered it, added a sprinkling of herbs, rolled it tightly, then laid it in on a bed of glowing embers in the fireplace. She turned it with the fire tongs and, unwrapping it, served what seemed to be the best fish we had ever tasted. Foil-wrapping any kind of meat and most vegetables with a bit of moisture (oil or water) and simply tossing them into glowing embers works very well – we know.

Instead of using the smaller fireplaces in the ice-cold bedrooms, we brought down our sleeping bags, zipped them together to make a double bed, and slept in front of that library fireplace with Shulu close on one side and our two cats on the other.

When conditions were improving, we walked out to Woody Hill Road at the end of our lane. There were no tire tracks – not a single car had passed to break the ice. We plodded back through the gathering gloom to our totally dark house.

So was this what it would be like to live here in the eighteenth century, or perhaps during some other more serious future disaster, we wondered. Even with lots of matches, dried wood, candles, tin foil, and good warm sleeping bags – so much of our time had been spent that week just surviving. We had been existing by hauling firewood, feeding and watering ourselves and the sheep, and doing everything else in complicated ways. There had been no telephone but neither had there been time for phoning, nor writing and certainly not for lazing around to think. Life in early Canada and New England must have been jammed full of chores for everyone. It took a hard ice storm in winter without power to show us how very changed and modern we had all become.

67

Lambing

Birthing in our barn was a time of highest excitement as far as Alice was concerned. She had been introduced to sheep farming by her friend, Jill Thompson, who knew everything about it as far as Alice was concerned. Southdowns are the greatest of all sheep, Jill had told her, and the most delicious. But they can have trouble birthing. Alice took that comment to heart, and Jill showed her how she could help ewes with the process.

Lester appeared in my writing room in shock one morning and told me that Alice was kneeling behind a sheep with her sleeves rolled up and one hand deep inside the ewe, helping her give birth to twins. He said it wasn't the custom around here to do that. But Alice, following Jill's instructions, carefully helped the mother produce two healthy lambs, and she made sure they found out how to find the ewe's milk. This should happen within a lamb's first hour to prevent illness and avoid rejection by the mother, in which case the lamb will have to be bottle fed, a tiresome chore, I know.

Lambing time does not match well with the concentration needed to write a book, design glass for Steuben, or drive to New York. My best time for writing has always been in the early morning, which exactly coincides with sheep feeding time. Bearing two buckets of water, I would hurry down to the barn in the late winter blackness, always accompanied by Shulu. He was very fond of all the ewes and lambs, but had become mistrustful of Big Virgil, who had butted him an awful smack in the ribs for paying too much attention to the ram's personal flock of ewes.

Once I had watered the sheep and spread their grain out on the long, wooden trays, I would stand back in the pale bulb light and watch the lambs. They seemed to be changing every day. Of course, they had been born over a two-week period and were all in various states of development. The ones who were a fortnight old would stand looking around at their limited-sized world beneath the barn, then suddenly, as though on springs, one would leap stiff-legged straight into the air, then go springing across the sheep pen. Seeing this, another one would try it. Then perhaps in imitation of each other, most of them would begin prancing and springing in a spectacular kind of dance, which I found endlessly fascinating. So did Shulu.

I often say that *Ghost Fox*, my second adult novel, which was published in 1977, took by far the longest time to write because of the necessary historical study about the French and Indian Wars. But I do honestly admit that the power of the lambs first springing in the barn and later joyfully rambling in our green pastures also took its toll on my daily writing.

Lamb

I've had the luck to live in a lot of different ways. But for me, pretending to be a New England farmer while earning daily bread in other ways was one of the most satisfying experiences of all.

I tried, with lots of help from Lester, to assemble an old farm tool collection in our barn, gathering many pieces at New England antique shows including an elegantly shaped and stenciled, one-horse winter sleigh. We whitewashed two barn walls behind the tool display and adjusted soft overhead lights. It all looked as grand to me as a Currier and Ives.

When we finally sold the farm, I gave almost all of that collection to Lester. About the same time, we gave most of those well-known characters that were our flock of Southdown sheep, together with our bold ram, Buckeye, to the University of Rhode Island. We left that wonderful farm life, for we planned to travel more, which is a costly thing to do if you also have a farm with animals. We wanted to spend more time writing and salmon fishing at our cottage in northern British Columbia.

The farm had been ours and we had loved it for thirteen years. I must confess that it was profitable to sell the place. We received almost four times the price that we had paid for it. The new purchasers, who have remained good friends, were much to our liking, and just as keen as we had been about the farm.

When they bought it, I said to them, "You've yet to find this out, but Lester Lewis is the best thing about this farm."

A year later, they phoned to say that I was right about Lester. They added that while driving from New York to the farm, their six-year-old son Oliver had coughed then said to his parents, "I hope I'm not catching a cold. I wouldn't want to give it to Lester."

68

A Toast to Canada and the U.S.

In the mid 1970s Jack McClelland, the president of McClelland & Stewart, Canada's most prominent publisher, became my publisher in Canada and a lifelong friend.

After an exciting war as captain of a motor torpedo boat, Jack joined the family company and by 1952 was running the house. Soon, with a blend of showmanship and good publishing taste, he had made M&S the most prominent book-publishing house in the country, with a list of excellent authors. Jack was widely known as a bon vivant who, with his friends, Farley Mowat and Pierre Berton, gave countless interviews on TV in praise of Canada and the writing trade. Margaret Atwood, Mordecai Richler, Margaret Lawrence, Sylvia Fraser, along with many others, were also friends of Jack, some a little more conservative in their ways. I always enjoyed Jack's company immensely.

One year, Jack, with his wife, Elizabeth, came with Pierre Berton and his wife, Janet, to stay with us at the farm and to attend the Westminster Kennel Club Show next day. We had a splendid celebration that evening with wine, of course, and I proposed a toast, first to greet them, then to honor our still-new, old colonial house. Dinner was in the keeping room at our long table before the fireplace that was almost large enough to walk in upright.

Since I designed for Steuben Glass, I proudly raised my glass in a toast to the guests, drank it down then flung my handiwork grandly into the fireplace as I had seen done in those royal, old Hollywood movies.

Jack's glass immediately went crashing in after mine. An ominous silence filled the room. Janet stayed Pierre's hand and Elizabeth and Alice gave us two true, merry toasters a withering look. But, hell, it was worth it. Who gets to have drinks with the likes of Jack McClelland these days? I haven't, alas, for several years.

When I think of it, how better could we have toasted Canada and the U.S.A.?

For years Jack and I were both members of a club in New York called The Leash. If he happened to be in town, we'd often meet there.

Some say The Leash is the most desirable of all clubs in New York. It was perfectly located halfway between Steuben Glass on 5th Avenue and my garden apartment on East 69th Street. It was said to be the only men's club in New York where one could sleep and have three delicious meals served every day. That was especially important to any New Yorker who got into a little or a lot of marital trouble and was desperate to spend some time at his club until things blew up totally or cooled down at home.

The Leash, as its name suggests, is a dog fanciers' club, and many of its members own champion field trial dogs or show dogs, most of which are kept on Long Island or elsewhere in the country for their health. The club had been established in 1925 during Prohibition, a period that had caused the formation of a number of clubs so men could drink with friends.

Beside the bar, (which doesn't look like a bar) one whole wall of the lounge has dozens of small, oak-paneled cupboards. Each has a sturdy inset lock and a tasteful brass plate with the name of a dog engraved on it. Yes, these are The Leash cupboards where our fellow club members keep their dog's leash, and as you can see there is also room for a few bottles of Canadian bootleg gin, or whisky, and even perhaps some bourbon.

Collar and leash

The older members could remember Prohibition. If this club of ours was raided, they said, the house man would open our door immediately and welcome in the police. During their thorough inspections, they always demanded to see what was hidden behind the small, locked cupboard doors. When they found gin and other forbidden treasures, they would demand to know, "Who owns these cupboards?"

"Look, Officer, the names are on each door. See – Brownie, Plunger, Lady, Bones – all of them are dogs. I guess those purebred mutts like to drink a little after the shows."

"Who owns these dogs?"

"We don't know, Officer. Now, Lady was a famous pointer belonging to Dr. Weber, but he died and so did his dog, Lady. The dog leashes and those bottles in the cupboards belong only to the dogs. That's a house rule and we're very serious about house rules in this club. Would you like to visit with us a while? Probably Lady or our friend the doctor wouldn't mind sharing a little of that gin with all of us."

"Would you like your martini straight up and very dry with an olive or a twist, Officer," the house man would ask. "Do you have a dog?"

69

Ghost Fox

The *White Dawn* was my first novel, and some say that everyone has a first novel hidden deep inside themselves somewhere. For this one, I had to do very little research because I had already lived the circumstances in the Arctic for a dozen years at the place where the events had actually happened, and I had already done all the necessary questioning and reading. The book was a great success and changed my life forever.

This is all going to be easy, I thought. I used to write and illustrate children's books at a speedy rate, nothing should stand in my way. Or could it? The second historical novel was entirely different.

I decided to write this new book about an Indian captivity because we were living in our old New England farm house, built circa 1750-55. I had started to become interested in the French and Indian Wars, which had been raging at the very time when our farm was built. My interest grew when I read a small account of Mary Jemison, who had been taken from a similar colonial farm and marched north with other captives by the Abnaki Indians into Canada. Jemison led an extremely perilous yet fascinating life among the Abnakis. She was married to one of them and had a child before she was recaptured by the British in the course of their attack on the Abnaki village.

At this point, I felt that I really could not understand the feelings of the two desperate women who appear in *Ghost Fox* and who were determined to escape their pursuers. I worried for a while, then taking our car, I drove to Vermont's northern border to the place called Canadanskawa, not far from a beaver swamp. It was an early spring evening with an ominous, overcast sky.

When I arrived, I bought a hamburger and ate it slowly, waiting in the car until it was dark. Faintly through the clouds, I could see the bleary half face of the moon. I waited until long after midnight in the warmth of the car. Then, working up the courage, I forced myself to walk forward into the darkness of the unknown swamp that had been swollen by waters from the snow runoff. I began wading. My ankle-high L. L. Bean boots filled with water as I kept slipping into holes and catching my feet under sunken roots. It was very dark and I hated being thigh deep in the icy water. Almost immediately I began to sense the dark terror and shivering pangs of the indomitable Deutsche woman and young Sarah as they tried desperately to escape by night, leaving no trail for their ruthless trackers. It was, I think, one of the two most miserable experiences I have ever had in my life.

After far too long in the icy black water, I saw the outline of a good-sized, dead apple tree, not tall but rugged-looking, with thick, low branches. It was easy to scramble up – anything to get myself out of that damned water. I wondered what my two main characters would do under such conditions. Having walked all day into the night, they would have been dead tired, and would have tried to sleep. But I feared for myself up there. If I shifted position, I might fall face down into the dreaded swamp. I had seen a leopard sleeping in a tree while we were on safari. It lay on its belly with its four legs dangling down on either side of the branch to keep its balance. I managed to do the same, uncomfortable as it was, and tried to go to sleep. Impossible. I was too cold, too wet, and too fearful of the bleary darkness. But I'll bet those women slept, bone weary as they must have been. I heard a beaver splash and a night bird squawk as I waited in misery for dawn to come.

Leopard in tree

I must have dozed off for a minute because when I opened my eyes there was more light around me. A movement in the water made me turn my head. Not far from me stood a man in a thick, plaid jacket, wearing hip boots and carrying a deer rifle. It was not pointed at me, but I certainly had his full attention.

"Good morning," I called to him in a shaky voice.

He didn't answer right away then said, "What in the name of God are you doing up there?"

"I'm, I'm . . . a writer, writing a book about . . ."

He snorted. "I'll bet you're some son-of-a-bitch escaped from Sing Sing Prison or a lunatic maybe out of a New York state asylum."

"No, no," I answered. "I'm coming down so you can point me the shortest way out of here. You know where I can buy some hot coffee? Have some breakfast?"

"Get going," this stranger said. "I'll keep right behind you. I'll take you to the diner. Kenny must be there by now for donuts. He's a cop. He'll take care of you. Go ahead. I'm right behind you. You can explain to Kenny why you were hanging in that tree."

The squad car was parked outside the diner and Kenny, the police officer, sat in a booth inside. He checked my damp pockets for a weapon before we three sat down, with me jammed on the inside. I ordered coffee, three sausages, two eggs and toast. The heat was coming up the diner wall beside me and the shivers were leaving me. The waitress stayed beside us to hear my excuse.

When I got to the part about Mary Jemison's escape into the beaver swamps near Canadanskawa, the waitress told us she had read all about that old woman in a magazine story and that Mrs. Jemison had lived just north of Canadanskawa with Indians about 250 years ago. Both the policeman and the deer poacher, who had hidden his rifle behind his coat at the entrance to the diner, seemed interested in the waitress' tale, and began to treat me more like a crazy author than a crazy felon.

Though I was somewhat worried that my story would be too well known, I wrote the book. My main character, Sarah – or Ghost Fox as she was called by the Indians – led a wild and dangerous life, even after she was released and taken south by various soldiers. She was returned to her parish and was paid the church reward for freed captives. But then, discontented with farm life, she returned to spend the rest of her days with her Indian husband in the north.

In the diner, I promised, as authors always do, to send these three new friends a copy of *Ghost Fox*. Much later, the waitress sent me a card from the diner saying that they had all liked the exciting way I told Mary's story. I swear that night in the beaver swamp taught me just how awful those two tired and starving women must have felt. I tried to reflect that in various chapters of *Ghost Fox*. After almost thirty years, it's still in libraries, still in print, and doing well. If you'd care to read it, I'd recommend you do so in a warm, dry bed.

The rest of my research for *Ghost Fox* was rewarding and more enjoyable. It took me more than four years in all, including traveling to the Newberry Library in Chicago, where most pamphlets and accounts on Indian captivities are housed. I did research in the Hudson's Bay Company archives in Winnipeg, Manitoba, and in other library collections, learning about the English and Scottish regiments serving in America including the Black Watch Highland Regiment and the *Régiment d'Infanterie La Sarre* from France who all fought desperately during those bloody years of war.

When *Ghost Fox* finally appeared, it was very well received and went into many translations, recordings, and printings. We sold the screen rights three separate times to various film companies. This, in itself, can be profitable if you put a limit in the contract as to how long the buyer may retain screen rights to the property before it automatically returns to you. The worst of those negotiations is that three times *Ghost Fox* has come close to production and just failed to get the financing necessary to make it into a major movie. I keep hoping that it still may happen. They may be waiting until I'm no longer around to love or perhaps hate the final film results. Who knows?

70

Sighting Authorities

In the 1960s I had worked with NBC to turn some of my children's stories into an illustrated TV series that seemed to work pretty well. In 1969 they got in touch with me again, this time about something very different from my animated children's films. Craig Fisher called me to say that they were thinking about doing a pan-Arctic show that would include Alaska, Canada, and Greenland, as well as a mid-winter journey in the Soviet Arctic across northern Siberia. "Would you like to come with us?" he asked.

"You bet," I said. "When?"

"We're going to decide our timing at a luncheon next week. We'll be bringing in a variety of people to discuss that. Tuesday, one o'clock, can you make it?"

"Sure," I said, already trying to remember my desk calendar and all the things I had sworn that I would do during the coming winter.

We all sat down to lunch at a boardroom table. There were about twenty persons gathered, and from the buzz of introductions I learned that there were many professors and the Russian ambassador among the dignitaries. I recognized the director of the North American Arctic Institute, an Alaskan musk-ox expert, and prominent biologists, anthropologists, glaciologists, museum curators, and archaeologists. I was proud to be included in such distinguished company.

Throughout the luncheon, our hosts from NBC asked us questions concerning weather, wildlife, art, and humans living on the Siberian taiga and the Russian Arctic coastline. They asked about the Soviet political climate at that time, and they asked whether the eastern Siberian herders and hunters should be automatically considered as distant early relatives of Eskimos of North America and of the Lapp-Sami tribes living in northern Norway, Sweden, Finland, and the western part of the Soviet Union. Some at the table agreed they were, and others doubted that.

Now came the tough question – when had the land bridge used by North American Indians crossing between Asia and the Americas disappeared beneath the Bering Sea?

There was a lot of mumbling round the table about dates and times of crossing. A man seated next to me spoke up. "The arrival of those we now call Eskimo began about five thousand years ago, evidenced by the recent Alaskan dig at Onion Portage."

That date didn't sit at all well with me. I'd been reading on that very subject and I felt certain his date was wrong. I kept quiet until coffee came, then leaned toward him.

"Can your dating on the earliest Eskimo crossing be correct?" I said smoothly.

"Well, it is," he answered, staring hard at me.

Everyone was watching. Very calmly, I played my trump card. "Dr. Froelich Rainey, now at the University of Pennsylvania, would never agree with that!"

"Froelich Rainey?" He grunted, then gasped. "FOR GOD'S SAKE, MAN, I AM FROELICH RAINEY!"

An Arctic silence hung over those who sat near us at the table. I tried to swallow my too-hot coffee.

He laughed. "Well, at least you picked a good authority!"

"Forgive me," I said. "I missed your name at the introductions, but I've read many of your papers."

He smiled and whacked me on the back – a friendly gesture I knew well, used frequently between Eskimo hunting companions. As it turned out, the filming dates were a conflict and I couldn't go to Siberia with NBC as I had hoped to do. But John Bockstoce, an anthropologist from Yale, went in my stead and said he had a helluva good time. And I did learn to listen to introductions more closely.

71

Aurora Borealis

Northern Lights, "Aurora Borealis," are spectacular, an ever-changing display sometimes seen in northern skies. Inuit claim these mysterious lights are caused by a great kickball game played by giant spirits in the sky. On some nights, you can see them shimmering like pale ghosts gliding along a darkened hall. But on other winter nights, they burst forth strongly like countless searchlights, probing downward through the skies, undulating like curtains of electric green moved eerily by some cosmic winds. You must whistle, blowing on your fingers, if you wish to let the spirits know you're watching the game.

One wintry morning in New York in 1974, I received a phone call at the office. It was the architect for the new Glenbow-Alberta Museum in Calgary. He said that they were interested in installing a major piece of sculpture in a central location in the new museum. They had thought of me, he said, and of glass because of its reflective qualities, and they wondered if I would care to apply to submit a design.

"You bet," I said.

"When could you get out here?" the architect asked me.

"Just hold the line a minute." I leaned out my door and called to our famous secretary, Big Linda. "Have you arranged my flights for Alaska?"

"I've got them here," she answered. "You're leaving Kennedy Airport tomorrow morning at 7:00 a.m."

I counted the two-hour time difference backward for Alberta's time, then changed forward to my flight time. "I could be in Calgary at 9:00 a.m. tomorrow morning."

"My God, that's fast!" the architect gasped. He was an Englishman and they still expect everyone to say, "Oh, I'll probably be able to get out there in a month or so." Here I was, already sounding like a jazzed-up New Yorker on the run.

He gave me the new museum's downtown address and I was in the building at 9:30 a.m., having merely stopped off en route to my long-arranged meeting concerning Inuit art at the university in Fairbanks, Alaska. The large, new building, perfectly located, was only partly finished at that time and huge areas of the gray concrete structure were as yet unroofed, with heavy plastic covers stretched over most of it like tents in an attempt to retain minimal heat and keep out snow. It was an unusually cold month in Calgary.

"Here's where the central staircase will go," he said, unrolling a sheaf of plans. "We were thinking your sculpture, if accepted, might go in here."

I looked up at the dark circle of open sky above. I couldn't see stars or the Northern Lights, but they came instantly to mind. "How high will that ceiling be?" I asked.

"Seventy feet, twenty-two meters," he answered. "But, of course, you don't have to reach that high. It's four stories."

"Well, I'd like to," I said. "I'd like to make a huge, shining sculpture that rises all the way to the roof. Maybe I'd call it *Aurora Borealis*."

"That didn't take you long." The architect rolled up the plans and shuddered. "Let's go next door and have some coffee and warm up."

As I flew on to Alaska and later on my way back, I made dozens of drawings in a sketchbook. I have always been hypnotized by triangular prism forms in glass. They throw light like a mirror. I wanted to make each of them look as long and slim as a model on the catwalk, but I knew that few glass furnaces anywhere could accommodate a length like that. I also worried about the spearlike nature of these prisms. I wanted not the slightest risk of any of them falling down and shattering in a public area. Acrylic, I knew, would not do that. So, reluctantly, I changed my thinking from glass to the very best quality of clear, stable plastic, a wonderful type of material that polishes and shines like crystal.

I knew a good structural engineer, John Martin, doing work at Yale, and another man, a stage designer, who taught there. I enlisted help from both of them, and John perfected the fits and structural strength between the thousand narrow, six-foot prisms that spiraled down irregularly from the arms of the metal structure.

A scale wooden model was needed to replicate the large stairwell inside which I trusted the sculpture would stand. Alice phoned the airline, asking if they could carry this large package to Calgary. She inquired about the width of their freight doors to make certain that the model would squeeze inside. When this model staircase was delivered, I set it up around my five-foot model of the sculpture, carefully lighted on the inside. With the miniature museum stairs curving around the lighted model, it looked to me like an Arctic fairytale.

Donald Harvie, head of the Glenbow Museum Committee, came to view the model. They agreed to have me do the sculpture. What a day that was! One doesn't receive a commission to undertake a seventy-foot sculpture in a new and beautiful art museum every day.

One of the great problems that concerned the Glenbow Board from the day they agreed to take the sculpture was how the staff would ever manage to clean and polish this seventy-foot giant. Its three thousand separate surfaces, some very awkward to reach, boggled everyone's mind. I was worried, just as worried as they were, for it is important to keep clear reflecting surfaces clean. We worked out a system with the building's architects whereby four small boatswain's chairs could be lowered on thin, steel cables through hidden holes in the ceiling, allowing cleaners suspended between the arms of brushed aluminum to maintain each shining prism.

We took particular care with computer-driven, moving lights that beamed upward from the base of the sculpture. To this I also added music – Claude Debussy's famous *Snowflakes Are Falling*, played through a moog synthesizer arranged by that Japanese musical genius, Tomita.

But first there was the awesome question of getting the thousand parts of the sculpture to Calgary.

72

Running West

A thousand clear, acrylic prisms – three inches by three inches by three inches by five to seven feet long, each one sharp as a pencil point on each end – had to be transported almost across the continent from Rhode Island on the Atlantic, where we had made them, west to Calgary, Alberta. How to get them there?

I called my son, John, then a student at Yale. "Will you help me," I asked him, "during your winter break?"

"Sure, Dad," he said, "how are we going to do it?"

"By truck," I told him. "I'm going to rent a U-Haul truck."

"Whooh!" said John. "Have you ever driven a truck?"

"No," I said, "have you?"

"Not yet," John admitted, "but I guess we'll learn while running west."

John came down to Rhode Island, and we loaded the one thousand prisms plus ten emergency replacements, all very carefully wrapped, into the covered truck and cushioned them tenderly in everything soft that we could find. Next morning, we set out in the dark down our farm lane, then onto Woody Hill Road and Interstate 95, heading toward the wider world.

John studied the map. "Let's go through the United States," he suggested. "I've always wanted to see Chicago and Sioux Falls and Fargo, North Dakota, and Bismarck, and Great Falls, Montana, and Missoula."

What a trip! We both knew the look of Canada from the Great Lakes across the prairies and into the foothills of the Rockies, so we had agreed on the southern route of the U.S., just below the banana belt.

"John, you sleep while I drive the first four hours. You look tuckered out. Have you been losing sleep because of exams? What do you do in that small room with that enormous waterbed?"

I admit I didn't like driving a truck or the stiff floor shift, but what the hell, we had to get there somehow. I kept glancing over at John, who kept peering into the sideview mirror and never closed his eyes. We stopped for lunch and talked a bit. When it was my turn to rest, I thought, *this kid has never driven a truck!* So I, too, kept my eye on the sideview mirror at an eighteen-wheeler treading on our tail. I never slept a wink.

We stopped at a gas station, then a motel that served an awful steak dinner while the jukebox played too loud. We went outside and walked and talked, then set the alarm for 6:00. I slept hard.

John looked better in the morning when we started out through a light frisk of snow that blew in swirls along the black-topped highway.

"I could do the driving, Dad. I'm really rested now."

"No, no, you catch some sleep. I'll wake you at lunch."

We talked some more, but John, I noticed, never slept a wink and seemed relieved to do the afternoon driving as I nervously watched the road, dreading any frost heaves in the highway and what they might do to our costly and sharp-pointed load of prisms.

Next morning at dawn, when we passed through the outskirts of Chicago, John said, "I better do the driving near the cities, Dad. Cities seem to make you nervous."

I pulled over and he jumped out, peed, then ran around, kicking the tires and laughing, grateful, I suppose, to be getting the steering wheel away from me. With neither of us sleeping in the truck ever, we drove until dark, then found a motel and conked out like hunting hounds at night. We made it slowly north to Fargo in snow and had the feeling we were getting nowhere. John had to get back to Yale when the term restarted, so we decided to drive throughout that night. At one point on the highway, cleared of snow by a strong wind, we saw in our headlights half a dozen black Angus cattle. We barely avoided hitting them. John nodded off to sleep during our breakfast of bacon and eggs.

Then we were on to Great Falls, Montana. Staring in sleepy wonder at the Badlands, we took the highway north. We watched herds of antelope running gracefully across the plains and pausing only to crawl under ranchers' fences rather than spring lightly over them as one had always imagined in dreams. Oh, I was worried about the one thousand pencil-tip points on the sculpture's prisms. How many had snapped off when we so violently hopped the railroad tracks just outside of Chicago?

John was looking tired again – even worse, I thought, than when he'd left his waterbed at Yale. It was almost midnight when we eased the U-Haul into Calgary and found the parking lot beside the new Four Seasons Hotel and the all-but-completed Glenbow-Alberta Museum. John's ticket back to New Haven meant that he would have to leave the hotel for the airport at 6:00 a.m.

The following morning I hugged him, thanked him, and said good-bye. U-Haul in Calgary took back their Rhode Island truck. John phoned when he got back to Yale and said he'd slept his way east during the flight across the country and that the whole journey had been a great adventure. I know that we both knew and liked each other better for it. He admitted that he was glad to get out of town before the prisms in the truck were unpacked and I discovered the damage. John suggested that I phone him, especially if I had good news.

I fancied I could hear his waterbed gurgling in his room when, next evening, I was able to tell him the splendid news that not a single tip had been broken by the violent railroad crossing or the countless frost heaves in the roads. John gave a whoop of joy, and I heard a high, girlish giggle besides. I didn't have the heart to mention his studies. John had always done so well at school.

Driving for five days across America, talking about this and that with John, was an important event in my life. Not all fathers have the chance to talk privately and at length with their college-aged sons. I've felt a greater closeness to John ever since. Nowadays, he's usually off making big movies somewhere around the world. I'm proud to have been able to help John make his start.

73
Calgary

On opening night at the Glenbow Museum in September 1976, a large crowd gathered, and there was a great deal of ceremony. I excitedly ate the caviar and drank the champagne, for all of this was happening during Alberta's richest oil boom, and the feeling of a city already expanding, shifting into overdrive, was all around us.

The music and the moving lights on *Aurora Borealis* gave the huge, soaring sculpture more magical reflections than I had ever dreamed would really happen. It could be seen from all four floors of the museum.

Dropping in to see the sculpture a dozen times after that glorious opening, I generally feel as moved as I did on that opening night. I still receive hundreds of letters from school children who have read my books and are taken to visit *Aurora Borealis*. They send drawings of how it looks to them. They're the ones who will decide whether that sculpture will be kept alive.

There is one favorite letter from Calgary, which I often quote:

Dear Mr. Houston:
     I have read your book *Tikta'liktak*. It is the best book I have ever read. It is the only book I have ever read.
                                        Love, Wendy

One day in Calgary a few years later I happened to be staying at the Palliser Hotel when Canada's Prime Minister, Pierre Elliott Trudeau, tried to leave by the front door, but was driven back by a crowd of angry businessmen who were enraged by his new National Energy Program. I slipped around the edge of the crowd, noting that these tanned, heavyset men were dressed in expensive cowboy boots, tight whipcord trousers, leather ranch coats, and wide-brimmed Stetson hats. And they were angry. It was east meets west in the worst kind of way.

Not long after this oil tax was announced, television showed giant U.S. oil rigs pecking their way south to cross the Canada-U.S. border like huge, long-necked, mechanical toys. Trudeau's new tax had emptied Alberta's vast oil patch of its drilling rigs, and these American big birds never really returned, signaling the sad end of that particularly profitable oil boom.

74

Montreal

When I was a teenager growing up in Toronto, we heard great tales of Montreal and thought of it as a kind of heavenly Mecca, unimaginable to those of us used to the beer parlors in Presbyterian Toronto. We wanted desperately to go to Montreal to see the liber-ated dancers, carouse in the cabarets, and ski in the Laurentians at St. Adele or Mt. Tremblant north of that great city. Oh, yes, the politics in Quebec were known to be very different. The Premier, Maurice Duplessis, was a legendary iron man with the kind of control that would have been greatly feared in some countries other than Canada. Mayor Camillien Houde of Montreal was even jailed during the war for his strong anti-Canadian sentiments. But none of that stuff could tarnish the city for us in those days.

To us, the French- and English-Canadians seemed to get on well enough in Quebec for about 250 years. They intermarried with great frequency. During the years I lived among them in Montreal and later in Grand'Mere, Quebec – where I had a small log studio and a highly intelligent young schoolboy named Jean Chrétien delivering proof prints on his bicycle – I enjoyed our relationships very much and always thought of the French in Canada as more sensitive and more fun than many of the English-Canadians I knew.

Then came René Lévesque, who had honed his communication skills in the American army during World War II. He almost managed to separate Canada. He would have done that, I believe, if it had not been for the Prime Minister, Pierre Elliott Trudeau, the leader whom that crowd of Calgary oil men so disliked, who stood solidly against the Separatist movement in the referendum plebiscite and kept the country together for another twenty years. Then René Lévesque died, and a new pair of Quebec Separatists leapt onto the scene: Jacques Parizeau and Lucien Bouchard. In 1995, a period of even greater Canadian anguish began. Once again a referendum was held.

I was in Montreal at a prominent hotel on Sherbrooke Street to witness this tense event as the votes came in that evening. Sherbrooke, an always busy street in downtown Montreal, was like a graveyard. No cars or taxis moved in the street; no people walked there. Everyone in the whole of Quebec, the whole of Canada, was transfixed in front of a television set. As the results were coming in, Parizeau, who appeared to me to be quite drunk, resigned and passed his power to Bouchard, but not before he had said on TV that the ethnics in Quebec had voted the wrong way and should be blamed for the failure of the French Separatists to win. The number of votes that allowed Canadians to keep the country together was very narrow indeed. I consider the outcome of this important plebiscite attributable in part to the determination and skill of another French-Canadian Prime Minister, Jean Chrétien. Twice the right man has been in the right place during a grave Canadian political crisis. Let all of us Canadians from sea to sea and across the Arctic help defuse this national problem before it flares up again.

75

New Arctic Housing

Back in the days when I lived in the North, the Canadian government asked me in their annual mail to send them my concept of a suitable Inuit house that could be supplied to those west Baffiners in need. I asked four of the brightest male and female Inuit among the Sikusalingmiut to join me in designing such a family house.

"First of all, we'll have to be able to build it, then take it apart when we have to travel," said these nomads who lived by the hunt and scarcely knew at that time that a government existed or that its staff would all but faint dead away at the idea of a house you could carry on a dog sled without too much weight.

We based this house on two-foot by eight-foot lengths of three-quarter-inch plywood and a bundle of precut two-by-fours that could be bolted and unbolted to form the floors, walls, and roof beams, all fitting neatly on a *kamutik*, even with a short door and one sturdy, plastic window to fit its frame.

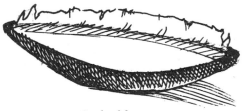

Seal-oil lamp

The house we designed, with the approval of everyone in Kingait, was sixteen feet long, eight feet wide, and six feet high at the roof peak. My Inuit friends thought this would be like owning a Rolls Royce; it would be a sturdy dwelling small enough to heat with their own stone seal-oil lamps, yet plenty large enough for a family (an average there was five). We had carefully made drawings and a sturdy scale model of our nomadic dreamhouse. Full of hope, we sent it out to the government at shiptime.

Sometime during the following spring, I received a radio message from Ottawa saying that they were thinking of a considerably larger house, something with at least 500 feet of floor space. Our design had had only 128 square feet, but these Arctic nomads could heat it with their traditional seal-oil lamps and could remain a hunting society, easily moving the house to wherever the game roamed during the year.

Living in a treeless country eliminated that common source of building materials and of fuel. So that year, I helped Inuit redesign what came to be called the 512 – because it had 512 square feet of floor space. If you measure the same in your house, you'll still think it mighty small. But it is certainly a house so large you couldn't move it, and that's the most important point. Wherever such a house was built, the owner became a captive to it. Where were you going to get the oil to heat such space? And how could you get oil without having money?

Slowly, the government encouraged – almost unknowingly, perhaps – these wandering, hunting families to settle down after God knows how many years and begin to live a more stationary life. It was, in a way, like bringing them to heel and chaining them to our imported, fifty-gallon fuel drums. This simple housing decision changed them from a nomadic hunting society to town-dwellers, part of a fuel-consuming, taxpaying, snowmobile community. It sometimes seems to me that we can't stand people in North America who enjoy more freedom than we do, and we take it away from them.

76

Alarm Bells

On one of my early trips back to Cape Dorset for the Canadian Eskimo Arts Council, I was asked to speak at the new school that had been erected there since my departure in 1962. I was eager to do this. These would be the children and grandchildren of some of my dearest friends, kids whom I had seen scampering around a few years before, timidly clutching the long-tailed *amautiks* of their mothers. The young principal had given me his regrets that he could not be at the school since he had gone out on the plane that brought me in.

When I went inside the school, pandemonium had broken loose, with Inuit children shrieking and rushing up and down the halls and in and out the classrooms as though the school were totally ruled by them. This new school had a library where I was to give a talk and display my newest books about the Arctic and make drawings on large paper for the children. Inside that library, there was an incredible, undisciplined, unstoppable roar of noise. I believed this was just excitement and that the children would settle down, or that their two teachers would soon demand quiet, or at least partial quiet, but this never happened. I, myself, was speechless, literally, with surprise. The children of Kingait, when I had known them only a few years earlier, had been quiet and respectful to all elders. Now everything seemed to have been turned upside down. Eventually, I had to leave the school without being able to speak at all. The two teachers and the librarian came to the door with me and apologized, saying that the children were excited by my visit and that the principal was away.

Was this part of the transition from the nomad way of life I had known in the late forties and the fifties when everyone living here moved in thirteen widely separated camps out away from Kingait? Had all these new ways happened too fast? And also, had it not been at least partly my fault? I had supported, when asked by Inuit parents, the idea of their quiet, orderly children settling down in one place and going to school. And now I had returned to observe the results of our new ideas.

I have no doubt that, for better or worse, whole families and societies in many parts of the world can change in a few years almost beyond recognition. What a pity! Canadians from the South, who had nothing but good will toward these nomadic, Arctic people and their decent, Spartan way of life, helped, as I did, to unhinge their delicately balanced system of living.

Can we help them to regain their balance as we flood our goods, our ideas, and our people increasingly into the Canadian Arctic to live among them? I doubt it. The greatly increased suicide rate among young males should worry all of us.

It will be interesting to notice over the next twenty years what effect the creation of Nunavut – "our land" – will have. There is a somewhat parallel model for this experiment in neighboring Greenland; I hope Canadian Inuit will benefit from studying its successes and be aware of its mistakes.

77

A Hunting Society

Some years ago I stayed with an Eskimo family while I was at Prudeau Bay on the northern slope of Alaska scouting for the Ford Foundation, assessing the possibilities of Eskimo art. Yes, people in Alaska gladly refer to themselves as Eskimos. They realize the value of that hardy, well-understood, and honorable name, which is respected worldwide.

There I heard a young bulldozer operator speaking to his grandmother on the telephone.

"Sure, I'd like to come back to Point Hope this springtime. Sure, Granny, I'd like to see you and everybody else around there, but I can't come home right now 'cause I got a damn good job here paying great and if I have to leave now, they'll fire me."

There was a long pause with a lot of talking from the other end of the telephone.

"Are you sure Alex is leaving here now, Granny, going back to Point Hope for the whaling? Is that what he told his grandmother? Well, maybe if he's going back, I guess I'll have to go along with him."

A minute later, he said, "Yeah, we can catch a plane. I know, Granny, you want a bowhead whale just like the one given to your mom and grandma every spring when the crews went out in the *umiaks*. Yeah, I'll probably be there to get you your *muktuk*, Granny. You say you've made new skin boots for me? Great! See you soon," he said, hanging up the phone.

"I gotta go," he said to all of us and shook his head.

One member of the family spoke up. "They told us over at the office that anyone skipping off work won't never get their goddamned job back. That's for sure!"

"That's true, but, still, I gotta go back for the spring hunt."

"Do your people really need that whale meat?" I asked him.

"Sure, they do!" he said. "That's a real Eskimo tradition to my grandmother. Young men in our family gotta go out with the older men in the skin boats and learn how to shoot and to harpoon the whales. Granny said if I don't hunt the whales, I'll be no better than a goddamned white man, sitting up on top of one of their big yellow monsters scraping the snow away for them.

"Well, I'll look up Alex and we'll fly back together after payday. I hate like hell to lose this fuckin' job, but I know the office will never take me back. After the whaling, I'm not going to hang around Point Hope, not by a long shot. But maybe I'll go down to Anchorage, yeah, I'll go down there."

Most people outside of the Eskimo world like to say that that world is coming apart, because of the young people who don't respect their elders' ways. But, in a way, I'd say the fault up here is partly that of the elders, like that grandmother, who have not yet fully perceived the enormous juggernaut of civilization that is steadily rolling their way.

78

Working with the NFB

I met John Feeney again recently in New York. He's a New Zealander. We had lunch together at the Century and got to laughing at one of our last escapades during the making of a Canadian National Film Board documentary film entitled, *The Living Stone*, on west Baffin Island.

The National Film Board didn't work like other film companies at that time, thanks to John Grierson, that free-wheeling Scottish genius. The NFB simply wanted to make a 16mm, half-hour documentary film about Inuit art. Grierson sent in John as director and Paddy as the excellent Irish cameraman he was to Cape Dorset to figure out what to do and how to do it. I helped them safely install themselves in what we called the Wildlife House, partly because of what went on in there, but also because it was occupied by homeless scholars on a variety of wildlife grants. They needed somewhere to store their stuff and live, not necessarily in my house.

After his arrival in Cape Dorset, I asked John what he wanted his film to portray and he said he didn't know and that it might be a good idea if we two prepared a script together. Of course, at that time I had never had anything to do with any kind of film, and had never really thought about a documentary or about the necessary preparations for anything of that sort. Over several weeks, while I did all my other usual chores, like hunting with my friends all day, John and I slowly began to develop a story around a well-known Inuit myth that old Paar loved to tell. He was an interesting-looking old man who had not yet revealed all the artistic talent that the world would come to see in him. We selected Niviaksiak, one of the very best carvers, to act the part of Paar when he was a younger hunter. Finally, when the rough shooting script had been prepared and I had alerted the male and female leads and extras we had selected to perform the dances and various small parts, Paddy got his camera out.

I could not believe how long this painstaking process seemed to take. Feeney wanted endless retakes, sometimes inside my big traveling tent and sometimes out on the open tundra, with rugged Kingait, the fiord and mountain, as the background. Inuit have immense patience, born, no doubt, from standing waiting over seal holes, and the women perhaps gain theirs from waiting for their husbands to return home with the meat. None of them seemed to mind one whit that both Feeney and Paddy took forever, but I quickly lost patience with the whole process and rushed off to buy stone carvings or to help the artists with their latest series of stone block prints. Summer was upon us by the time Feeney declared that the thirty minutes of 16mm filming was all but done. After that, the two of them had time on their hands because the government icebreaker that would take them out was not due to arrive for at least a month.

Feeney was starting to worry about the sounds he would use in the film to accompany the music and the voiceover from the rough script that we had written. "Do you know of anything special we might use," Feeney asked me, "beyond the calling of geese, the sounds of the sea, and that old button accordion Ilisuusi's mother traded from the whalers?"

"It will soon be the right season to hear candle ice," I told them. "Candle ice," I explained, "has that name from when the sun melts snow and makes shallow pools on top of the ice, causing the ice to crack quite evenly, like varnish on a painted canvas. The water running down through the ice creates long, icy, candlelike shapes. When a soft breeze blows, the water opens near them and the candles of ice collapse sideways into the water, striking together to create the most beautiful sound in the world."

"Oh, we must record that," John and Paddy agreed. "How far away is that lake," John asked, "and when can we go there?"

"As soon as the weather turns a little milder," I told him. "We'll take a small tent because we may have to wait up there a few days until conditions are just right. A light breeze is important. I'll send Osuitok up tomorrow morning early to check on the ice. He can put up the tent. Then when he comes back in the evening, we can decide what to do."

Osuitok had taken with him Alisa, a young hunter, using a second, smaller dog team. Alisa came back alone and told me that Osuitok had said conditions were perfect and we shouldn't wait but come right away that night. Osuitok had stayed, he said, because the country farther north was covered with snow geese, and he needed quite a few to share with people living here.

Young Alisa, always game for anything, said he wasn't tired and that he was ready to take us back to exactly the right spot on the frozen lake to hear the ice fall over. I remember thinking, *that's one helluva lot of dog-team traveling for Alisa.* Even though he was young and strong, he had been awake for nearly two days and nights of hard, active work without sleep.

Feeney and Paddy were ready and excited, shrieking and running in and out of the Wildlife House. It was 10:30 at night before they had their camera loaded and their sound booms and tape recorder wrapped and taped. At that time of the year, it stayed light all night.

We decided to carry the camera and sound-recording boxes down through the rugged tidal heave of barrier ice that jammed the coast. We wanted to make sure that nothing got broken. Then we tightly lashed it all onto the long sled. The dogs were leaping with excitement, and we took off with Alisa up on the grub box doing the yelling and the driving.

Sled

We turned into the long ice passage that points toward Tessikuakjuak. There were many pools of azure blue water spread across the ice, which looks terrifying to a novice traveler, especially when they see that the dog-team driver plans to drive the dogs straight across them.

As the dogs entered a pool of water belly deep, Paddy grabbed me by the arm. "Are you sure this is going to be okay? I mean, John and I would gladly walk behind."

"No, no!" I laughed. "Alisa knows when the ice is strong enough."

They nervously clung to the sled until we left the water.

An hour later, I was sort of nodding on the sled, when I noticed a particularly large pool of water before us. Paddy and John seemed confident now, for we had been through many melted pools on top of thick ice. The dogs were running steadily. I looked up ahead at Alisa's back. He had his hood up and seemed very much in control.

Nevertheless, I hopped off the sled and ran a few yards forward. Looking back, I saw that Alisa's eyes were closed. Worn out from all his traveling, he had fallen asleep. The dogs went plowing out into the shallow water, then seemed to slow a little, looking at us. Just before them lay a large black hole.

"Alisa!" I yelled, and he leapt off the heavy sled.

One on either side, we grabbed the sled, trying desperately to keep it from continuing its slide forward on its own momentum. John and Paddy jumped off, too, and dug in their heels in.

"Pull back! Pull!" I yelled.

We all four tried to pull it back, just as the two curved front deals of the *kamutik* broke through the forward edge of the rotted ice. Sea water sloshed up over the grub box as the front of the sled sagged downward.

"Jesus, help us! Save the cameras!" Paddy shouted.

"And all the sound stuff!" Feeney yelled.

We all four heaved back frantically as the sled teetered on the brink. Our fourteen dogs had rounded or swum across the ominous black hole and were now waiting for us there, not pulling.

Alisa ran splashing around the dreaded black opening. He shouted as he chased the dogs to the left, then started to use them to help us right the partly submerged sled with its irreplaceable cameras and equipment. We all used herculean efforts, and finally the dogs, with help from us, slithered the heavy sled up onto somewhat firmer ice.

But we were still not free. As we moved forward, the back of the sled began to sag down into the freezing waters. Things were so bad I went to cut the *ipiutak*, that short, strong, braided line that holds the fan hitch of dogs to the front of the sled, for I was afraid they'd get dragged down and drown. But before I could get to the front of the sled, Alisa, screaming at the dogs and pulling with all his might, suddenly jerked the *kamutik* into motion. In no time, we were away and onto solid, snow-covered ice again.

"I'm afraid to look at that poor, fuckin' camera," Paddy said after we had all caught our breath again. "I wrapped and taped it in a rubber sheet, but I'll bet there's sea water inside."

"It's the sound equipment – that's what worries me," said John. "Remember, we've come out here to gather those tinkling sounds."

"*Naalungmiuraluak*," Alisa apologized many times for going to sleep. We were all so excited by our near call that we thought of little else until we reached the barrier ice and could hear the rush of water at the little falls as the melting ice water tumbled out of the higher lake down into this narrow arm of the sea. We had good, smooth traveling across the lake, and in the mists I spotted the bread loaf shape of Pokaritaktok, the mound of granite near the place where I liked so much to stay in spring to fish.

As we drew near, I asked Alisa where Osuitok had put up the tent. He said he didn't know, that he had headed back to Kingait before Osuitok had started.

John and Paddy looked grim as they went pawing through their wet equipment, groaning now and then when a soggy reel of new film was unwrapped.

"It seems Osuitok has gone goose hunting further up the lake," I admitted sheepishly.

Feeney and Paddy snorted, then shuddered in that cold that comes before dawn.

"I'll make a kettle of tea," I told them, and got out the Primus. I tried to look through the damp mist formed inside my binoculars, but couldn't see him. My watch said half past two. Fortunately, it was still light and there was little wind.

"Sorry about the tent," I said. "I thought it would be up and waiting for us. But Alisa and I can't find it. Well, we've got our sleeping bags." Mine was half wet, but theirs were only damp. "Unbutton and spread them out on the gravel over there. This rising wind may dry them. The three of us can sleep under one spread over us," I said as we drank tea. "We can toss a knife for who gets the middle. The outside two will be colder than stone by morning."

Alisa, at my suggestion, took the team and went up the lake to find Osuitok. *What could he have done with that damned tent?* I thought. I really felt embarrassed, for between us Osuitok and I had usually been able to put up a good show of efficiency for any outside types, but now we'd gone and blown it all. I was kind of fed up with the whole day's events, but a mug of hot tea and the sight and sound of flocks of snow geese soaring in and landing on the tundra edges of the lake soon rocked me off to sleep.

In the morning, I was cold when I became conscious, being one of the two unlucky outside bastards under the bag that had been dragged away from my side. When I opened my eyes, to my amazement the tent was up and taut over our heads, its dozen tent lines neatly anchored to big stones. How could this possibly have happened? How could those two hunters have raised a tent over us without waking anyone?

I hurried outside the tent, but I could see by their sled tracks that they had come and gone again without a sound. The time showed almost ten o'clock on my wristwatch. We made porridge, had heavily sugared tea again, and shared a large wedge of cheese. The slight breeze was still blowing, and there was not a cloud in the wide blue sky.

We explored the granite cliffs behind the sharply rising hill and watched a rough-legged hawk chase a hungry raven away from her nest in the crags of Pokariataktok. When evening came, we returned to the tent. I could see open water rippling against the rotting ice.

"Listen, listen. You can hear it now," I told them.

We hurried to the edge of the ice that was still attached to the land. A soft, clear sound like a thousand Oriental wind chimes came gently drifting to us.

"Get the sound gear, Paddy." Feeney waved his arms in glee. "This is what we damned near drowned for."

Paddy returned with the soggy, muff-wrapped microphone and held it out toward the thousands of vertical candles of ice as they slowly collapsed together along the edges of the open water, then rose like icicles and, tapping gently, drifted away.

It was the true beginning of the Arctic summer. I could see both dog teams returning, like faint gray pencil lines drawn just above the surface of the frozen lake.

Two years later, when I was in Tokyo, I finally saw the film, *The Living Stone*, for the first time. I was credited as technical advisor. But oh, God, you'll never know how grand I felt when I heard that clear, tinkling music of the candle ice. Everything had gone a bit zigzag on that journey, just the way it often does in the Arctic or down here in the banana belt.

79

Gift Exchange

While the *Sculpture Inuit* exhibition was on tour to Paris, Berlin, Copenhagen, Moscow, and other cities – which other Inuit visited with other escorts – I had the pleasure of escorting my old friend and master carver, Iyola, around London and the exhibition in the British Museum. He was enchanted by much of what he saw, particularly, it seemed to me, the Burlington Arcade with all its shops. He told me he was eager to buy a present for his wife.

I helped him achieve this, then asked him what kind of present I could buy for him. He thought this over for a while, then chose for himself another item that would be used only by a woman.

I said I was surprised by his choice.

He answered, "*Opinani*, it's no wonder. You always had it a little bit wrong with us. You gave Zippo lighters to the men and brightly-colored headscarves to the women. You should have given those gifts the other way around, so that each person who received those wonderful presents could have given them a little later to the person they cared for most."

Imagine my having to have a simple thing like that explained to me after all those years among them, twelve years after moving from Cape Dorset. Probably most of us have wished for that same thing, but we've never been very practical as a people, certainly not as practical as Iyola and his people.

80

Glassmaker Extraordinaire

Dale Chihuly, I'm pleased to say, has been a friend of mine for a very long time. No one, in my opinion, has been more innovative or successful in the whole process of making glass. When I first knew him, he was a professor at the Rhode Island School of Design and often used to visit our farm not far away, accompanied by our mutual friend, the graphic designer Malcolm Greer.

I was asked to lunch in Providence with Dale and Bayard Ewing, then head of the Board of Trustees of RISD, to discuss the future direction that glassmaking at the school should take. I was all for a very practical approach to making glass, with the idea that the students, like Inuit artists, would enjoy a kind of apprenticeship that would prepare them to go out after their graduation and actually make a living by designing and making art glass. Dale did not share this view. He believed that no commercial taint should be involved in the teaching of glassmaking. He won that round with Bayard, who seemed to agree with him – you know the old saying, 'Art for art's sake, art for God's sake.'

Ironically, a few years later, Dale became so overwhelmingly successful at making marvelous, very expensive art glass, selling it to collectors, and showing it in art museums, that he began touring the whole world endlessly, often forming glass teams in other countries that would then create highly saleable Chihuly glass in his name and theirs combined. Now Dale Chihuly, in my opinion, has become the most daringly creative and financially successful glassmaker in the world. And, like Pablo Picasso, he has not been afraid to change and develop new art styles – even if he still believes in teaching art for art's sake, only.

81

Bill Blass

It wasn't every evening that we went out to small dinner parties in New York with well-known celebrities like Bill Blass, the fashion designer. We did so at the home of Grace Mirabella, now editor of *Mirabella* and newly married to her doctor husband and my friend, Bill Cahan. It was summer, his birthday, when we gathered in the Cahans' walled garden and had drinks, then dinner inside with the French doors open to let in the night air.

Alice was seated next to Bill Blass, a strong, hearty-looking man with a ready smile. The dinner conversation was lively, the dinner excellent. The salad was served after the main course so that its oil and vinegar dressing would not sully one's taste buds for the dry white wine.

Alice, sitting across the table from me, was in some deep discussion, but also eyeing a large cherry tomato on her plate. It was too large, she thought, to pop it whole into her mouth. Then came her fateful decision. I saw her try to cut it. A stream of red juice shot away from it across the arm and chest of Bill's cream-colored suit.

"Oh, dear, I'm so very sorry!" she gasped as they both tried desperately to wipe away the long, pink diagonal stain.

They salted it as best they could, but the stain would not disappear. Here was the very embodiment of a man who lived by fashion, marred at a summer dinner party by my wife.

"Oh, well, forget it," Bill smiled bravely at Alice, then at his hostess and the other guests.

Alice, trying to minimize the damage, said, "Oh, Bill, at least I take some comfort in knowing that you have many other suits."

"Yes, but not here," said Bill as he tried to rearrange his necktie to cover the stain.

It was not what Alice considered her finest hour.

82

Giraffes

Fourteen Inuit men and women, artists all, came to visit an exhibit of their work in the United Nations Gallery in New York City in June 1989. Some had never seen southern Canada before; none, I think, had ever been to the United States. It was billed as a worldwide Inuit art exhibition, but there was so little from Alaska, Siberia, and Greenland that it turned out to be an Inuit art exhibition with 90 percent from Arctic Canada. It was splendidly mounted in that gallery with each piece of sculpture caught in the glow of a halogen light.

Boutros Boutros Ghali, then head of the United Nations, opened the exhibition and a dozen Canadian carvers stood somewhat nervously behind him as the cameras flashed. They had flown in late in the evening, and I didn't have a chance to talk with them until five o'clock the following day. They were already full of first impressions.

"What do you think of this country?" I asked.

"*Piungitukassak*," they said. "A bit bad."

"Why?" I asked.

"The money," they answered, "it's all green. Not like Canada. *Atouasiks* – green, *mukos* – brown, *tidlimiuts* – blue, *kolits* – purple, big fifties – pink. That's how we best know them, by the color."

"What was the biggest surprise to you?" I asked them.

"All the lights when we came in over this city, so huge, so many cars moving like bugs following each other."

"What was the worst surprise to you?"

"Escalators!" they agreed. "Like moving ice beneath your feet just before it drops you through."

"I tried to run down against it," one of them said, "but all the rising people started screaming at me."

"What was the very best?" I asked them.

"Giraffes!" they agreed, smiling at each other. "Oh, the long necks on them, the long legs, the big brown spots."

"Tell me," asked one of the hunters, "are those long-neckers good to eat?"

83

On Safari

We went on safari with the Explorers Club to east Africa in 1974. Not a hunting kind of safari, which was slowly going out of style, but on a drawing/photographing journey along the Olduvai Gorge, where the very earliest traces of mankind had been found.

Each day we traveled to new places in Land Rovers, sometimes across wide grasslands, plains with no roads at all. Sometimes we moved through game parks and often we camped beyond them, setting up a new camp each evening, trying to look and think like characters out of a Hemingway novel. It was a wonderful adventure with great herds of animals – wildebeests, zebra, giraffes, elephants, rhinos – with crocodiles sunning themselves on the riverbanks and hippos wandering in the moonlight.

Our two guides – traditionally called white hunters, although one of them was black – became very friendly. When I asked about fishing, the English white hunter said, "There's a jolly farmer living further along this road with a very pleasant wife. You and Alice should stop off and have a cup of tea with them. This man is mad

for fishing," he said, "and will tell you all about fishing in Africa."
Our hunter stopped when we reached the farm and introduced us
to the farmer and his wife, who quickly asked the two of us to tea.
Then the pair of khaki-colored Land Rovers drove off toward the
hills, our white hunter having told the farmer where he planned to
pitch our camp that night.

The farmer and his wife seemed to be just our kind of people.
During tea, he told us all about the local fly fishing, mostly for
rainbow trout that had been brought to Africa from Canada,
possibly from the Nass or the Skeena River in northern British
Columbia. We discussed the different kinds of flies we used to fish.

Thomson gazelle

As sundown came, we had some gin and bitters while sitting
on their long veranda, watching countless numbers of Thomson
gazelles grazing on what I like to think of as the farmer's immense
front lawn. Beyond the scattered herds of elegant gazelles, distant
pairs of giraffes were feeding off some thorn trees. We watched the
darkening sky over Mt. Kenya sending long, gray funnel-shaped
tornadoes down to touch the plain, raising pale white dust storms
as they moved across the vastness of the African savannah.

"Another for the road," the farmer suggested. "Darkness comes
down jolly quick here on the equator. I'll give you a drive."

A drive back to the safety of our camp, wherever it was, sounded
good. His wife came to the car with us. Behind his house, he kept
a small English two-door sedan that was deep into its second
decade. It hunched slowly across the plain with much gear shifting
until we reached the edge of the forest. He stopped at a rutted road
that looked more like a twisting path.

"Your camp's down there," the farmer said, pointing down into the already darkening valley. "Damned pity I can't take you. This little car of mine would go down, but I feel absolutely certain it never ever would find its way back here again. Terribly sorry."

"Oh, that's all right," said Alice brightly. "We can walk."

The farmer looked at her intently, then opened his car's glove compartment. "Yes, well, maybe you should take this little torch." He tried it. "Oh, damn, the batteries aren't up to snuff." The pale light died.

We thanked him anyway, and he said, "It isn't very far, if they're camped where Ian said they would. Good luck." He smiled and waved as he turned the wheezing little car around and disappeared into the darkness, pierced by his one good headlight. Suddenly, it seemed very dark, and the bush around us rustled with strange noises.

"I wish to God we had a flashlight," I told Alice.

"Oh, we'll be all right," she said, taking my hand. "He said it wouldn't be far. Wasn't that a lovely tea with all those gazelles so close to us?"

"Yes," I said, "let's go. Damn, I wish we'd picked a moonlit night."

It was truly dark now, and as we started down the heavily forested hillside, our only guides were the two pale ruts in the road. We had descended perhaps a quarter of a mile in darkness when we heard a loud scream much too close and to our left.

"What was that?" asked Alice, tightening her grip.

"I don't know," I told her. "This is Africa, not the goddamned Arctic."

The good thing about the Arctic was we always traveled with a rifle and a dog team or a boat.

"I feel naked, absolutely naked out here," I told Alice. "That sounded like a bloody leopard to me."

With binoculars, we had seen a big one in a tree the day before, and the memory was all too vivid in my head. Clutching each other like Hansel and Gretel, we moved fearfully down through the intolerable darkness. It seemed to take forever. I listened and often looked behind us, but the scream did not come again.

"Look!" said Alice, stopping dead.

A faint light far below us was moving slowly upward, blinking and swaying through the growth of trees.

"There's two headlights, it's a truck coming up this track." I looked behind us, afraid I'd see a leopard's spots. Then we hurried down toward the lights.

The black hunter got out and said in his English accent, "We certainly missed you two. Hop in." He moved his rifle behind the wide front seat. "Sorry, I'm going to have to back down until we reach an opening in the bush where I can turn this vehicle around."

After that, he drove carefully down to the pitch-black floor of the gorge.

"We're camping not too far from here," the driver said. "You can see the glow from our fire among those trees."

We were home at last – well, not home, but, believe me, the little cluster of tents looked and felt to us like home.

"I expect you two could use a drink," our other guide said cheerfully. "Damn long trek down that hill at night."

He was right. We told our fellow travelers about the leopard's scream and had a second drink. Looking behind our small circle of humans hunched around the blazing fire, I saw a glowing ring of eyes, small animals that had gathered close to watch us perform our nightly pageant for them in the heart of Africa.

84

Alice, the Navigator

My wife, Alice, is an excellent navigator. I swear she has some kind of compass built inside her head, so she always knows instantly where north, south, east, and west are located. She had Tokyo figured out in no time. That great city has few streets named as we do or even house numbers, but Alice studied a map and could take me almost anywhere. She is also a skilled driver, but she can be distracted from all these virtues by a strong desire not to miss anything that interests her, especially in any art discussion.

Mame Jackson, who has a Ph.D. in art and anthropology, is a friend that we both enjoy and admire. She first held a professorship at the University of Michigan at Ann Arbor, then for a time moved north to Canada's Carleton University in Ottawa to be closer to Inuit artists who take part in her favorite subject, printmaking, and to make it easier to reach the printmakers on Baffin Island.

After attending a conference on Inuit art held at the University of Vermont, we offered to drive Mame to an additional conference we were also to attend, which was planned to take place in Kingston, Ontario, the following day. I suggested that Alice do the driving, while I sat in the back seat with Mame to discuss Inuit art, without the distractions that traffic and road maps usually bring to me.

We proceeded in this way to the Canadian border and handily cleared Customs. Mame and I were deep in a discussion concerning the remarkable artistic talent of Kenojuak, our mutual friend from Kingait on west Baffin Island. Alice knew Kenojuak, too, and had a weather ear cocked, not wishing to miss a word of the back seat conversation.

After an hour or so and a number of twists and turns, we found ourselves once more lined up for a border crossing, this time back into the United States.

"Alice, what the hell is going on here?" I demanded. "You must have lost your way."

"You said Kenojuak had fourteen children," Alice protested. "I've always heard she had seventeen."

"Listen," I said, "you're supposed to be doing the driving. Mame and I are having an Inuit art discussion back here. What's happened to your sense of navigation?"

Halted in the U.S. once again, Alice examined our road map. "Oh, I've got it now," she said. "We're all right."

We took off again while Mame and I moved onto the subject of the artist, Pudlo Pudlat, his unusual life, and Mame's early encounters with Pudlo when the Canadian government had loaned her the Wildlife House while she did her research. Less than an hour passed before we made a zigzag turn and entered Canada again!

"Lord, God, woman, where are you taking us?" I asked.

Alice seemed ashamed to admit anything when the Customs inspector asked, "When were you folks last in Canada?"

We all three started to laugh hysterically, which seemed to put off the official.

I'll cut this account right here by saying that Alice is still capable of being a good navigator. But as a professor's daughter, she really does prefer to gather facts – especially from someone as lively and reliable as Professor Mame Jackson.

85

Stonington

Stonington, Connecticut is a truly famous New England town. We decided to move there from the farm because we had started to zigzag more and more each year, often traveling to give lectures or hear them, and to do research for art and writing projects. Farm costs are exactly the same, whether you are in residence or not. We know now that we should never have developed Letfern into a working farm. We didn't really mean to do it. But, hell, Alice had never experienced any domestic animals and she seemed to have an endless longing for sheep and ducks. One thing grew into another, and soon enough we had two Southdown rams and forty ewes and lambs, two cats, a springer spaniel, a barn full of pigeons, and wild mallards landing on our pond.

We were not using our small apartment in New York so much. Whenever we did want to go into town, inevitably John or Sam, then two eligible young bachelors – Sam from Aspen, John from some distant movie location – would phone and say, "Dad, hope you're not planning to use the New York apartment this weekend. I'm counting on bringing the most wonderful girl in the world into town. I hope we can use it."

"We've been thirteen years on the farm. Let's move somewhere else in the world," I suggested to Alice one day as we drove into New York.

"What about the sheep?" she said indignantly.

"We'll give them to the University of Rhode Island for their agriculture program, take the pets with us, and sell the farm."

Alice looked thoughtfully out the window until well beyond New Haven before she asked, "Where would we go?"

"How about Nantucket?" I said. "That's an island we both love."

"Well, winter fogs on the Atlantic make that a hard place to fly to and from. How about Stonington, Connecticut?" she said. "We've already got some good friends there."

"It's an attractive village," I admitted, "twenty-five miles closer to New York, should be an easy move. Alice, why don't you get someone to help us find a house there."

When we returned from New York, I went on drawing, writing, and designing glass, while the indefatigable Alice went house-hunting in and around the borough of Stonington. It is an ancient seaport with two main streets running down a long finger of land that juts out into Long Island Sound, just adjoining the Connecticut-Rhode Island border. Alice came back one evening to the farm and said, "I've had the right person house-hunting with me and there's only one house I want. That's the Captain Amos Palmer house. From the upstairs east windows, we'll have a wonderful view of Little Narragansett Bay, and from the west windows we'll see Stonington harbor, with all those beautiful sunsets. Whistler's mother lived in that house. Her sister was married to a Palmer."

To cut a long story short, we sold the farm to a New York family who are still our friends. But even so, Alice cried that night and told me that the farm had been the best home we'd ever have in all our lives.

We moved into the circa 1780 Stonington house in October, right after the salmon season was done in British Columbia. The huge furnace was so old we had to heave it out and buy a new one. Our corner house, built in 1780 on the foundation, on top of an earlier Palmer house that had burned, had had a massive, central chimney and six fireplaces. It was built on a small hill to avoid hurricane or flood damage, for the location was on this long, narrow point of land. Highly visible from the water, it has the appearance of a colonial period house from outside, with a staircase of welcoming arms in front, and strong, paneled, storm shutters, still called Indian shutters, to be pulled from inside the walls.

This house, like the others in Stonington, came under direct gunfire on August 9 and 10, 1814, during the War of 1812. The British attack was led by Sir Thomas Hardy, who was famous for receiving the last words of Admiral Lord Nelson at the Battle of Trafalgar, heard as "Kiss me, Hardy."

Captain Amos Palmer, a loyal privateer who had built and lived in the house, was Chairman of the Committee for Public Safety for the town during the war. When *Ramillies*, a British ship of the line, with seventy-four guns, accompanied by *Paetalus*, thirty-eight guns, and the bomb ships *Terror* and *Dispatch*, twenty guns each, with giant mortars mounted on their decks, sailed into Stonington harbor, Captain Palmer went out halfway in a small boat. He met and negotiated with the British, whose long blockade of Long Island Sound had left them short of supplies, so that they demanded a large number of domestic sheep, hogs, and cattle as well as corn flour. Palmer and the Committee refused their demands. The British answered that their naval bombardment of Stonington would begin within the hour. They advised Palmer to return and clear the town of women and children. Captain Palmer, also in charge of Stonington's magazine, rushed to open it, rolling out kegs of powder and two large cannons (now in Stonington Square). These were horse-drawn down to the battery to protect the harbor.

By good luck, Stonington had a master gunner, Jeremiah Holmes, who had been forced into naval service on a British man-of-war for seven years during battles in the Mediterranean. He now took up a position with several other young American volunteers acting as gun crew.

Cannons

Paetalus opened the barrage against the town while she lay beyond reach of the Stonington guns. But the bomb ship *Dispatch*, with her two dreaded mortars that would send fire bombs and stink bombs into the town to burn it, came in close enough to the harbor front for Gunner Holmes. A direct hit was made on the bomb ship, which put her out of action.

The British, who had not expected such strong resistance from the little town, moved around the point of land at night and attacked at dawn from the Little Narragansett Bay side, their barges loaded with British marines. Several of the barges were hit with smaller cannon fire, which caused great damage. The Amos Palmer house, rising from a small hill and being highly visible from the water, was mistakenly judged by the British to be the center of the town. Many rounds of cannon fire reached it, destroying the large, central chimney, scooping out the lower south wall, and driving a cannonball in the back door and out through the front door. It is said that Captain Amos Palmer, who had been watching the battle from his door stoop, ran after the spent ball as it rolled in the street. Though the cannonball was still hot, he carried it in his hat to the gunner, Jeremiah, and had him fire it back at one of the barges.

After this attack, the British ceased firing and withdrew, leaving, by the burgesses' calculations, fifteen tons of iron shot. Having won the battle and helped starve the British off New England's coast, Stonington whooped it up in the streets that day. Although the British during that war had been able to burn down the White House in Washington, our little village of Stonington successfully defended itself.

After the battle major repairs were required for the Amos Palmer house and many others in town. Following the style of the time, our house was altered inside to reflect the newer Federal Period. Central hallways were built on all floors. The huge fireplace that one could walk into in the living room had to be dismantled, and two smaller ones replaced it.

When we bought the house, it once more needed quite a lot of work inside and out, but we felt then and now that it was more than worth the trouble. We soon discovered that we were surrounded by interesting neighbors who, like ourselves, had spent or were still spending part of their lives in New York, a two-and-a-half-hour drive south. Others came from Boston, a two-hour drive, or Washington, D.C., an hour's flight.

It is so easy to give or attend a dinner here in town where most of your guests go home after the party. On the farm, we used to have to keep New Yorkers and other out-of-towners for the weekend. We had beds for twelve. In the Arctic, of course, I might have had to keep them with their dog team for maybe a month or so, depending on the season and the weather.

Not long after we had left the farm and were established in this Stonington house, I turned on the television and saw Buckeye, our younger ram from the farm. He seemed larger and much more ramly, with his head held high, for he was now the mascot of the University of Rhode Island's football team. He was prancing proudly across the field right in step with a beautiful, long-legged cheerleader who was holding him by a leash. I saw Buckeye glance out through the TV tube at us, then give me a kind of bachelor's wink! I knew it was Bucky's way of thanking me for allowing him off the farm to enjoy those grand rewards of a damned good university education.

Whistler's mother, who had borne the painter, James McNeill Whistler, had occupied the southeast, upstairs bedroom. There was said to be a peculiar ghost in the house, one we never saw. Persons sleeping in the opposite guest room reported regularly that they heard a rocking chair creaking in the room, used by Whistler's mother for her sewing, then the sound of someone weakly humming *The Battle Hymn of the Republic*. Others said they heard a kind of old and dusty giggling as a glass bottle slipped to the floor. These ghostly hearings – not sightings – distinguished our house for about ten years, but now seem to have faded. Perhaps old Mrs. Whistler simply could not stand the docility of the current tenants in a dwelling whose history boasts so many stories of war and privateering, and whose foundation and walls still bear the marks of British cannonballs.

From our point of view, the good neighbors in the borough and at nearby Mystic seaport bring us shared pleasures, along with two good libraries, fine restaurants, and the sea around us. Who could ask for more?

86

Shattering a Globe

In 1987, the art director of *National Geographic* magazine called me from Washington, D.C., when we were at our writing and fishing hideaway – or should I more honestly call it our cottage – on that glorious river in the Queen Charlotte Islands, a retreat for salmon fishing, drawing, and writing. Howard Paine told me that the National Geographic Society was about to celebrate its one hundredth year of publication and wished to create a special centennial award for some of the most important living persons of this century. He thought of Steuben glass and then called me.

"I don't want this one to look like so many other awards that are given these days," said Howard. "We want something unusual. Why don't you try to think of one while you're busy waving that salmon rod of yours over the river? And further," he half whispered, "if it's a real zinger of an idea, we just might use it as our centennial cover."

It sometimes happens that I do have some of my best design or book ideas while wading, crotch-deep, in the chilly river flow while waiting for the salmon to come up with the tide. One morning I had the strangest feeling that I had the right idea. It was near the end of that day's run and the light was rising, so I was busy changing to a small, brown hackle fly. Suddenly, I hooked a good one. Then, after a twenty-minute struggle and without a net, as the Scots love to say, I grassed the salmon. In fact, I had to pebble-beach this hen salmon with small bubbles surging all around her. The bubbles – aha! That was the very image I was looking for in this award design.

I hurried home, all four fingers thrust through the gill of the heavy fish. "She'll be full of eggs," I called to Alice, who was fishing across the river.

"I'm coming over right now to start the caviar," she called out as she reeled in her fly line. "Don't you clean her. I'll do that." She waded out of the river and crossed the small white bridge.

It was a gorgeous, deep blue, autumn morning, with not a breath of wind disturbing the spruce trees where bald eagles so often perch. *Design, new design*, thought I, so eager to get my hands on pencil and paper that I was scarcely able to haul my waders off.

When Alice had finished removing the salmon roe and cleaning the fish, she came back to the true hideaway. That is my little hut at the end of our yard, my drawing and writing room, away from our telephone, and from any strangers or visiting evangelists out trying to recruit Haida and anyone else around. It is half hidden from anyone who might stop their car or dismount their bicycles and head toward our front gate, scarcely giving me time to leap out through our back door. This time, Alice, all alone, was carrying two mid-morning cups of coffee.

"What do you think of these?" I said, bringing the two best design drawings out onto the small front porch of the hideaway to give us better light.

A wide cedar plank that we used as an outside seat was still too wet to use after the night's rain. Still standing, we examined the drawings.

"That one's not too bad," said Alice. I considered that high praise from a professor's daughter of Scottish decent who had been warned since birth against giving students overblown ideas of the merit of their work.

"It's going to be great," I told her with all the boundless hope and nerve that had somehow been instilled in me by my own Scottish parents.

I went on polishing and improving the piece in my imagination and in my drawings for the rest of the day. Then I phoned Christopher Hacker, Director of Steuben's Design Department in New York, and asked if he could find some special kind of light box that would give off a pure white light and yet was smaller than any in use in the world. Every day as I went salmon fishing, I kept thinking about the award design, with an image of the magazine's centennial cover looming in my mind. I was eager to find something that would work for both the award and the front cover.

Chris called and said he'd managed to find someone who could white light the little silver box I had in mind. I kept thinking about the rising bubbles around the salmon and the global nature of the *National Geographic* magazine. Finally, after rendering it very carefully, white and silver on black paper, I called Howard in Washington and said I was sending my design to him and to Steuben.

"Will I receive it tomorrow?" he asked.

"From where I'm sitting, you'll be lucky if you get it in a week or more," I told him. "And at that, I'll have to have someone hand-carry it south from Sandspit, our local airport, to the airport in Vancouver."

Both Steuben and Howard liked the design. It was almost the end of the autumn salmon run. We closed up the cottage, locked the hideaway, and elaborately hid our fly boxes and our trout and salmon rods – by far our most valuable items on the northwest coast.

Back in the USA, the project continued to take shape. Ladislav Havlik and Roger Selander did the skillful copper wheel engraving of the world on our carefully plotted, four-inch crystal globe. The globe stood on a six-inch-tall square step of crystal enclosing a multitude of small glass bubbles representing stars in frozen space. Both the globe and the stars were caught in the small, hidden light. The silver base of each award was engraved with the name of one of the winners.

The centennial presentation of the awards in Washington in December 1988 was a major event to honor the skills and fortitude of the following people: Senator John Glenn, Sir Edmund Hillary, Jacques Yves Cousteau, Dr. Jane Goodall, Dr. Mary D. Leakey, Richard E. Leakey, Dr. George F. Bass, Barbara Washburn, Bradford Washburn, Dr. Frank C. Craighead, Jr., Dr. John J. Craighead, Dr. Harold E. Edgerton, Thayer Soule, Dr. Robert D. Ballard, and Dr. Kenan T. Erim.

The centennial cover of *National Geographic* for December 1988 showed a hollow Steuben globe of the world at the instant it was struck by a high-speed bullet. My plan was to have the image ask the question, "Can man save this fragile earth?" The bottom side of the glass is in the process of bursting out toward the reader.

Shattering globe

This tricky piece of hologram photography was done in a science laboratory in California with five special, high-speed cameras taped to a piece of two-by-four lumber. As the bullet exploded from the muzzle of the gun, all the cameras focused not on it, but on the flying glass. As an impressed visitor to the lab, I thought the camera setup would look like something from some future outer space era. This one looked like something from a kid's tree house.

"No need to make it fancy," the scientists explained. "We'll do special tricks like this only one time."

A holographic image is very complex. No ink is used. There are microscopic ridges – twenty thousand to the linear inch and visible only with a powerful microscope – which are electroplated on pieces of pure nickel. For the magazine cover, the hologram was put onto clear plastic, then metalized in a vacuum, depositing a film of aluminum on the plastic. This wafer-thin, foil-like material was then laminated to the magazine cover's paper stock. When moved under direct light, the hologram is beautiful and exciting to see. And, I later learned, that special *National Geographic* cover hologram was seen by ten million people around the world.

87

Mission Schools

We as Canadians can all thank God that the mission schools – where Inuit and northern Indian children were sent to board away from their families – stopped short at the Mackenzie River Delta and did not come much farther east, except for a few schools on the west coast of Hudson Bay, north and south of Churchill. These schools raised a level of bitterness among the students who attended them that is hard to imagine. Yet it is so universally agreed by former students as having been a horrible experience that one has to wonder at the methods. The use of their native language by the children was absolutely outlawed in school, in favor of French and English, and the message was reinforced by beatings. Sadly, this was a method that did great harm to the ongoing cohesion of family groups, as kids returned home barely able to speak their parents' language. The underlying idea seemed to be to change hunters, trappers, and fishermen into farmers or business folk, even where the lands were unsuitable and few real business opportunities were likely to occur for perhaps half a century.

To add insult to injury, the mission schools sometimes held on to money they were supposed to spend on the children: I know this because I did the school Inspection for the old Department of Mines and Resources. In the cases I remember the boarding schools not only took the government money to spend on feeding and clothing the kids, they demanded that the father of each child forced into school supply the mission with enough caribou meat and hides to completely feed and clothe the child. This amounted to – if I remember correctly – about forty caribou per child per year, and the parents naturally set out hunting to make sure their kids were fed. I raised some hell about this, and like to think that I may have helped prevent the mission schools from spreading eastward.

It's hard to believe, but the mission schools, financed by the government, set about destroying a culture that had survived on its own for thousands of years. The government, I hope, gave little thought to what they were doing, for surely they would not knowingly have allowed such destruction to occur to the native Indian and Inuit groups, each a society within Canada's borders.

The next fifty years will be absolutely critical in the determination of what kind of lives Inuit in their vast new territory of Nunavut will live. Fortunately, Inuit still have their language in the eastern and central Arctic. But will they be able to retain it against that great and ever-increasing blizzard of satellite television? How will the new agreement to create Nunavut in 1999 help them to survive that cultural onslaught, when we in the South have been unable to protect our own children from it?

88

The High, High Arctic

Barentsburg is in that group of Norwegian islands north of the Arctic Circle known as Svalbard. On a long-term lease arrangement too dangerous to break, this piece of the largest island of Spitsbergen was made a part of the Soviet Arctic and is an important place to Russians for the mining of coal. Foreign ships had tried to visit, but had always been refused. In 1989, the USSR, however, was poised for astonishing political change.

We flew from Oslo to Longyearbyen. The plane cut down through a cold, dense fog, refueled, and took off, leaving our group there. Few among us had ever been so far north. We looked out the small, military airport windows at the brown tundra and occasional rock that faded away into a wall of fog like some close-up picture of the surface of Mars. We were about 80 degrees north, all but level with the top of Greenland and Canada's northern tip, Ellesmere Island. It was after noon. Boarding *Polaris*, the cruise ship we were joining to tour these northern waters (me wearing my lecturer's hat), we sailed down the fiord to Barentsburg.

An ancient, khaki-painted bus came and took us on a kind of tour of the town. We saw hydroponic gardening and then a large pigsty, dirty beyond belief and smelling inside in a way that made you want to lurch outside (as many of our party had already done), for there are few smells on this earth like old, lye-smelling urine and pig shit, especially if the odor has had to be kept inside, unaired throughout the Arctic winter.

The almost total shabbiness of Barentsburg was hard to believe – the people, the buildings, everything. Yet these Europeans had learned to suffer and to survive in this bitter, lonely place near the top of the world. This was nothing like the Inuit/Eskimo world. This was said to have been a kind of remote gulag camp throughout the Stalin years and later, with prisoners wrestling the coal out from the primitive mines to ship it south during the brief period when the ice began to move, making shipping possible. Still, necessity, the mother of invention, had caused this small colony of miners and their families to raise vegetables out of beds of gravel and sustain themselves in ways that few other societies had ever managed to do.

We returned to our Scandinavian ship, showered and perfumed away the pig smells, and gratefully met for drinks in the ship's lounge, where we examined our watches while discussing the shock of the pig farm. We were eager to get another, kinder view of Barentsburg. Down at the loading dock at the end of our ship's gangway, the old Soviet bus waited, its two drivers glowering resentfully as though they loathed letting us into its tattered seats again.

As we rode uptown, I thought again, as I had in 1962, *Imagine us being terrified of a Cold War enemy as clumsy, vodka-soaked, and broken down as the USSR. Thousands of costly shelters had been built against the imminent threat of their launching an atomic war.* But had this same broken-down, pig-smelling Soviet Union not flown a satellite in space before we could? Had not this poor, shabby lot of people exploded an atomic device long before we thought that possible?

Surely the U.S. must have known exactly how weak and rundown this economy was. I had spent some time in the Soviet Union

from 1961 into '62. I could see it all around me in Leningrad and
Moscow. I could smell it like a broken toilet in Moscow's best
hotels, where the tiles were falling off the walls of the shower stalls
and the faucets dripped rusty-colored water. I believe that the U.S.
chose to cast a shadow over this, chose to go on building its military hardware, which was good for business and good for the government's giant defense contracts.

The bus jerked to a halt before a long, low building that had a
special air about it, a bit like an overly decorated Swiss chalet. We
trooped inside the fluorescent-lighted interior and were shown the
place to hang our parkas; then we were conducted to our seats at
long banquet tables. Old-fashioned, cheerful polka music was
playing. At our table, there were ten visitors and two interpreters.
The young russet-haired Russian assigned to our end of the table
smiled and shook hands heartily with each of us. He told us his
name was Yuri. He was tall and appeared to be about twenty years
old. He asked each of us our first names and he remembered every
one of them. "What part of the world do you come from?" he asked
us, and remembered everybody's country, state, and city.

When I said, "Toronto, Canada," he shuddered.

"Must be a place like this. I've heard it's kinda cool in winter."

"Yeah, cool," I laughed, "but nothing like this."

A master of ceremonies arose. The music stopped and he greeted
us, welcoming us to the glorious Soviet Peoples' Republic. "Here's
a toast to all our countries," he said, his microphone crackling,
booming, distorting his words.

Yuri pointed at the fifth of Stolichnaya vodka that had been set
beside a glass at every person's place. We rose, filled our small toast
glasses, and drank to the greatness of the Soviet Union, the United
States of America, other countries, and oh, yes, Canada! The food
was bland – pork chops with hydroponically grown radishes, potatoes, and Brussels sprouts covered with a thick white sauce. Halfway
through the dinner, the master of ceremonies proposed another
toast and then another round of vodka before the tapioca pudding,
followed by another toast.

Alice moved to another seat, and Yuri came and sat between
Keith Shackleton and me.

"You like the place? You like the food?" Yuri asked us.

"Oh, sure," we said, "it's great."

"You get better food in the United States or England?"

"Sometimes better, maybe sometimes worse," we two foreigners agreed politely before the toastmaster raised his vodka glass to the futures of all our countries.

"I know you got lots of political and racial troubles in the U.S. besides the food," Yuri nodded wisely. "I knew you were going to get in trouble a long time ago."

"How did you know that?" we asked him.

"Because of that President Jimmy Carter. No decent president would let the people call him 'Jimmy.' That name's got no respect. Can you imagine," he whispered to us, then looked around behind him, "can you even dream of somebody calling our leader, Comrade Stalin, 'Joey Stalin?'" He laughed, then shuddered. "You want to finish off that vodka before we go? Your Swedish captain has asked us all to come back and visit on his ship."

It was light outside, of course, though the long, white night was heavily fogged over, and rain was driven by a cold wind that swept in over the harbor. The dock beside the ship was tight-packed with what appeared to be every citizen of Barentsburg. As we foreigners made our way up the gangway, some still humming the powerful Soviet national anthem, the crowd just stared at us in silence as they watched their *komissar* and his few uniformed officers followed by the coal mine manager and his staff. None of them were women.

They gasped at the luxurious interior of the ship as we led them to the lounge. Some of us had remarked about the ship seeming somewhat worn and austere, but now, seeing it through the Soviet Arctic eyes of Barentsburgers who probably had never seen Moscow or Leningrad, we suddenly felt proud of our free world opulence.

Our captain was long and lean, a splendid, blue-eyed, blond-haired Scandinavian, and we were proud to have him represent us on this rare and very special occasion. He and the *komissar* stood up and faced each other, smiling, standing military straight in their formal uniforms, hats on. Our captain called for a fresh bottle of the best French cognac, and the ship's stewards scuttled among us, taking orders for free drinks, compliments of our captain and the ship. He proposed a grand Swedish toast to the *komissar* and the workers at Barentsburg. It was interpreted. They drank. We all drank as comrades.

Then the *komissar* proposed his toast to the captain and all of us aboard his ship. We waved and sang as we drank to that. Now came the first grand gesture. The captain removed his visored cap with the elegant Scandinavian gold crest and gave it to the *komissar*. Another toast, then the *komissar* removed his wide-brimmed, gold-laden official's hat and placed it on our captain's head. A roar of approval filled the lounge and the stewards quickly recharged our glasses.

Both captains were now swaying a little, although the sea seemed calm. Our captain ripped his navy jacket off and handed it to the *komissar*. Tears appeared in the *komissar's* eyes as he, too, pulled off his jacket and helped our captain into it. Wow! This certainly called for another toast! This time, the Russians called for vodka. I could scarcely believe my eyes when I saw both great men kick off their boots and then pull off their trousers.

"Oh, Jesus, look!" yelled Pete Puleston, supporting himself against the ship's bar. "The *komissar's* got on pink undies. He's wearing women's stuff."

"My God, Pete's right!" I nudged Alice. "He's in pink ladies' underwear. What do you think of that?"

Alice leaned over to the Christiansens, our friends from Washington, and said, "It's my guess that the poor devil lives alone up here and he's thrown his underwear in the washing machine with a red sweatshirt or pair of socks."

"That's right." The women laughed, then yelled at us in triumph, "It's not what you men are thinking."

"It's just a typical male mistake, an accidental pink," Alice insisted.

The incident of the pink underwear would have been the best story of the voyage, but our own women had to go and screw it up.

Badly in need of fresh air, we went out on deck to see the *komissar* appear to his crowd of workers dressed as a Scandinavian captain, and our captain transformed into their *komissar*. They let out a cheer. "Friendship, friendship," several of them called to us in English.

Yes, they and we could tell something new was happening. The world was about to change. And, by God, it did, just two years later.

89

Old Relationships

Long ago and up to the present day, old Arctic missionaries have liked to revive ancient matters with persons who have at one time or another lived near them in the country. In the Arctic, of course, "near" often meant that there were endless days of dog-team travel between. Not long ago, a missionary friend of mine whom I had known from those far-off days sent me a letter including a photo-copied photo of a handsome Inuk girl. He said that a fellow missionary had lent him the original photograph. He planned, he said, to use this picture in his new book. He asked me straightaway, as missionaries love to do, "Wasn't she the girl you had an affair with years and years ago?"

A long silence on my end of the line.

"Is that not correct?" he asked again.

"Never!" I answered. "You're getting her mixed up with her sister." Then I told him, "You must be getting old. You're starting to forget the most important things in life."

90

Marie

I went to Aupaluktuk and stood on the very headland at Kingait where I had waited in the rising October light to see any signs of smoke from the vessel that had been told to pick me up. This one small Arctic ship on which I traveled in the mid-1950s had a remarkable story to tell. But I feel certain now that the captain, his first mate, or crew will not be the ones to tell it.

The government had urged me to board this ship and head south during a season when it was almost impossible to travel because of ice. Although saltwater in the strong tidal waters of the Hudson Strait had remained open, our shore ice in the fiord at Kingait extended out for almost half a mile. It was late October, a time when Inuit rarely undertook a journey, for the water was not open enough for boats and not yet strong enough for dog-team travel.

Pingwarktok had had his small trap boat propped up for winter near the point at Aupalukluk that year. But he was keen to help. "I know how to get it out over the shore ice if you really need to go," he said.

So I arranged by radio a rendezvous with this particular ship to take place out on the Hudson Strait. We received a radio message from the ship to be there at 7:00 a.m. They would wait for me a while if the weather would allow.

I did not go to bed that night because I was so excited. Pingwarktok and four other strong young men came in the pitch darkness that is special to the Arctic on moonless nights before much snow has fallen. There was not a breath of wind. When we reached the old trap boat, Pingwarktok had already prepared it, checked the engine, filled it with the government diesel fuel that I had given him, and removed the blocks and props that would hold her high and dry for winter.

We put all our muscle into it and slid her down the oil-greased boards onto the ice. Yes, it was solid beneath our feet, but would not remain so for long. We started skidding her, trying to keep her upright on her keel as Pingwarktok urged us to go faster, faster! We wanted to have all the momentum we could get before she broke through the ice. All six of us were running, pushing hard with both hands on the trap boat's gunnels, ready to jump as I felt the ice begin to sag beneath my feet. We ran on through the terrifying darkness. The bow went down and Pingwarktok yelled, "*Missikkiat!* Jump!"

I, like the others, heaved myself up onto the gunnels, then into the trap boat. We were afloat, but with a huge sheet of inch-thick ice before us.

Two young Inuit got up in the bow and started trying to break us out of the ice, while the others pushed us forward with ice staves. Pingwarktok began to whirl his flywheel until the cold, old-fashioned make-and-break engine began to cough, then slowly chugged into life. The ice was thin enough and we had enough weight in the trap boat for her bow to break the sheets of ice and send them sliding on top of each other like giant playing cards.

Here again the Inuit had done what I had considered impossible in launching this boat over half a mile of thin ice, using the running power of men where nothing else would have worked. We headed out into the Strait with the east light of dawn creeping around our heads and lighting the world enough for me to see the faces of the other men who crowded in the boat with me.

"*Umiakjuak*, big ship," Iyola called, pointing eastward.

There, I, too, could make out the dark silhouette of the small cargo vessel, hove to but with no lights that we could see. Then we heard a dull hoot on the ship's horn and I took out my flashlight and signaled toward the ship. In fifteen minutes, we were running alongside the rusty hull. A rope ladder came swinging down and Pingwarktok grabbed it.

I shook hands hard with everyone in the boat, shouldered my pack, and started shakily up the ladder. I hate climbing hanging ship's ladders, especially in soft, sealskin boots, but it wasn't far. Hands grabbed my wrists and pulled me over the side. I felt the iron deck beneath my feet. *"Tavvauvusi ilunnasi,"* I called to my friends in the boat, who were already falling behind. They waved as the trap boat sheered away and headed back to Dorset.

"Come in and have some coffee with us, Mister," an unmistakably Newfoundland voice called to me. Once inside their mess room, I eased off my pack, pulled off my parka over my head, and sat down at their oblong, bolted-down table and benches that all but filled their small messing quarters.

"Jesus, we never thought you'd make it out here over all that fuckin' ice. Them Eskimos," the mate said, "they knew how to bloody do it."

I shook hands first with the captain, who was taking his place at the head of the table, then his first and second mates and engineer, who shared the mess.

"We offloaded cargo at Chesterfield Inlet after waiting for the goddamned ice and we're on our way home just now. As you got a look at this old bitch you've boarded, you've seen that she's no ice-breaker, and we're looking to stay away from heavy ice. You must be in some helluva goddamned hurry, Mister, to have bust your ass out through all that ice. Even a Newfie sealer wouldn't try a trick like that."

I drank the thick black coffee and eyed the captain. His jacket was ragged and unbuttoned, turning mildewed green, with both elbows out. Like his crew, he hadn't seen a woman close up for a long time.

The food aboard was terrible, and the room I had was about the size of a clothes closet, which caused me to step out into the companionway to pull my pants on. The crew consisted of rough and ready cribbage players, surprisingly full of affection for each other and the world. They all had earned rich names like Tiger, who looked like anything but that, and the Grinner, who did grin a lot, and Tithead. It was wonderful to live among these east coast shipmen who were so contented. Mind you, that contentment could have come about in part because the captain had brought aboard two dozen cases of overproof Barbados rum, all duty-free, which he doled out daily to his crew as though they were still in the Merchant Marine in wartime, running supplies to British ports. "Splicing the main brace," they called it, belting down four ounces under the watchful eye of the mate. That double-powered rum made the lot of them sing like orioles, with me joining in. The captain and the first mate, while in the old man's cabin, placed no such rum restrictions on themselves or me.

On the day of my arrival aboard, the old man, as the captain was called, invited me up onto his covered bridge. There was little ice in Hudson Strait, but it was snowing big, wet flakes against the windows by the wheel. I noticed something in the dark corner of the bridge – something big and alive, head up, with shining eyes examining me.

"What's that?" I asked the captain. As I spoke, this unknown creature turned into a seal that hissed and with teeth bared came humping heavily out of the gloom and straight toward me. I'll bet she weighed two hundred pounds.

I stumbled backward, trying to hide behind the captain at the wheel.

"Go back, *recule*, stop, *arrête*, Marie!" he yelled at her.

The seal stopped and looked up at him and then at me.

"She's not likely to bite you," he told me. "She did nip the gunner's ass once when he was at the wheel, but she's tamed down a lot since then. She's been a helluva lot better friend to me than any goddamned dog or cat."

He reached down and stroked the seal affectionately on the head. "She's a harp, a harp seal," he said. "I got her off the ice in March. She had a white coat then, a pup no bigger than a young lamb, with big eyes and pretty as a picture. Me and the mate, we fed her on that thick, sweetened, condensed milk out of a baby's bottle and did she grow! We were caught in ice off Resolution Island coming north and I kept the Grinner jigging for Tom cod over the side and soon enough, she was eating fish and starting to lose her baby's coat of white. Underneath it was that slick-looking, shiny silver coat that she's got now. Notice the good-looking saddle markings she's got on her back? Now doesn't that look just like the shape of a harp to you? They say these kinds of seals got the name of harp because some of the first Irish immigrants coming across to live in Canada saw a big herd of them off southern Greenland and shouted, 'Faith and b'Jesus, it's the sea angels lugging their harps!'" He laughed. "Well, they weren't so wrong about that. Marie here has been a great salvation for me. Why don't you go down and get the mate and I'll join you in my cabin when the watch changes. We can have a nip or two of rum and play some cribbage."

Marie, the seal

The mate unlocked the old man's cabin and let us in. He knew exactly where to find the key to the rum cupboard. "I got quite a start up on the bridge," I said, "when Marie came leaping out of the corner at me, hissing and showing her teeth."

"Oh, that's just part of her showing off while she's growing up, I guess." He laughed. "Marie won't hurt you, and God knows she's straightened out the old man's head."

"What do you mean by that?"

"Oh, he was in a terrible mess last year."

"Why?" I asked.

"Because his old lady, well, she wasn't old, she was his wife, Marie Thérèse, died. He knew she wasn't well when we left, but he never dreamed she would go and die. He took to grieving something awful and drinking way too much of this blessed, overproof rum. We tried to hide it from him, but we couldn't. Sometimes he'd stay locked in this cabin for days, moaning and wailing and drinking, with only that young, white coat, seal pup near him. He'd sneak out after dark and get food for her and him. I saw him once or twice and he looked terrible. I had to run this ship myself, which wasn't hard, for we've got a goddamn good loyal crew aboard. One night when I passed this cabin, I heard the old man drunk and singing, and, honest to God, Marie – that's what he calls her – she was singing along with him. Well, you know, not really singing but sort of howling like a young dog or maybe a wolf, trying to imitate a human. I knocked on the door, but he wouldn't answer. Still, something serious must have happened, for I could hear that he, and she, were starting to feel a whole lot better.

"Ever since we entered the Hudson Strait on our way to Churchill, you could tell that everything had changed with him. He was eating with us at the mess room table again – and just a little drunk, mind you, not worse than some of the rest of us. Oh, young Marie, she had changed entirely during this, her first voyage. She was gaining size and weight and her new coat was getting smooth and slick. We couldn't always stop to catch the rock cod, so the captain took to ordering a big bowl of oatmeal porridge up from the galley every day. He'd put some condensed milk in it, and evenings he'd lace the porridge with rum. He said Marie coughed a bit at first, but then he said she came to love it and refused to eat her oatmeal unless he'd put in plenty of rum.

"Well, you saw Marie today and you'll believe it when I tell you that me and the old man rolled her onto the kilo sealer that we got in the hold and Marie weighed just over two hundred pounds. That's about what the old man weighs. I know, I weighed him and her both at that same goddamn time. 'She's like a sister to you, Captain,' I says. But he winked at me and says, 'No, Mate, she's a helluva lot better than a sister.' That's when I started to get suspicious of what was going on.

"You haven't heard me play the button accordion yet, and I do not go winning any contests, mind you, but I'm not too bad, they say. The old man took to getting me here evenings in his cabin with the squeeze box and asking me to play, oh, maybe, "Lead, Kindly Light." Well, Marie was crazy about that hymn, and she would sing along for quite a while, then slide down off this same settee and eat her porridge, which the old man had swimming with rum, and he and I would drink another round with her and I'd play maybe "Jesus Loves Me," which was one of her favorites and mine, too.

"Believe me, the old man was coming out of his funk really fast. I hadn't seen him drunk or tearing up in a week. One night when I came in this cabin, it was just reeking with some kind of cheap *eau de cologne*. I guess it was some he'd bought in the Hudson's Bay Store in Churchill as a going-away present for his wife. Anyway, he'd shaken it all over Marie as she lay kind of half drunk on his settee, smiling at him, at both of us."

"Then what happened?" I asked.

"Well, this went on and on, rum and porridge, every night, the two of them yowling and singing, and then he'd draw that old wartime blackout curtain across his porthole and the two of them would be more or less silent in there. I'd have to chase away some of the crew, who used to stand by the old man's door and listen. They knew they were on to something strange.

"Now the captain started looking tuckered out each morning and Marie looked tired as well, both of them with the smell of rum on their breath, that and the perfume." At that moment, the mate went silent as the captain came into the cabin with Marie close behind him. She expertly heaved her weight over the captain's high ship's transom. I was a witness to that night's party – lots of rum in Marie's porridge and several manly rounds for us. Then the accordion came out and all four of us began to sing together. The old man put a pink ribbon around Marie's neck and sprinkled on the cheap cologne. The mate gave me a high sign and the two of us rose to leave. The captain sighed and lay down on his settee beside Marie, wriggling his hips to make her give him a bit more room.

Outside on the deck, the mate stopped and we leaned against the starboard rail. "We're still off the coast of Labrador tonight," he said, "but this sort of thing" – he nodded his head toward the captain's cabin – "it's just got to stop. I'm telling that to the old man in the morning. Jesus, I've got to. We'll be in port in a week's time if this weather holds for us. I'm counting on you to help me, Jimmy," he said. He'd called me Jimmy since the moment he'd met me.

"How do you mean help you?"

"Well, I don't want the crew to get mixed into this whole thing any more than they are, and we've got to get rid of Marie before we heave into port or, by Jesus, you'll hear the tongues in there start wagging."

I, being just a passenger, went to bed near dawn and slept till noon. The mate hurried up to me and said, "He's agreed to do it, but we'll sure as hell need your help."

"How?" I asked.

"Listen to this," he said. "The old man's willing to call the crew forward and give them a talking to of some kind, and the two of us will grab Marie and roll her up on two wide planks, then in off the stern."

"How are you going to get her back there?" I asked him, thinking of her two hundred pounds and remembering the time she'd tried to bite me.

"Rum and porridge," he said, giving me a sly glance. "That'll do the trick."

Porridge with rum

When the captain was ready and in place to call the crew forward, the mate started to rattle Marie's enamel dish. As she watched him, he poured in a double shot of rum, then took a long, straight shot for himself out of the neck of the bottle and passed it over to me. He placed the dish halfway up the two oak loading planks that led up to the ship's rail, and Marie climbed them neat as any circus performer. When she was finished, the mate began to stroke the beautiful harp on her sleek back, then with a helpful heave from me, we rolled her off and into the waiting arms of the sea. These were harp seal waters that would soon be familiar to Marie.

But to our alarm, Marie came swimming after the ship and calling. She was singing what sounded to me like "What A Friend We Have in Jesus." I felt bad, the mate felt worse.

The old man stayed impossibly drunk until they dropped the hook in port and the owner and the agent came out to take us ashore in the launch. They may have noticed that the captain looked a little hung over, but there was nothing strange about that.

I flew to Montreal, then Ottawa, and did my government business. When the ice up north was strong, I flew back to Frobisher on Baffin Island, and from there made my way home to Kingait.

I got a letter from the mate in the annual mail next summer. He had a good, square-handed way of printing that was very legible, but short and all too brief. He wrote that all was well with him and with the old man, but that the big news was that the captain had met a wonderful young girl named Marie – he'd forgotten her last name – and they had married. The mate said he and most of the crew went to a party at their new house, and on the wall was a framed photograph I'd taken of the original Marie, the porridge lover. This new wife loved rum with ginger ale, but had no use at all for oatmeal porridge. I never met any of that wonderfully good-hearted crew again, but, believe me, I'll never forget them.

91

A Gourmet Feast

In Paris in the autumn of 1961, when I was waiting for a visa to go to Russia to visit the Soviet Arctic and Antarctic Institute, I was hearing more and more about the ancient cave paintings at Lascaux, in the Dordogne. Those drawings and paintings on the large chalk white walls inside had been discovered by two young boys in search of a lost dog during the war, but the cave's entrance had been a well-kept secret from the Germans, and visits to view them were still not widely available.

The local Abbé, Henri Breuil, because of his overwhelming interest in the caves from the outset, was considered their most knowledgeable and well-respected guardian. In the autumn of 1961, he invited some artist friends of mine to come down and view the caves with him. They were kind enough to encourage me to join them.

Abbé Breuil, a notable gourmet in the grand French tradition, was not a well man at that time and he died within a year. Could that fatal date have been set forward by the fabulous gastronomical delights of the famous local restaurant that he so greatly favored? Certainly, when he planned our journey south, well in advance he decided with the chef the two major meals we would have in the Dordogne. Each was a nine-course meal with an aperitif, six wines, and naturally afterwards coffee and Armagnac. In the smallish, homelike restaurant, the walls were decorated with written, illustrated menus of gourmet feasts that had been enjoyed by previous special guests. Along with our *pâté de foie gras*, we had – can you believe it – red champagne.

Like everyone who had seen these caves at Lascaux, I was bowled over by their scale and brilliance. Not long after our visit, they were closed again to all but scholars because of the adverse effect the breath of human viewers was having on the atmosphere inside the caves, with the alarming result that the vibrant colors of the drawings on the walls appeared to be fading.

In the years since that unforgettable visit, my interest in French and Spanish cave drawings has increased, for I believe that there may be similarities between those Paleolithic drawings and contemporary Inuit art. Twenty years later, in February 1981, Alice and I set out to view the caves in northern Spain. We visited *El Castillo* and another dozen caves with prehistoric drawings. Some of them had entrances so narrow you had to crawl in on your belly, squeezing through the narrow entrance on some privately owned property, following the farmer's son who held the flashlight and would later collect the fees.

The French and Spanish cave drawings have been examined by many experts and have been declared genuine, drawn about 15,000 to 17,000 years ago. But the newly discovered large cave called Chauvet in southeast France is exceptional. Radio carbon testing on the charcoal and red ocher used by the artists has enabled experts to confidently date the drawings at 30,000 to 40,000 years old, making them the oldest known paintings in the world. Most surprising of all, these newly discovered drawings in Chauvet show an understanding of perspective, and seem to have been created by certain individually talented artists.

Cave drawing

Thank God for nature's landslides and the cautious secrecy of primitive man that have allowed these drawings the time to be varnished over by natural calcite and hidden from light for all those centuries. This allows us to start trying to fit together who we are and whence we came as part of the human family.

Alice and I rented a little Spanish car and drove bravely south to visit our Ottawa friends the Robertsons, moving through the splendidly austere winter landscape of northern Spain. I say drove bravely, for the Spanish drive at a helluva clip and their roads are ruled by plenty of heavy lorries that are not in the habit of giving ground to a small car even on deadly mountain curves. After Toledo and Malaga, we arrived in Nerja at night and were allowed into the Robertsons' solid, stucco-walled protection by a guard. This was largely a British and Canadian compound near that wonderful town with a wide view of the Mediterranean.

On Sunday, a group of friends decided to drive up into the surrounding hills and have lunch at a restaurant they favored in a small, white-washed hill town. A memorable meal of roast goat, rice, and cheese, black olives and sharply brittle Spanish wine was served at a narrow table that had been set for the dozen of us. Jutting outward from the restaurant, it stretched halfway across the road, its white linen cloth fluttering in the afternoon breeze. The sky was a deep winter blue and the sunshine turned the house walls a brilliant white, making the shadows seem to glow in their contrasting blackness, and making me feel that Spain is one of the places where I'd like to have stopped to live. Perhaps another zigzag may take me there.

92

Up the Orinoco

The two great rivers of South America, the Amazon – largest in the world – and the Orinoco, have fascinated me since childhood. I used to get a thrill just running my finger along their long, twisting courses in an atlas, to marvel at the fact that they both well up from the same source in the upper highlands of Brazil. That was a world I had never dreamed I'd have the luck to see.

Suddenly, out of the blue, came an invitation in 1997 to join a cruise on an elegant, Norwegian-registered ship. I have lectured aboard cruise lines before, but always in the Arctic. What could I say about South America? "Talk about making Steuben glass," was the answer I received. "We'd like you to bring your wife and sail with us. Speak about the designing of glass, and we'll take along a dozen or so sculptures you've made for the passengers to see."

What a thrill! We'd been hanging around Paris, life drawing and eating, when the invitation came. We quickly flew home, gathered summer clothes, and flew south through Miami to Curaçao. There we boarded and set out on an unbelievably luxurious cruise ship, anchoring at remote places like Tobago on the off side instead of the larger island of Trinidad. My speaking of Steuben was limited, usually just before cocktails.

Then, zingo, we were on our way to Venezuela and up the dream-like Orinoco River. We saw exotic sea birds and drew whole families of Indians in dugout canoes who were so tanned they looked like parts of their handsome watercrafts.

One morning before 5:00 a.m., we set out with native guides in their dugout canoes, soon to disappear beneath the leafy canopy of the jungle covering a narrow tributary. We heard howler monkeys that screamed at dawn, and the awakening bird life. I had always thought of this part of the world as a malaria-ridden forest, but we used very little mosquito repellent and no head nets. At that hour of the rising dawn, the temperature was comfortable.

As the canoes weaved their way up the ever-narrowing tributary, we saw many flights of dovelike birds. Parrots took off from the tree-tops, flashing their scarlet color and streaming tails. We saw big-beaked toucans in flight. The roots of the trees on the riverbanks were like witches' fingers with their roots probing downward into the dark, reflecting waters, where we looked hard for alligators.

Toucan

One could imagine the early Spaniards, sweating in their breast-plates and their beautifully engraved metal helmets, paddling up this narrow waterway in search of gold as Indian eyes stared out, watching their every move, wondering if they were gods or demons. Our fellow passengers, having solved the golden riches problem in other ways, were more than content to catch the merest glimpse of a pair of red eagles.

The water began to widen, the forest receded, and our canoes moved into a lakelike opening. Suddenly, we saw a rise, as a pink dolphin rolled and then another. These dolphins were really pink – it was not just the light of dawn breaking over them. We saw more pink dolphins rising, and our Indian guide showed no surprise.

Suddenly, we heard a yell from our shipmates. Looking over, we saw small, shining fish, more than hand-length in size, leaping over their canoe. As we drew closer to them, these fish began to jump across and into our canoe. More than a dozen actually landed in the boat – which made me wonder at the abundance of this country and how well it had provided for its native people. We stopped for a last look right before we turned to go back to the ship that was waiting for us in the deep center of the Orinoco River. Lying behind us was the enormous height of Angel Falls, with its narrow white plume of falling water and the native homes along the river.

Spanish helmet

Do I wish that I had been one of those conquistadors going up this unknown river five centuries ago? Yes, I do, crazy as that may sound, I do. It's something hard like that that has always thrilled my bones, such as when I was dog-team traveling long ago.

A young anthropologist was invited aboard our ship. He seemed Spanish at first, but claimed all Venezuelans are at least part Indian. He said he had spent time with a remote Indian tribe that lived in the jungle far upriver.

"How do you manage to contact them?" I asked him.

"It's easy enough," he answered. "Just go along the edge of the jungle in a canoe, then strip off every stitch of clothes you're wearing and leave them all behind. Then start into the jungle and keep walking for days and days, until you see some human sign – footprints, maybe. You follow them and start singing softly, maybe whistling a bit, but not like a bird. And after they have taken several days to watch you, they'll leave you a sign or two. Then one by one, you'll see them. They move in slowly and feed you something and try to talk to you a little. After a few months with them and their families deep in the forest, you'll discover that there are no better, kinder people in the world."

Imagine two such remote and different people as these jungle families and Inuit I used to live with, both treating a helpless stranger with the same kindness. Do either of them really need our improved way of life?

93

Art Profits

Because Inuit art speaks to everyone across great chasms of distance and across the boundaries of language, it has proved to be very popular, and has earned a lot of money. The Americans worried that perhaps Canadian Inuit were not getting their fair share of money from their carvings because they had always heard about earlier traders shortchanging American Indians. The Canadians, on the other hand, worried that the Inuit were getting far too much money. And, since Inuit, they feared, didn't know how to handle the returns, it would ruin them and spoil the major art markets in the South – i.e. Toronto, Montreal, Vancouver – for other more formally trained artists.

Probably there is some accuracy in both views of the situation. But on the whole, I believe that all the Canadian Inuit artists have handled their success well. They have bought snowmobiles, tents, fancy rifles, electric sewing machines, their children's clothing, televisions, etc. They have enjoyed having enough money to give some away to their friends and relatives when they are in need. This is the Inuit way, though not exactly our way. In their culture people who earn money usually find various ways to dispose of it. What's wrong with that?

Inuit have never had or understood our kind of banking system. When I encouraged Osuitok to keep some of his money in a bank account in the first bank at Frobisher Bay, he confessed to me that having money privately and secretly hidden away from others in a far-off place seemed wrong to him. Relatives of his were perhaps in need and he should gladly share the money with them to buy necessities. He explained that money should be like meat that the fortunate man took in the hunt and fully shared with his relatives and neighbors. If they hadn't done that, whole camps would have starved to death. Greedily hiding away his money was a situation that worried Osuitok, so much that he said he dreamed about it. After all, in Inuit opinion, the worst thing that could be said of a Baffin Island hunter was that he was selfish with the meat, that he wouldn't fairly share it.

So here we have a real conflict in our very different ways of thinking. Putting money into a bank account or buying relatively safe stocks or bonds is seen as nothing but virtuous in our eyes. We believe it is the prudent thing to do. Inuit think that constant sharing of meat or newly purchased goods from the Inuit co-op store or Northwest Company to give to others is a compassionate way to live. And since goods and gifts and meat are constantly being given back to you, it is an ancient system now largely outside our own, but it works for Inuit people, and everyone feels the joyful pleasure of giving

94

In Praise of Inuit Art

I believe that many Canadians have been surprised by the success of Inuit stone and bone carving and by later Inuit originality in the predominantly women's field of printmaking and tapestries. They almost seem to feel that the worldwide recognition of this old, new art that has held strong now for a period of fifty years was somehow wrong, a trick perhaps. *Canadian art has never been so quickly and widely accepted*, they thought.

Well, there was no trick about it. Inuit are immensely clever human beings, at first unsullied by our accepted scholastic systems of formalized art education. When their art first came out of the North, it appeared fresh and oh, so real, on the world art scene. To be sure, Inuit had good help in marketing their work from art galleries in Canada, the U.S., and from art dealers around the world. But, remember, each of these stone or bone carvings is one of a kind in a world where that sort of single sculptural expression has become extremely rare. Much of the art created in the South today is usually cast or lithographed and then sold in somewhat limited editions.

I've been privileged to watch Canadian Inuit sculptures carefully for fifty years. I've returned to various parts of the Arctic twenty-six times since I departed from Cape Dorset in the spring of 1962 after living there for nine years. It is amazing to me that the quality of Inuit art has held up so well as it passed before our eyes through three generations of Inuit carvers. Major Inuit stone carvings are being sold today in the better galleries of Canada, the U.S., Europe, and the Far East for prices ranging from $18,000 to $38,000, and a good many more in the $2,000 to $8,000 range. Fortunately, smaller ones may still be found for only a hundred dollars or so.

Like many collectors, I have predicted that the market for Inuit art, both carvings and stone block prints, would soon collapse. I've been worrying about this, and wrongly predicting it, for forty years. But, to tell you the truth, the market today for both old and new works is showing signs of even greater strength. There is a whole new enthusiasm for Inuit art. Collectors, particularly out on the southwest coast, have evaluated the genuine North American art objects being created today, and that's why they are buying Canadian Inuit art – and so am I.

In 1968, I was asked by Arthur Laing, the Minister of Northern Affairs, to make a survey and report on Canadian Northwest Coast Indian art to see if there were any possibility of a resurgence of that art, as had happened in the Canadian eastern and central Arctic as well as Arctic Quebec. I reported to the minister back in Ottawa that I saw a great potential there and, of course, thirty years later it has turned out to be more than true. Some old-fashioned dealers at that time were just starting again to go from house to house on the many British Columbia reserves, offering handfuls of cash for old potlatch gifts, masks and carvings, and traditional hunting and fishing objects, totems, painted boxes, coppers, cedar root hats, and Chilkat dance blankets. They were then paying twenty-five to a hundred dollars. Those same masks and ceremonial paraphernalia are selling for $15,000 to $70,000 today, and, I believe, will go much higher.

Good Inuit art may experience a slump in the future, like sharp-pointed men's shoes, and lie dormant for years, like Haida and Kwakiutl and Tlingit art, but I believe its quality guarantees that it will come roaring back again.

The much maligned George Swinton, who has observed and written about Inuit art for years, has taught at the University of Manitoba and sometimes in Toronto or Ottawa. In his book, *Sculpture of the Inuit*, Swinton has made a good selection of the kind of carvings that have so powerfully become a part of the art mix of this country. In Greenland and in Alaska, I see Canadian Inuit prints and stone carvings being quietly passed off as local native work. I know for certain that the Inuit art success has exercised a direct influence on many Indian communities across Canada and in the U.S.

Nunavut Territory will become a reality in 1999. Some tried and truly profitable aspects of Inuit history should be encouraged to go traveling forward with Inuit there. Documentary filmmaking, for example, could be a coming thing in the Arctic, and some thought should be given to producers, directors, and actors. Some Inuit still possess an ancient wellspring of power, cleverness, and drive that will surprise and delight anyone of good heart who comes into any lengthy contact with them.

Over the years, there have been many important tours of Inuit art to major cities of Canada, the U.S., Mexico, Britain, France, Italy, Denmark, Germany, Russia, Japan, and Korea. There are plans to do that again in the huge, new Inuit territory of Nunavut and beyond. We have many master carvers and printmakers, old and new. This is a Canadian cultural marvel. If cared for, it will bring

Inuit and Canada future fame. As William Blake wrote in his Proverbs from *The Marriage of Heaven and Hell*, "What is now proved was once only imagined."

For all the artistic excellence of their work, Inuit hunters and artists are nothing if not practical. As you'd expect, Inuit carvers don't like to work with any stone that is too soft, for it can break while they are making the piece. Once, a somewhat famous carver I knew was working outside on a good-sized carving of Sedna (some Inuit call her Taliillajuuk). When I came up and knelt down beside him on the tundra, it happened, as though I were a shaman bringing a curse. One of Sedna's arms broke off.

"Too bad," I said as we looked at the broken arm now lying between our feet.

He thought for a while before he said, "In the old story of this half seal, half woman, in a big storm her father and his hunting companions had to throw overboard first the walrus meat, and then his daughter. When she tried to crawl back into the boat, her father had to cut off her arms at the elbows. So this undersea woman, if she lost her other arm, would seem the same as that sea spirit after she had her arms lost."

"You're right," I said, and he promptly knocked off her other arm and started to turn them both into flippers.

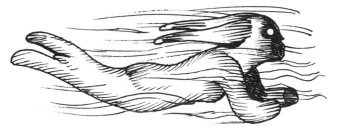

Sedna, the sea goddess

95

Inuit Prints of Canada

An isolated hunting existence has given Inuit art a very special form and character. Like most hunting societies, Inuit consider living in harmony with nature as their art. The objects they carve, the surfaces they decorate, are to them merely reflections of the life around them. Even the killing of food has been for them a religious experience.

Each print is a personal, as well as a shared, expression of the spiritual linkage between man and nature, itself an evidence of ancient, shamanistic perceptions that continue to affect Inuit life, as I know from my own experience with them.

In their best and most evocative prints, Inuit artists transcend the barriers of language, distance, and time. Through their art, we can feel their needs and joys, their ingenious perspective on human and animal life. We come to realize that their prints and carvings embody much of what all of us share, however disparate our cultures and experience.

The means whereby this remarkable vision is expressed – Inuit printmaking – was first used at Cape Dorset on west Baffin Island in 1957. The five hundred residents of this huge Arctic region called themselves *Kingarmiut*. Descendants of nomadic Asiatic tribes, they are warm, generous, family people who possess a strong and abiding sense of community. They are sea hunters, skillful carvers, singers, dancers, practical people with a powerful sense of survival. They are among the last of the hunting societies that have preserved a keen, insightful sense of observation.

This insight, coupled with a long, formidable tradition of artistic expression – in stone carving, in the incising of bone and ivory, and in the important women's art of skin appliqué – enabled Cape Dorset artists to adapt with great alacrity and intelligence the principles of block and offset printing once it was introduced.

The Cape Dorset printmakers employ three techniques in their art: stone cut, the stencil, and engraving. To make a stone cut, the process whereby their unique prints are made, the Inuit carefully flatten and polish a large stone, then carve in low relief the forms and figures they desire to print. They ink the block and place a sheet of fine, strong paper on it. By gently rubbing with their fingers or a small sealskin tampon, they transfer the inked impression onto the paper. This method is slow and painstaking, but produces the most sensitive results.

The Inuit artists usually follow the early European and Far Eastern traditions wherein the artist creates the design, and his work is then cut into the stone block and printed by an expert printmaker. For this reason, the signatures of both artist and print-maker appear on each print. A small symbol is usually added to identify their location. The igloo represents Cape Dorset. Other settlements producing prints are Baker Lake, Holman Island, Pangnirtung, and parts of Arctic Quebec.

The creation and distribution of prints and carvings are very important to Inuit at this time, for apart from providing a necessary source of income, these activities band the community together in an Inuit-controlled adventure. How fortunate we are to live at a time when famous Inuit prints are being created by living artists. It is like Paris at the time of the French impressionists, when museum treasures of the future were available to all at modest prices, though only a few had the wit and daring to acquire them.

For the Inuit, printmaking boldly expresses the importance of traditional Inuit life even as it becomes entwined with a new and swiftly changing world. The prints are historical reflections of human feelings, wondrous elements in the rarified, enchanting atmosphere of the Arctic world.

For the children of Nunavut, it will not be so easy. Inuit family life is now assailed on every side by countless outside influences. Because of the new snowmobiles and improved rifles, the mammals, birds, and fish of the Arctic are for the first time in need of protection. Whether the coming generation will be able to carry forward any of this natural artistic heritage, whether the Inuit will remain in harmony with the animals around them, remains a serious question for the future.

When I was living in Cape Dorset, I came to realize that Kenojuak was a very special person. One of my earlier unachieved ambitions was to arrange a meeting between Kenojuak and Oonark, the extraordinary woman artist from Baker Lake, the settlement just inland from the west coast of Hudson Bay. I so much wanted to be in the same room when these two remarkable women might meet. Alas, these two geniuses lived far apart, and in the older days, no Arctic east to west air transportation was available. The traveler from Cape Dorset had to go by charter aircraft east to Iqaluit (Frobisher Bay), then south to Montreal, west to Winnipeg, then north again to Churchill and charter from there to places farther north along the west coast of Hudson Bay. With the changing weather there were always complications on top of the immense cost.

Oonark (later known as Jessie Unark) drew her best images with great discipline, possessing a design sense highly suitable for sewing and equally adaptable to printmaking. I had the luck to meet her on an early Central Arctic Patrol in late spring 1955 when the schoolteacher at Baker Lake alerted me to the fact that an excentional woman folk artist was living out at the Inuit hunting camp on the Kazan River. We were introduced and I saw a sheaf of Oonark's astonishingly original drawings. The teacher, who became our go-between, remained in contact. I asked her to select and send some of Oonark's drawings to Cape Dorset with the understanding that the West Baffin Eskimo Co-operative would pay the going amount of money for any drawing if it were decided to do a print series from it. When the drawings arrived, we decided to print two of them in the 1960 group using the name Una, Kazan River. The prints were *Tattooed Faces* and *Inland Eskimo Woman*. Also in that catalogue were ten prints by Kenojuak, including *Complex of Birds*, *Dogs See the Spirits*, *Woman Who Lives in the Sun*, and *The Enchanted Owl*. It was a remarkable year.

In Cape Dorset in the earliest years of the printmaking project, there was much excitement in the co-operative's workshop. We often worked together until eleven o'clock at night cutting stencils, inking stones, rubbing prints. I was thrilled with the art created by Kenojuak, now fully recognized as one of the most famous Arctic artists. Kenojuak made gloriously complicated drawings that became prints where each form and line connected with another. Once I tried to imitate her mystical drawing of *Complex of Birds*, but found it totally impossible. I hope you'll try to do a similar drawing in her connected style, for example, of birds and dogs – you'll see what I mean.

When I once asked Kenojuak how she drew her compositions, she told me that a small blue line seemed to be moving just before her pencil, showing her where to go. This takes us into the realms of shamanism where few of us would dare to venture.

96

Life Drawing and Life

Life drawing in Paris is very old, indeed so old that it was an exciting thing to do even during the French Revolution. Over the years, nude models have become famous, some of them as famous and sought after as the works of their painters.

L'Académie de la Grande Chaumière is on the Left Bank of Paris in Montparnasse on the *rue de la Grande Chaumière*, which the dictionary describes as a place of thatched roofs. This is no longer the case, but the buildings in this part of Paris are far from new. *L'Académie*, for instance, has marble steps in its hallway that are worn in a central groove so deep that each step runs into the one below. Every part of the building has the worn, dusty, dirty look about it that is a must in all of the old French institutes of study.

L'Académie, I should explain, is not a school in which one learns to draw. There are no instructors there. You are supposed to have more or less completed your art training before entering the *Académie*. It is understood that you have returned to have the use of a live model while perfecting or perhaps revitalizing your drawing skills with the hope of gaining some new personal insight into art. That certainly has been the reason why I have returned to Paris frequently since 1947.

The entrance to *L'Académie*, surrounded by some of the best old-fashioned art stores, leads past a bulletin board plastered with paintings of male and female models for private hire. The afternoon's drawers are of every age. Along with them you walk in, turn left, and push through high, dark doors.

Inside, there is a large, single room. Gray dusty light seeps down through historically grimy skylights and tall north windows. Three ancient, shaky, wooden drawing bars, vaguely the same as those used by ballet dancers, stretch around the raised model's stand to support everyone's large, individual drawing board. The front two rings are usually already occupied by the earliest enthusiasts when I arrive.

I try to pick a suitable three-quarter drawing angle on the outside of the circle or on the back bar. Then I search to find the best three stools from among an angular wooden forest of incredibly rickety perches. I choose one of the highest stools to support the bottom of my drawing board, a lower, sturdier one to sit upon, and a third very low stool to hold my pencils, pens, and watercolors. Over the years these old, ill-shaped roosts have developed humped corners to gouge into your ham bones and keep you lively and awake for the three full hours of a session, the *croquis*. These stools would have long since fallen apart except that some amateur chair-fixer years ago had in desperation repaired them with loose fencing wire.

There is a limited amount of friendly greetings at *L'Académie*. Those persons gathered to draw the model speak many different languages and are at first preoccupied, arranging their various chairs and tools and planning with what medium they will approach the subject on this particular afternoon. Talk is not exactly encouraged. During the pose, gray-haired men and women hiss like snakes if anyone talks or scrapes a stool while others are drawing. Old men grunt and groan, then argue violently and often stomp out from the session if anyone dares to turn on the lights over the model to cut the evening's gloom.

In the eighties and mid-nineties, many East Asians attended the drawing classes as their national economies rose. Now those eastern economies have taken a hard turn and we notice sadly that certain Hong Kong, Japanese, and Korean friends have not returned. We also miss some other older faces, those of dedicated drawers, not seen in recent years. Unemployment is currently high in France – some say more than 14 percent – and perhaps that, too, has caused a new sense of seriousness in the classes. Or is it me? In the good old days (as old days have always seemed), Picasso, Matisse, Giacometti, Maillol, and countless other artists drew at *L'Académie*. On the same floor as the amphitheater-style room, Zadkine had his sculpting studio and pounded without cease. The unanswered telephone rings on and on as though waiting for him to stop.

Among the drawers, the quality of the many models is much discussed because they vary greatly. Artists are not perhaps so interested in the face or figure of the model, male or female, as they are in the model's ability to strike interesting poses and maintain them until time call. That ability, in itself, I consider an art.

It takes a certain skill and sense of presence to be a model suitable for life drawing. The very best of them, male or female, quickly establish a strong rapport with those drawing in the room. In fact, a model can change the entire dynamics of a drawing session, and they very often do. At first, we watch them struggling to remove their clothing behind a tippy Japanese screen. We can only see the tops of their heads, with their eyes glued to the clock, usually one minute before the pose begins.

We, the drawers, ranging in age between twenty and eighty, rearrange our messy little boxes full of charcoal bits and watercolor pans, feathered quill pens or cheap ball points, and large pads of white or natural-colored papers. We drawers are ready to take any kind of impression that at the moment suits our fancy. A deadly silence reigns during the sittings. Some models come in looking the worse for wear, perhaps having had an overly active night. They may decide that the first pose should be lying comfortably flat. "*Ne dormez pas!* Don't go to sleep," the more serious drawers shout at them, for sleeping models twitch.

Once in a while a wandering drunkard provides excitement as he tentatively eases open the tall door and staggers in to view the middle of a pose. As he stands there swaying, staring at the nude, the older women drawers hiss at him. If that fails, the model screams at him. The drunk – a real one or perhaps a sly voyeur – reluctantly turns and reels outside. Ahh, Paris!

Nude

97
Life Plus Life Drawing

Today, the talk around me at *L'Académie de la Grande Chaumière* is almost exclusively French. When things are going well, friends tend to sit beside friends so that they can chat briefly between the sittings. Other years, when other countries were experiencing greater financial success, the whole atmosphere was different with the sound of different languages in the room. The Orientals laughed and seemed quite open. You could see their drawings improve year by year. Not that you could always see everyone's work. Unfriendly types would sometimes take up a position directly behind you, so that they could see what you were drawing, but you would not see theirs, not even later on request.

After a week's solid life drawing, you begin to develop very special senses. You suddenly start to notice more in the human forms around you: subtle colorations in each person's face, the bony planes of the forehead, the exact angle of the nose and its proportions to the face, the neck, the mouth and chin, the whole shape of the head, and especially the eyes.

This makes my 6:00 p.m. ride home on the bus along *Boulevard Montparnasse*, starting in front of the restaurant *La Coupole* and going to *Duroc*, a constant thrill of observation. I see how deep the French eyes are set, how wonderfully strong and prominent is the Gallic nose, and note the various head shapes, and styles of hair. The French passengers do not look at me. They look at no one, except perhaps the person they are with, and more commonly they look out the window in a sort of trance. I like to think they are playing classical music or making intellectual arguments in their heads.

I know from past years that these art-sharpened physical observations will slowly drift away from me with time, and I will become an unobservant person again – that is, until the same time next year when my senses will come sharply alert as I study the width of a passenger's cheekbones.

But I daydream on as I walk along *rue de Sèvres*, remembering those aristocratic-looking girls who made eyes at you in the George V Hotel or the Ritz, trying to make a living somehow, and any decent young ex-soldier felt a duty to help them solve the troubles of their past. Those were joyful days in Paris for all the allies and for the French who had triumphed in the war. We were not afraid in those days to go up a dark alley with a male friend in the breaking dawn to trade American Express checks, watching very cautiously for a quick, safe trade for francs. The amount was almost twice what we'd receive from a hotel or from a respectable French bank.

Changes have come year by year. In 1947-48 with World War II just ended, all the models were young and noticeably lean, made strong from riding bicycles throughout the war. They were anything but shy, and would sometimes come naked down among us between drawing sessions. They would lean on a drawer's shoulder and tell what they liked about your work, and sometimes ask what you were doing later on for dinner. These young girls, so experienced with life in Paris, would sometimes forget who they were seducing and would break into German instead of English. Ah well, it was only two years since the German army had departed. Who cared? The war was over. The lights were back on from the *Étoile* to the *Marais*, and while soap and nylons were still rare, they were back to stay.

There was a great air of camaraderie that gave flavor to the evenings on the *Champs Elysées* in spring. Scores of young foreigners of school or army age would crowd the tables over on the Left Bank at *Deux Magots* to discuss their unholy gains. When the *International Herald Tribune* began to publish the daily black market prices, it lost some of its danger and excitement.

The *Académie*, reflecting the feeling of all France, had been on an overwhelming quest from the 1950s onward to capture all that was shockingly modern. Their academicians tried to forget all academic drawing. Now the younger generation is trying to do real, honest-to-God life drawing again, a bit of rebellion against the old rebels.

Fifty years later, I prided myself as being the longest lasting drawer at *La Grande Chaumière*, but I was wrong. In March, 1998, a woman seated next to me asked to borrow my knife, and during that exchange, I learned that she was from Montreal and had been going to the *Académie* since 1939. She had married a Frenchman and spent most of the rest of her life near the center of France, a beautiful part of the country, she told me, where the wine is good, but the people are far too political and no longer seem to care about art or most other pleasures of life.

My new friend had visited her hometown of Montreal a few years ago and said the politics of Quebec made her glad she didn't live there now. But she said that she was truly envious of Canada's low cost of food. It's true that restaurant prices in Paris seem almost out of hand. Fancy meals can cost more than a thousand dollars and truly reasonable ones are hard to find.

In the sixties, by contrast, there was an artists' café called Rajah's where one could have a thick, rich soup and a knuckle of pork with a glass of house wine for a reasonable few francs. But Rajah's closed before my very eyes, and I doubt that we will see its likes again. We loved to go to Rajah's for lunch with the print-making girls we were working with in the atelier. If we took them to better restaurants, old ladies sitting nearby would loudly whisper, "*Mon Dieu, regardez les mains sales des femmes!*" The truth was that the black printer's ink would not scrub off their hands. That saved us lots of money in the end.

Bill Hayter's famous Atelier 17 was where I did some engraving in the winter of 1961. It was oriented to printmaking and turned out dozens of masterful people: Krishna Reddy, Sergio Gonzalez, Adrienne Cullom, Jeremy Gentilli, Pat de Gogorza, Benita Sanders. There were other outstanding characters there as well, only partly French because it was run by the talented Bill, a famous British chemist who taught students all there was to know about the almost magical art of full-color intaglio printing. Before he died, Bill became Sir William Hayter, knighted for his tireless efforts in the arts.

When we from the Atelier 17 wished to have a party, we would go to the local police station in our district and sign papers to receive permission to hold the party. Then, if by chance we left the windows open and in our exuberance made too much noise, the police would be prepared to handle the phone calls and complaints from the incensed neighbors on the narrow street. If old women appeared in their windows in nightdresses and shook their fists at us, we would usually fire a champagne cork over into their window. If one laughed and yelled, "*Vive la France!*" which they quite often did, we would send a pretty girl across the way to offer them champagne and our apologies. Life was wonderful in Paris in those days and nights in a recovering city full of optimism.

98

Steuben

In my mind, the clarity and brilliance of Steuben's glass make it like no other sculptural material in the world. You can see through it perfectly. It magnifies. And nothing can be hidden, as often happens in colored glass and all other sculptural materials. A glass form that gives its designer the greatest hope for success may utterly fail because of this clarity and see-through quality. On the other hand, it may totally surprise the designer and turn out far beyond his greatest expectations.

The first formalized piece of glass I ever made for Steuben, *Partial Eclipse*, included metal, as has my most recent finished piece, *Green Heron*. I have had thoughts of animals moving in nature, and been impressed by the close relationship between clear, fiery, hot, malleable glass freezing into a metal and being hard as ice. I am thrilled by the frosted, Arctic-like appearance of deep engravings on glass.

The kind of pieces I most often try to make are usually connected to storytelling. I am always excited by the possibility of designing from a story that leaps over the boundaries of words and even languages. The King Arthur legend of *Excalibur* is a perfect example, since the piece of glass may be viewed and the legend then immediately recalled, as is the case with *Rip Van Winkle*. *The Goose That Laid the Golden Egg* is a piece I have often presented to Steuben in design meetings, and although often accepted, I found it impossible to make. Now I have found the way and it shall soon appear. What a perfect storytelling piece.

Working with a glassmaking shop on the factory floor of the blowing room and later with the Steuben cutters, then on to the engravers, has always held a special thrill. I find that one of the best moments in the glassmaking process is the excitement of thinking up and drawing and redrawing the object one hopes to create. But more thrilling is to work with a really good gaffer and the others in his shop while trying, sometimes dozens and dozens of times, to create the object one hopes to achieve. Hot glass, alive and beginning to take shape on the end of a cherry-red iron, provides a thrill that can never really be duplicated. Yet, that same piece of glass that later turns to an ice-cold brilliance is exactly what we want.

Glassmaking, like almost every other aspect of my life, is changing. I am proud to belong to the old school. After all, I knew Frederick Carder in Corning when he was over a hundred years old. This pioneer, who originally created Steuben Glass, and Arthur and Jack, and Dale Chihuly are men who have opened the modern road.

99
Nude Models

In the Queen Charlotte Islands on the banks of the Tlell River, there are, if one were to look for them, some wonderfully gnarled tree roots. The big moon tides have washed the soil and gravel away and left the trees naked of bark and beautifully exposed. I've had fifty years of life drawing off and on, including time spent in Paris at *L'Académie de la Grande Chaumière*. Now I ask myself, *isn't it appropriate that you settle down in your old age and really draw these tree trunks?* They have stripped limbs and torsos that twist and turn as interestingly as a human spinal column. They have thoracic cavities, clavicles, femurs, bones of wood. The changing light of day causes them to delineate themselves in marvelous lights and shadows. These models on the riverbank move very little out of pose, nor do they ever tire and require a twenty-minute break.

Locked trees

Yes, I'm in my tree stump drawing phase whenever I'm living beside the river. I draw on rich, Italian paper of beautiful, muted, earthen colors. I've saved most of this paper since I purchased it in Florence soon after the war. For many years, I had the feeling that it was too luxurious to draw on, that I'd save it for some future subject that was really worthwhile. But now time flies. *What the hell,* I say to myself, *use up that gorgeous paper you've been hoarding. Draw* on it. No, not on both sides, you miser. Take another sheet. Splash on the watercolors. Use the heavy Arches 140-pound weight paper. We'll none of us be here forever.

I have a comfortable, three-legged stool, and I stand my fly rod against a shady cedar close beside me. I'm doing something more appropriate to my age. I ask myself, Who needs Paris when you've got this river and these marvelously contorted tree roots with their naked limbs?

Of course, I'll miss the human side of things a bit: the crowded classes of English, Koreans, Japanese, Germans, Scandinavians, Swiss, the odd North American, and lots of French. Being in an academy means being in art classes where there is no teacher. Who would dare to try to teach other artists such as Picasso, Matisse and Giacometti, who have all been drawing at L'Académie during my time? In my mind's eye, I see a model hurrying in from the hall, wearing drab, ill-fitting Paris street clothes. She then reappears from behind the battered Oriental screen as a thing of startling beauty, all grace and curves. Next day a male model with fabulous back muscles might appear. I try to forget all that, and the butcher shops of an earlier Paris with braces of geese, brown hare, and rough-haired, tusked wild boar hanging outside that always gave me the feeling of the Flemish painter, Breughel.

I'm on the Tlell River with all these trees. Yes, it's great, all right, but it doesn't mean I'll not go back to Paris to draw!

100

Hideaway

When the shad run in the Connecticut River is over, the cool weather starts to disappear and I start to dream of other non-humid climates that I know. My thoughts turn away from books, drawings, crystal sculptures and begin to focus on that other river. To prepare ourselves we usually drive to Fin and Feather in Rhode Island and buy a dozen new old-fashioned flies, the kind I used to tie myself a half century ago: Brown Hackle, Royal Coachman, and the like. I'll have to wait until we reach the other coast to buy the Umpqua flies. Oh, yes, we'll need new leaders, too. But we won't buy much else. Lord, no! Being a Scot and thinking of cutting a staff to help me down the river's bank, I feel that we've got most of the fishing gear we'll ever need, good graphite salmon and trout rods and reels that only improve with age.

On a much anticipated summer morning usually well before sunup, we prepare to depart from Stonington. Having removed the best of our household treasures (not worth that much, but impossible to replace), we phone our house sitter, throw the bolts, and carefully set the burglar alarm. Then before leaping into our car, we shout, "We're off!" hoping that our best friends and nearest neighbors, who loosely surround us in Stonington, will hear us and roll over in their beds, wake their partners, and together celebrate our departure.

We usually have the choice of going to Boston then flying up to Toronto and west. But it is really handier for us these days to drive to Providence, Rhode Island, and fly directly to Chicago, then take a connecting flight to Vancouver. It arrives too late to fly on to the Queen Charlotte Islands, now called Haida Gwaii. That delay always forces us to remain a day or so in Vancouver, one of the grandest cities in North America. We have good friends living there, the shops have wonderful Northwest Coast Indian and Inuit art, plus there is a distinctly British feeling about the place. The food, once dull, is now spectacular. We buy more suitable coho salmon flies and start to become truly excited. We are river-wading anglers, and a few twelve- to fifteen-pound coho, nicely grassed without a net, using the lightest tackle and smallest flies, will set us dancing for the rest of the year.

We rise early to have breakfast and taxi from the hotel to the Vancouver Airport, which isn't very far. We go to the one and only airline that flies north to the old military airstrip, now much improved, at Sandspit on South Moresby Island. An hour-and-a-half flight north along one of the world's most spectacular mountain ranges and a jig out over the Pacific and we're landing. We board a wee bus north and drive along the peaceful inlet to Alliford Bay, where we expect to board the ferry, which is small and sturdy. However, the ferry crew takes an hour off for lunch at noon, exactly coinciding with the time everyone wishes to cross. But no matter. We enjoy the bright or rainy crossing and arrive at Skidegate Landing.

There, we retrieve our dying island car. (Wiser travelers rent one for their journey, and so will we when this car's done.) We joyfully pat our ancient station wagon, which looks unloved and damp and mildewed from an overwhelming season of winter rains. Forget rain. Once wet-geared for fishing, who cares if it rains or shines? The moon is waning, and we talk with others about the salmon schooling in the estuaries, preparing themselves to come up the river to pass our house. We trust they'll come past by the dozens daily, without being too quick about it.

Now we go into the local store, the new Skidegate Haida Gwaii store, to stock up. We can never remember what we left behind last year, so we make purchases like paprika and toilet paper, just in case. Prices are wicked on the Charlottes compared to the mainland. I go out, open the back door of the old station wagon, reach in, and grab two hand-tall Sitka spruce and throw them out from the places they've grown in the earthy carpeting on the floor. This is normal enough for the Charlottes, which are known – because of dampness during the soggier winter months – to provide greater tree growth than any other place in North America, perhaps the world. Anything that's got the will to live will flourish in this damp, lush, island climate endlessly warmed by the Japan Current.

The car sags with food and Hochtaler dry white wine from British Columbia's Okanagan Valley, a jug wine that is reasonably priced and goes nearly as well with salmon as the Chilean imports. We fill up with gasoline by the liter that also costs an awful lot. As we drive north on the one main island road, cutting through the dark spruce shadows and patches of sunlight, I start thinking of the hideaway.

Tlell has been declared an unincorporated, almost invisible village that has left moldering evidence behind of Haida chiefs' houses, one on top of the other and God knows how old. Wooden houses, like totem poles, usually last less than a hundred years in the rain. Tlell stretches for several miles along a handsomely repaired logging road that's called the Yellowhead, named after a fast-flying flicker and a famous Iroquois guide. I close my eyes and try to recall the first exciting moment of stepping through our front gate in the early seventies.

In about half an hour, we see the white wooden bridge that crosses the Tlell River, and a fly-cast away stands our house. We squish along the mossy path and up onto the front porch of our cottage, treading cautiously. It has long fed an army of carpenter ants. It used to sag and creak, but it feels better now, a neighbor having fixed that problem several years ago. I poke around the corner and find the hidden key, then peek through the window before I unlock our red front door.

We stagger in with the luggage, then all the food. Kind neighbors of ours have been ahead of us to start the fridge and freeze water in the ice cube trays. One of them has laid a slab of fresh-caught spring salmon and some of this morning's hen's eggs on our cutting counter.

We sit for a moment, staring out the window, wondering again at the soothing quality of the tidal river. We're home. Yes, home. I think, *Put up the fly rods, hang out the hip boots and the waders, shake out the rain gear. Open the fly boxes. Tomorrow morning's coming.*

There's a smell of must and mold inside the cottage. A shriveled mouse carcass lies in a trap, his round black mouse turds scattered artfully around him. A large and lively spider is busy wrapping up a big blue fly, tightening it in his web in the corner of the river-viewing window. We fling open the doors to let the outer air come in.

After unloading the car and checking the well, I don't bother to go upstairs or even to look into the fish room. I go out to feel the soft, yielding moss beneath my boots. I want to look around for delicious king boletus mushrooms – our small, riverside property is famous for them. Then I check to see if the deer that hop our fence each night and the flights of migrating fish crows have cleared all the Saskatoon berries off our one large bush. Not quite. Alice doesn't have a garden at Tlell because we're almost never there when that garden should be planted. Mercifully, we have generous island friends, good fisher folk and gardeners who revel in the rich soil and abundance urged on by winter rain.

Stepping up onto the open porch of my hideaway behind the house, I unlock the rusty padlock with some difficulty, then push open the door and step inside the single room that is eight feet by ten feet, painted startling white. Everything looks more than right to me. Wrapped around my head is my favorite smell, the almost overwhelming scent of cedar like my mother's death-to-moths closet in Toronto, but here the scent is vastly stronger. There is the boxlike, cedar double bed folded tight against the side wall, and my homemade writing desk stretched beneath the window across the whole north wall. Through the windows above the desk, I can see the river curving away, glinting smooth as molten lead between the stands of spruce and cedar that shelter the hideaway's back wall. I sit down and eye the river, a source of so much action and so much fishing excitement. Of course, there will be no salmon in this river at this time of year, but trout, yes, big cutthroat trout, eager to take a fly. Cutthroats have been in short supply these last few years and should all be carefully released for the sake of the trout and their future in the river.

I try my modern Danish lamp above the desk; it works. I check to see the small electric heater in the cupboard beside the toaster and electric kettle. There is no plumbing in the hideaway, no telephone, no radio, just clear water from our well to make morning coffee or afternoon tea. I look back at the small, colored flag on the back of the cottage roof. Alice has pulled it up, showing all is clear. Alice lowers it sometimes to warn me that unknown persons are inside our gate. She runs up the flag when it's all clear. This does not, of course, include our friends. I stand up, stretch, and take another heavy whiff of cedar, then wander slowly back to our green shingled cottage, which is gently fading into the forest and blending with the evening's incoming fog.

Alice has cooked some back strap (filet mignon) from a plump, island blacktail deer given to us when we stopped in to hear all the local news about the fishing, Haida happenings, new loves, old feuds, big tides, and the violence of the winter rain and weather. Full of contentment just to be home again, free of our series of plane flights, I sigh and say to Alice, "We zigzag back and forth one helluva lot these days – east to west, or north to south. Do you think it would be proper to describe us as a pair of nomads?"

She pauses before answering, looking around her stove for mice in our sagging, cobwebbed cottage, precariously perched on the bank of this marvelous salmon river so naturally located exactly in the middle of nowhere. "Nomad is not quite the right word for you," she says thoughtfully. "Why not try 'hermit?' That's it, I think – we're a pair of hermits."

"We could stay here like hermits," I say, "stop zigzagging around and winter over again, maybe write the next book about . . ."

"About what?" she asks.

"Well, about this whole lovely Haida way of life."

Raven rattle

About the Author

JAMES HOUSTON, a Canadian author-artist, served with the Toronto Scottish Regiment in World War II, 1940-45, then lived among Inuit of the Canadian Arctic for twelve years as a Northern Service Officer, and the first Administrator of west Baffin Island, a territory of 65,000 square miles. Widely acknowledged as the prime force in the development of Inuit art, he is past chairman of both the American Indian Arts Centre and the Canadian Eskimo Arts Council and a director of the Association on American Indian Affairs. He has been honored with the American Indian and Eskimo Cultural Foundation Award, the 1979 Inuit Kuavati Award of Merit, and the 1997 Massey Medal, and is an officer of the Order of Canada.

Among his writings, *The White Dawn* has been published in thirty-one editions worldwide. That novel and *Ghost Fox*, *Spirit Wrestler*, and *Eagle Song* have been selections of major book clubs. *Running West* won the Canadian Authors Association Book of the Year Award, while his most recent novel, *The Ice Master*, will soon appear in Spanish translation. Author and illustrator of seventeen children's books, he is the only person to have won the Canadian Library Association Book of the Year Award three times. His most recent children's book is *Fire Into Ice*, about creating glass sculpture. He has also written screenplays for feature films, has created numerous documentaries, and continues to lecture widely.

His drawings, paintings, and sculptures are internationally represented in many museums including the St. Petersburg Museum in

Florida and private collections including that of the King of Saudi Arabia. He is Master Designer for Steuben Glass, with one hundred and ten pieces to his credit. He created the seventy-foot-high central sculpture in the Glenbow-Alberta Art Museum.

He and his wife Alice now divide the year between a colonial privateer's house in New England and a writing retreat on the bank of a salmon river on the Queen Charlotte Islands in British Columbia, where he has written a large part of his trilogy of memoirs, *Confessions of an Igloo Dweller*, *Zigzag*, and the forthcoming *Hideaway*.